Risk and reliability in ground engineering

Proceedings of the conference organised by the
Institution of Civil Engineers, and held in London
on 11 and 12 November 1993

Edited by B. O. Skipp

Thomas Telford

Conference organised by the Institution of Civil Engineers

Organising Committee: B. O. Skipp, Soil Mechanics Ltd (Chairman); D. I. Blockley, University of Bristol; K. W. Cole, Arup Geotechnics; R. Driscoll, Building Research Establishment; M. Jefferies, Golder Associates (UK) Ltd; W. M. Reid, Thorburn Ltd; N. A. Trenter, Sir William Halcrow & Partners Ltd

First published 1994

Distributors for Thomas Telford books are
USA: American Society of Civil Engineers, Publications Sales Department, 345 East 47th Street, New York, NY 10017-2398
Japan: Maruzen Co. Ltd, Book Department, 3 - 10 Nihonbashi 2-chome, Chuo-ku, Tokyo 103
Australia: DA Books and Journals, 648 Whitehorse Road, Mitcham 3132, Victoria

Classification
Availability: Unrestricted
Content: Collected papers
Status: Refereed
User: Geotechnical engineers and researchers

A CIP catalogue record for this book is available from the British Library.

ISBN 0-7277-1986-6

Published on behalf of the Institution of Civil Engineers by Thomas Telford Services Ltd, Thomas Telford House, 1 Heron Quay, London E14 4JD.

Printed and bound in Great Britain

Corrigenda

Risk and reliability in ground engineering
Edited by B. O. Skipp, Thomas Telford, London, 1993

Page 33. The following should be substituted for the text below Table I

RISK ASSESSMENT OF SLOPE STABILITY

A prime geotechnical application of risk methodology is in
the study of slope stability. A systematic audit of
uncertainty in a risk-based analysis of slope stability
exposes the need to elicit expert judgement across a broad
range of topics. Included in this inventory are the
evaluation of geotechnical data; formulation of a general
geological model; definition of model elements;
characterisation of the strength of materials; and the
formulation of a slope failure model. A practical test case
for the risk assessment of slope stability is given in
Paper 22.

In such a project many decisions have to be made, some fall
clearly within the definition of expert judgement, others
clearly can be regarded as engineering judgements. There
are also commercial judgements, management judgements and
judgements in the interpretation of regulatory
requirements. Many judgments which at first sight could be
assigned to the category of an engineering judgement can
with examination and perhaps decomposition are seen to be
properly expert judgements and are therefore required to
fulfil the logical canons. In Table II the suite of
decisions which have had to be made are listed and divided
into the two categories of judgement. It is clear that
where the parameters are concerned expert judgement has to
be employed and in order to assign ranges to these
parameters for which the number of tests on site does not
permit a frequency approach so Bayesian approaches are
appropriate. In making choices as to the failure model
which is assumed the choice is also amenable to the use of
expert opinion in that probabilities can be be assigned to
one or other models and logic tree formalism could then be
employed.

FAULT MODELLING IN SEISMIC HAZARD ANALYSIS

Exposure to nearby active faults can sharply ratchet up the
level of seismic hazard at a site. Active faults which
happen to pass through a site constitute an even greater
potential

Page 36, last paragraph
Line 3. *For* Table II *read* Table III.
Line 5. *For* Table III *read* Table IV.

Contents

Evaluating risk

Managing risk

1. To treat or not to treat abandoned mine workings: towards achieving a dialogue over risk and reliability

K. W. COLE, S. T. JARVIS and A. J. TURNER, Arup Geotechnics, UK

INTRODUCTION

The workload of a large multi-disciplinary consulting engineers' practice has provided many tens of projects with a mining element, and has given the authors the opportunity to evolve a consistent strategy for evaluating risk. This strategy provides the bedrock for the assessment of the need for treatment; whereas the technical justification may be logically derived and easily explained, there is need to communicate the risk of the mine and the reliability that represent it both in the untreated and treated states. It is in the dialogue between client and engineer, and the engineer and the certifying authority, that the meaning of the terms needs careful explanation. The method needs to be comprehensive yet simple and transparent.

All projects commence with a site investigation, which includes investigation of the mine(s) and a report is written for each project. Given that the Client has provided the opportunity (i.e. the time and money, see Site Investigation in Construction, 1993) for a comprehensive and adequate investigation of the ground around and above the remnant mine cavities (Cole et al, 1986; Braithwaite and Cole 1986), so that sufficient technical evidence is available upon which make engineering judgements, there should be a clear exposition and evaluation in the appraisal section of

i) the nature and condition of the mine(s)

ii) the forms that collapses of the mine(s) may take e.g. crownholes, areal subsidence, shaft collapse; each collapse giving rise to disturbance of the overlying ground is termed a hazard event.

iii) the likelihoods of various hazard events

Table 1

RELATIONSHIP BETWEEN POTENTIAL AND RELATIVE LIKELIHOOD OF COLLAPSE

Range of relative likelihood, l	Potential P	Rating
10^{-1} to 10^{-2}	0.8	High
10^{-2} to 10^{-3}	0.4	Intermediate
10^{-3} to 10^{-4}	0.2	Low
$< 10^{-4}$	0.1	Very Low

Table 2

Typical values of I and I_s; the Importance of land use and Importance of structures and services

	Value of I, I_s
1. Public open space, farmland, tidal land.	0.3
2. Domestic houses (single family occupancy), secondary communications network/roads and railways, small factories and small places of assembly.	1
3. Domestic multiple occupancy, places of assembly, medium to large factories and offices, main roads and railways.	3
4. Essential services, valuable and/or costly property.	10
5. Structures or services giving great danger if damaged.	30

FIGURE 1   Consequences of a hazard event and severity of consequences for the Subjects of Life Property and Money

Subject at Risk	Severity of Consequences		
	Total Loss	Impairment	Inconvenience
Life	Death	Injury	Common cold
Property	Destruction	Roof damage	Door sticking
Money	Bankruptcy	Credit cards lost	Purse mislaid

FIGURE 2   The "field" of risk; Degree of Risk and Likelihood for the Subjects of Life Property and Money; from Cole, 1987

ANNUAL LIKELIHOOD OF A TOTAL LOSS EVENT			
Degree of risk (nomenclature)	To life Annual risk of fatility	To Property Annual risk of destruction	To money Annual risk of bankruptcy
Very risky	1 in 100	1 in 10	1 in 1
Risky	1 in 1000	1 in 100	1 in 10
Some risk	1 in 10 000	1 in 1000	1 in 100
A slight chance	1 in 100 000	1 in 10 000	1 in 1000
Unlikely	1 in 1 million	1 in 100 000	1 in 10 000
Very unlikely	1 in 10 million	1 in 10 million	1 in 100 000
Practially impossible	1 in 100 million	1 in 10 million	1 in 1 million
* NB These statistics applied in 1987 and may not now be true	1 in 95* The overall death rate	1 in 2000* The overall destruction rate	1 in 130* The overall bankruptcy rate

iv)   the risks that various hazard events will impose, taking account of the importance of the use of the land and the vulnerability of the structures and services.

v)   the treatment methods (if required), and their respective cost-benefits.

A consistent approach to identifying hazards, and evaluating likelihood and risk has been maintained.   This has been essential, as the responsible representatives of many clients have remained associated with the projects for many years. Table 1, which is Table 307 in the Report on the Study of Abandoned Limestone Mines in the West Midlands (Ove Arup & Partners, 1983a) shows the assessed relationship between potential for collapse and relative likelihood of collapse. The range of the risks considered in Table 1 are shown on Figure 5, and can be seen to be similar, although there is no differentiation between events causing destruction and damage.

The early work on evolving a risk strategy concerned abandoned coal mines (Cole, 1980), but it was the opportunity to assess the risks posed by the huge abandoned limestone mines in West Midlands (Ove Arup & Partners 1983(a) and 1983(b), and Cole, Turner and O'Riordan, 1984) and more recently by the salt mines in Northern Ireland (paper in course of preparation), that enabled the concepts presented to develop.

The state of knowledge at the time of preparing the Report on the Abandoned Limestone Workings in the West Midlands (Ove Arup and Partners 1983(a)) only permitted assessment of the relative risk of hazard events, see Table 1.   An early step towards a comprehensive risk assessment strategy was made in the paper "Building over abandoned shallow mines; a strategy for engineering decisions on treatment" (Cole, 1987).   Risk was identified as the consequence of a hazard (hazard event) and the severity of consequences were recognised as a factor in the degree of risk, see Figure 1.   The "field of risk" was displayed in a numerical form (Likelihood of 1 in 10, 1 in 100, etc., was chosen arbitrarily, but has subsequently proved to be a happy choice) with ranges displaced by an order between the "subjects" of Life, Property and Money, see Figure 2. The degree of risk was also expressed verbally and as will be seen, the expressions chosen (Very Risky through to Very Unlikely) have proved to be "anchor points" in the method.

The difference between public (involuntary) risk and private (voluntary) risk (after Starr, 1969) was recognised in the 1987 paper, but could not be expressed numerically with the simple array of Figure 2.   In addition, the expressions for Degree of Risk were evidently descriptions of both the Annual Likelihood and the Annual Risk, where risk is the combined likelihood of an event and severity of consequences (the words used in this paper are close in meaning to those suggested by

FIGURE 3   Hazard Events causing Total Loss (destruction); Degree of Risk, Annual Likelihood, Annual Reliability and Attitude to Reliability, for subjects of Life, Property and Money; from Cole 1993

Hazard Event Causing Total Loss

Degree of Risk	Annual Likelihood			Annual Reliability			Attitude to Reliability	
	To life	To property	To money	To life	To property	To money	Voluntary Risk	Involuntary Risk
Very risky	1 in 100	1 in 10	1 in 1	99%	90%	0%	Very concerned	Totally unacceptable
Risky	1 in 1000	1 in 100	1 in 10	99.9%	99%	90%	Concerned	Not acceptable
Some Risk	1 in 10 000	1 in 1000	1 in 100	99.99%	99.9%	99%	Circumspect	Very concerned
A slight chance	1 in 100 000	1 in 10 000	1 in 1000	99.999%	99.99%	99.9%	Of little concern	Concerned
Unlikely	1 in 1 million	1 in 100 000	1 in 10 000	100%	100%	100%	Of no concern	Circumspect
Very unlikely	1 in 10 million	1 in 1 million	1 in 100 000	100%	100%	100%	Of no concern	Of little concern
Practially impossible	1 in 100 million	1 in 10 million	1 in 1 million	100%	100%	100%	Of no concern	Of no concern

FIGURE 4   Hazard Events causing Impairment (damage); degree of Risk, Annual Likelihood and Attitude for subjects of Life, Property and Money; from Cole 1993

Hazard Event Causing Impairment

Degree of Risk	Annual Likelihood			Annual Reliability			Attitude to Reliability	
	To life	To property	To money	To life	To property	To money	Voluntary Risk	Involuntary Risk
Very risky	1 in 10	1 in 1	10 in 1	90%	0%	0%	Very concerned	Not acceptable
Risky	1 in 100	1 in 10	1 in 1	99%	90%	0%	Concerned	Very concerned
Some Risk	1 in 1000	1 in 100	1 in 10	99.9%	99%	90%	Circumspect	Concerned
A slight chance	1 in 10 000	1 in 1000	1 in 100	99.99%	99.9%	99%	Of little concern	Circumspect
Unlikely	1 in 100 000	1 in 10 000	1 in 1000	100%	100%	99%	Of no concern	Of little concern
Very unlikely	1 in 1 million	1 in 100 000	1 in 10 000	100%	100%	100%	Of no concern	Of no concern
Practially impossible	1 in 10 million	1 in 1 million	1 in 100 000	100%	100%	100%	Of no concern	Of no concern

FIGURE 5

Risk Description (Relative Risk)	Degree of Risk of Hazard Event	Annual Likelihood or Annual Risk (Annual Reliability)		Attitude to Annual Reliability & Degree of Risk		
		Event causing total loss (destruction)	Event causing impairment (damage)	Voluntary involvement (exposure) concerning both total loss and impairment	Involuntary involvement (exposure) — Concerning total loss	Involuntary involvement (exposure) — Concerning impairment
Prone*	Very risky	1 in 10 (90%) / 17	0.7 / 1 in 1 (50%) / 1.7	Very concerned	Totally unacceptable	Not acceptable
Very high	Very risky to risky	1 in 30 (97%) / 70 / [A] 1 in 10 to 1 in 100 / High	1 in 3 (70%) / 7 / [B] 1 in 3 (1 in 2 to 1 in 7) / Very High	Very concerned to concerned	Totally unacceptable / acceptable to not acceptable	Not acceptable to very concerned
High	Risky	1 in 100 (99%) / 170 / 1 in 100 to 1 in 1000 / Intermediate	1 in 10 (90%) / 17 / 1 in 10 (1 in 7 to 1 in 20) / High	Concerned	Not acceptable	Very concerned
Intermediate	Risky to some risk	1 in 300 (99.7%) / 700 / 1 in 1000 to 1 in 10 000 / Low	1 in 30 (97%) / 70 / 1 in 30 / 1 in 20 to 1 in 70 / Intermediate	Concerned to circumspect	Not acceptable to very concerned	Very concerned to concerned
Low	Some risk	1 in 1000 (99.9%) / 7000 / <1 in 10 000 / Very Low	1 in 100 (99%) / 300 / 1 in 100 (1 in 70 to 1 in 300) / Low	Circumspect	Very concerned	Concerned
Very Low	A slight chance to unlikely	1 in 10 000 (99.99%) to 1 in 100 000 (100%) / 700 000	1 in 1000 (99.99%) to 1 in 10 000 (100%) / 70 000	Of little concern to of no concern	Concerned to circumspect	Circumspect to of little concern
Negligible	Very unlikely	1 in 1 million (100%)	1 in 100 000 (100%)	Of no concern	Of little concern	Of no concern

* After Blockley 1993, previously called "vulnerable".

FIG 5. Hazard events causing either total loss (destruction) or Impairment (damage) to Property. Risk Description (Relative Risk) Degree of Risk, Annual Likelihood and Annual Reliability and Attitude to Reliability. Note: Inset 'A' is from Table 1 and shows the correlation with the assessments for abandoned limestone mines reported in Ove Arup and Partners 1983(a); Inset 'B' is from a report made in 1992 to the Department of Economic Development (Depart of the Environment) of Northern Ireland concerning the risks associated with the collapse of abandoned mines (Ove Arup and Partners, 1991 to 1993). The figures in the corners of the "boxes" are the Risk Numbers giving the "ranges" for the values in the boxes e.g. N_R = 30 has the range N_R = 17 to 70.

Blockley 1992 and presented by Blockley 1994, and have similar definitions).

RELIABILITY
The difficulties described above were removed by the introduction in the January 1993 paper in Ground Engineering (Cole, 1993) of numerical values and expressions for reliability, with step-wise presentation of the terms for Attitude to Reliability to account for voluntary and involuntary attitudes being different for the same Likelihood. The tables for severities of consequences of total loss and impairment are reproduced in Figures 3 and 4. A further table for the severity of consequence of inconvenience is presented in the Cole, 1993 paper.

RELATIVE RISK
For over 10 years a scale of Relative Risk (combined likelihood and severity of consequences) has been in formal use for limestone mines (Ove Arup & Partners, 1983), see Figure 1 and Introduction above, and related projects (eg salt mines in Northern Ireland, see Figure 5). This scale is applied to both consideration of the risk of an area of ground that might be affected by the subsidence (collapse) of the ground above a mine and the risk to individual structures. Ove Arup and Partners (1983(a)) noted that "There is no evidence to suggest that the incidence of collapse (of a mine) is related either to the area or inclination of a given mine"; there has been no further evidence to require amendment of that conclusion.

When the assessment takes into consideration the land use of the area of ground that might be affected, the Relative Risk ($R_{R(I)}$) above a particular part of a mine affected is given by:

$$R_{R(I)} = P.I$$

7

Table 3

Typical values of V_s; Structural Vulnerability

Type No.	Type of Structure	V_s
1	Structures designed to accommodate subsidence movements. Rigid frames with multiple redundancy. Ductile frames with an adequate number of possible plastic beam hinges.	0.7
2	Ductile coupled shear walls. Small building units with raft foundations	0.7
3	Ductile frames with an inadequate number of possible plastic beam hinges. Small building units with strip foundations.	1.0
4	(a) Single ductile cantilever shear walls (b) Garden walls	1.4
5	Shear walls or slabs not designed for ductile flexural yielding but having the ability to sustain a significant amount of movement. Major electricity services within infrastructure. Roads.	1.4
6	Industrial processes which are sensitive to movement.	2.0
7	Buildings with diagonal bracing capable of plastic deformation in tension only: (a) Single storey (b) Two or three stories (c) More than three stories	 2.0 2.5 3.0
8	Single storey cantilevered structures (a) Ductile columns of doubly reinforced load bearing walls providing restraint to the structure. (b) Boundary walls (c) Single reinforced load bearing walls providing restraint to the stucture	 2.0 2.0 2.5
9	(a) Shear walls or floor slabs other than as given above (b) Chimneys pipelines and tanks or reservoirs on the ground	3.0

Table 4

Typical Values of V_m; Structural Material Vulnerability

Type No.	Material	V_m
1	Structural steel or flexible pavement construction, thermoplastics	0.7
2	Structural timber: Shear-wall buildings Other buildings	 0.7 1.0
3	Reinforced concrete	1.0
4	Prestressed concrete (when used in elements which resist movements by flexural yielding)	1.4
5	Unreinforced masonry in panels exceeding 3m, cast iron, thermosetting plastics, glass	2.0
6	Unreinforced masonry in panels exceeding 6m and buried service pipes with rigid joints and no relief bends	3.0

Table 5   Methods of assessing Likelihood

Methods of assessing Likelihood

–	Historical evidence	–	records, maps, etc.
–	Field evidence	– –	internal change external change
–	Analogy	– –	natural examples limits to extent
–	Analysis	– –	probability theory fuzzy relationship methods

9

where

    P = Potential for collapse (Assessed Likelihood within a specific period of time (usually a year (annual)) of a collapse which affects a given area x scaling factor)

    I = Importance of land use (a non linear scale of values related to the importance of structures and services, similar to that adopted in earthquake effect assessments). The total area of land $\sum_o^n A_i$ to be taken into account above a mine will extend outside the mine by the "draw" (a distance usually about one third of the depth of the mine)

For the whole area of the mine the Relative Risk is given by:

$$\text{Average } R_{R(I)} = \frac{P_i . I_i . A_i}{\sum A_i}$$

For individual land uses and structures, the relative risk to a particular land use is:

$$R_{R(I)(V)} = P . I_S . V \text{ where } V = V_S . V_M$$

where

    P   = Potential for collapse (Assessed Likelihood x scaling factor)

    I_s = Importance of structure (or service) being considered (Non linear scale)

    V   = Vulnerability (Non linear scale expressing the relative degree of damage likely to be experienced). This term can be subdivided into V_s and V_m where

V_s =	structural vulnerability }	For simplicity vulnerability is
V_m =	material vulnerability }	considered to be independent of the type of hazard event

Values of I_s, and V_s and V_m for typical structures and services are given in Tables 2, 3 and 4.

RANGES OF VALUES

In the procedure for the assessment of risk described below, it will be seen that the columns and lines in Figure 5 provide a numerate form of "game board"; it is entered at an assessed value of Likelihood for a particular subject. This value is tested against the Attitude to Reliability, and then adjusted to take account of the Importance of the site or structure and Vulnerability of the structure or service and the material of which it is made. Some loss of definition occurs during the procedure, created (not the least) by personal prejudices, and incorrect "weighting" of factors. To account for this the examples in Appendices A and B introduce a simple range of values for Risk, from 0.1 to 10 of the value of the assessed Risk Number N_R; examination of the implications of the extremes of the "range" may assist in selection of appropriate preventative or remedial works.

CALIBRATION

The "basic" system of Relative Risk (Table 1) has been calibrated against Degree of Risk. This has been done by relating the numerical Annual Risk (R) to the Annual Likelihood (L) with values of Importance (I, I_s) and Vulnerability (V, V_s, V_m) set at 1.0 (typical value for "suburbia", the most widespread and uniform occupancy of lands normally also with extensive secondary communications network, and structures and services of average vulnerability). Thus "High" Relative Risk has been found to correspond to "Risky" Degree of Risk, see Figure 5, with an Annual Likelihood of a Hazard Event causing damage to property of 1 in 10. With an Annual Reliability of only 90%, a person involuntarily involved would certainly be "very concerned" as indicated by Figure 5.

At the other end of the "field of risk" a Very Unlikely Degree of Risk of a Hazard Event (corresponding to a "Negligible" Relative Risk), with an Annual Likelihood of destruction of 1 in 1 million (10^{-6}) will have an Annual Reliability very close to 100%, see Figure 5. Such reliability, with a corresponding Annual Likelihood of Loss of Life of 1 in 10 million (10^{-7}), see Figure 3, is sought for nuclear power stations (H & SE, 1992).

Calibration has also been made by considering examples where the input is varied widely, and the following examples are given in Appendices A, B and C.

Example A - Destruction of Property (see Appendix A)

Example A1   Likelihood of collapse of mine - High
                    Importance of use of area - Low

Example A2   Likelihood of collapse of mine - Very Low
                    Importance of use of area - High

The former example gives a Risk to the area, taken to be farmland, of 1 in 300 with a "range" from 1 in 170 to 1 in 700; this is an Intermediate relative risk and the Attitude section of Figure 5 shows that a person voluntarily involved would be concerned to circumspect about the risk of destruction of the structure or service under consideration. A person involuntarily involved would consider the risk not acceptable or be very concerned. Example A2 produces much the same risk as Example A1, of 1 in 600 with a "range" from 1 in 300 to 1 in 1000, and the voluntary and involuntary attitudes are similar. In both examples, the lower figure of the "range" (higher risk) indicates that it is unlikely that the situation would be re-assessed as being Risky (High Relative Risk) unless there is a change in the circumstances e.g. re-zoning of the land for use for housing development, or an increase in the frequency of hazard events over a period of several years.

Example B Damages to Property (structures, services)
(see Appendix B)

Example B1   Likelihood of collapse of mine - High
                Importance of use of area - Intermediate to Low.

Example B2   Likelihood of collapse of mine - Low
                Importance of use of area - Intermediate

In these examples the overlying structures and services are respectively those of "suburbia" and the centre of a small town. The Likelihood of collapse of the mine is some ten times greater in Example B1 than for Example A1, and this reflects in the high risk the mine is assessed to present; i.e. Risk of 1 in 10 with a "range of 1 in 7 to 1 in 17. Notwithstanding that this assessment is being made only in regard to damage (and not destruction), the attitudes to Risk of concerned (C) (voluntary involvement) and very concerned (VC) (involuntary involvement) might seem cavalier. The Risk Number N_R of 7 at the bottom of the "range" for a Risk of 1 in 10 lies on the boundary of "very high risk", at which it is judged a person involuntarily involved would probably state their attitude to the risk as being "very concerned" (VC) with an inclination towards it being "not acceptable" (NA).

Example B2 shows an annual risk lower than that in Example B1, with a value of 1 in 30 and a "range" from 17 to 70. The attitudes to risk of concerned to circumspect (C to Circ) and very concerned to concerned (VC to C) for voluntary and involuntary involvement are realistic, and could apply, for instance, to several places in the Black Country where limestone mining took place beneath conurbation centres. In the Black Country such Intermediate Risks see Figure 5 (which might range as high as High Risks in some areas) has prompted extensive treatment to severely reduce the risks or eliminate them.

Example C Destruction and Damage to Vulnerable Properties
(see Appendix C)

In this Appendix the previously described Examples A1 and B2, in which the Importance of the use of the land overlying the mine was considered, are taken as the basis for examining the effects of structure or service vulnerability. Examples considering "neutral" structural and material vulnerability i.e. with $V_S = V_M = 1.0$ would give the same output of Risks as Examples A1 and B2. The range of values of V_S and V_M in the examples cover the whole range of vulnerability foreseen, but there may be occasion to extend either range to take account of particularly susceptible or particularly resilient structural forms or materials.

The message of the examples in Appendix C is that consideration of quite common structural forms e.g. shear walls in multistorey structures to resist wind forces, blockwork garden walls, prestressed concrete and cast iron in certain modes, may lead to as much as doubling of the assessed risk from say 1 in 30 to 1 in 15. Thus in the circumstances where consideration is being given to the need to treat a mine, inclusion of the vulnerability of structures likely to be affected may significantly influence the outcome.

PROCEDURE
The assessment of risk is made in four stages.

Stage 1. The likelihood of a hazard event is predicted. This may be on the basis of one or more of the methods shown in Table 5. It should be noted that, roof falls in mine will commonly progress upwards (migrate) more slowly as time passes, and thus the progression to "chimneys" and crownholes might be expected to gradually slow down. There are, however, several case histories where the opposite is true, particularly where "chimneys" have reached weak overburdern or drift deposits e.g., at the Santon-Dragonby mine in Lincolnshire, where the water-logged weak sandstone layers in the overburden seriously increase the rate of roof collapse when they are intercepted by the chimneys (Arup Geotechnics, 1992). At other mines where the collapse mechanism involves "squatting" of relatively weak strata over pillars, collapses may well become more and more frequent after total quiescence for many years (Cole and Statham, 1992).

In the absence of meaningful data on which to make an estimate of likelihood, the best recourse is to analogy with mines in and overlain by similar strata. If the information from that is also unsatisfactory then notional (default) values of Annual Likelihood $\frac{1}{N_L}$ can be chosen. It is suggested that values of $N_L = 10, 100$ and 1000 are entered; $N_L = 1$ (annual likelihood of one event) would indicate that there should be signs of the effects of recent hazard events. At the other extreme $N_L > 1000$ (annual likelihood less than 1 in 1000) is becoming too remote for judgement to be realistic on the need for preventive works.

Stage 2. Calculate Reliability $(1 - \frac{1}{N_L})$. Check on Figure 5 for attitude to involuntary and voluntary involvement affected

13

FIGURE 6 Flow chart for deriving Risk of a Hazard Event caused by collapse of abandoned mine workings.

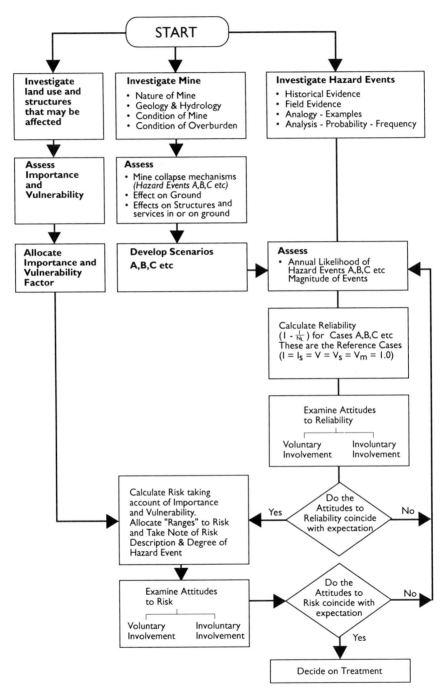

by a hazard event. The Attitude to Reliability of the system incorporating the hazard event at the given likelihood should compare reasonably with personal expectation eg. that a voluntary involvement in setting up an office over a mine with a likelihood of 1 in 100 of a hazard event causing damage would suggest you ought to be circumspect, whereas the local planning officer would be concerned. The indicated attitudes may turn out to be strongly at variance with the personal expectation of one or more of the parties to the decision on the need for and nature of treatment. In such a case the whole field of risk (Cole 1993) should be discussed by all parties to ascertain if personal prejudices are over-riding judgement on the basis of the facts.

Stage 3. From Annual Likelihood (likelihood Number N_L) calculate Annual Risk numbers

$$N_{R(I)} = \frac{N_L}{T} \text{ hence } R_{(I)} = \frac{1}{N_{R(I)}}$$

or
$$N_{R(I)(V)} = N_L \cdot \frac{1}{T} \cdot \frac{1}{V} \qquad \text{hence } R_{(I)(V)} = \frac{1}{N_{R(I)(V)}}$$

$$= N_L \cdot \frac{1}{T} \cdot \frac{1}{V_a \cdot V_m}$$

Stage 4. Obtain degree of Risk and Description of Risk from Figure 5. The Attitude to Risk columns should also be noted as they give an indication of the attitude that could be expected of persons voluntarily and involuntarily involved.

CASE STUDIES

CASE STUDY 1 - BLACK COUNTRY SPINE ROAD

The techniques outlined in this paper were applied in an assessment of the risks posed by mine workings known to exist beneath the proposed Black Country Spine Road in the West Midlands. This road formed a major part of the infrastructure investment programme of the Black Country Development Corporation.

The road corridor was divided into geological/mining history similar zones, termed Sub-Areas. This was not a particularly onerous task as these zones were essentially defined by the primary geological faults crossing the road corridor. The extensive mining that has been undertaken in the Black Country meant that every coal seam within each of the sub-areas could be assumed to have been worked. This assumption was confirmed by the site investigation that had been undertaken prior to our involvement.

Data for each zone included:

a)   depth and thickness of coal seams

b)   type and nature of working methods

15

FIGURE 7　Case Study 1 Black Country Spine Road, Assessed Annual Likelihood of Subsidence for Sub-Areas and Mineral Horizons.

Mineral Horizon	Area A	Area B	Area C	Area D	Area E	Area F
Two Foot Coal	0.01	<0.01	0.01	-	0.01	-
Brooch Coal	0.01	<0.01	0.01	-	0.01	-
Pins/Pennyearth Ironstone	0.01	0.003	0.003	-	-	-
Chance & Flying Reed Coal	0.003	Mineral horizon not present	Mineral horizon not present	-	-	-
Thick Coal	0.003	0.003	0.003	-	0.003	-
Heathen Coal	0.001	0.001	0.001	0.003	-	0.0003

FIGURE 8 Case Study 1 Black Country Spine Road, Annual Risk and Risk Description.

Mineral Horizon	Area A	Area B	Area C	Area D	Area E	Area F
Two Foot Coal	Intermediate (0.03)	Low/Intermediate <(0.03)	Low/Intermediate <(0.03)	-	Low/Intermediate <(0.03)	-
Brooch Coal	Intermediate (0.03)	Low/Intermediate <(0.03)	Low/Intermediate <(0.03)	-	Low/Intermediate <(0.03)	-
Pins/Pennyearth Ironstone	Low/Intermediate <(0.03)	Low (0.01)	Low (0.01)	-	-	-
Chance & Flying Reed Coal	Low (0.01)	Mineral horizon not present	Mineral horizon not present	-	-	-
Thick Coal	Very Low/Low <(0.01)	Very Low/Low <(0.01)	Very Low/Low <(0.01)	Negligible (0.001)	Very Low <(0.01)	Negligible (0.001)
Heathen Coal	Very Low (0.003)	Very Low (0.003)	Very Low (0.003)	-	-	-

17

FIGURE 9   Case Study 1 Black Country Spine Road, Relative Cost of Mineworking Treatment for chosen risk level.

Achieved Level of Risk	AREA A Structure	AREA A Road	AREA B Structure	AREA B Road	AREA C Structure	AREA C Road	AREA D Structure	AREA D Road	AREA E Structure	AREA E Road	AREA F Structure	AREA F Road	TOTAL COST Structure	TOTAL COST Road
Negligible	3.2	28	N/A	14	1	14	2.5	0	18	0	0	0	7	72
Very Low	3	27	N/A	13	1	13	2	0	17	0	0	0	6	71
Very Low/Low	3	27	N/A	13	1	13	2	0	17	0	0	0	6	71
Low	2	15	N/A	6	7	6	2	0	17	0	0	0	5	45
Low/Intermediate	1	7	N/A	0	0	0	0	0	0	0	0	0	1	7
Intermediate	0	0	N/A	0	0	0	0	0	0	0	0	0	0	0
High	0	0	N/A	0	0	0	0	0	0	0	0	0	0	0
Very High	0	0	N/A	0	0	0	0	0	0	0	0	0	0	0

NOTES: A) Costs do not include treatment of mine shafts

c)   geological setting of the coal seams

d)   voidage within coal seams

e)   collapse records within the general area of the road corridor

Using this data an assessment of the Annual Likelihood (L) of subsidence was established for each coal seam in each of the identified sub-areas.   The results of this analysis is presented in Figure 7.

Following the procedure outlined in Figure 6 the following were established.

    Importance factor (I) (Table 2)   = 3

    Structural vulnerability (Table 3)   = 1.4

    Structural material vulnerability (Table 4) = 0.7

These factors were used to derive the Annual Risk ($R_{(I)(V)}$) for each of the coal seams in the sub-areas, as shown in Figure 8.

The Annual Likelihood (L) and hence the Annual Risk ($R_{(I)(V)}$) can be modified by effecting treatment works such as grouting. The costs of these treatment works were derived which enabled the costs to be identified for achieving a particular level of Annual Risk and hence Relative Risk for any sub-section of road.   This in turn enabled cost-benefit decisions to be made for each road subsection as well as for the road as a whole.

This cost benefit analysis is given in Figure 9.   The costs have been normalized for comparative purposes.

It can be seen from Figure 9 that reductions in risk to Low/Intermediate are easily and relatively cheaply achievable, but the achievement of Very Low and Negligible levels require large expenditure.

The costs were split between carriageway and structures to enable the effects of a different choice of Annual Risk number to be applied between carriageway and structures.   This approach was subsequently adopted.

The risk proved by mineshafts was addressed separately and did not form part of this analysis.

CASE STUDY 2 - SALT MINES IN NORTHERN IRELAND
In 1990 an abandoned salt mine in Carrickfergus, Northern Ireland collapsed with little obvious warning (Griffith, 1991) resulting in major disruption of the ground surface with maximum surface settlements exceeding 8m.   Subsequent desk study and investigation of seven adjacent mines (the collapsed

FIGURE 10 Case Study 2, Salt Mines in Northern Ireland. Assessed Relative Risk and resulting action.

Mine	Mine Condition	Approximate Depth to mine Floor (m)	Relative Potential for Collapse [Likelihood]	Land Use (related to Importance)	Relative Risk $R_{K(1)}$ (Annual Likelihood)	Attitude to Reliability	Action Proposed/Implemented
French Park	Mine open flooded, many pillars dissolved. Shafts partly collapsed	250	High (main) Very high (Shafts)	Agriculture Road	Main- Intermediate (0.03) Shafts- High (0.1)	Concerned to Very Concerned Very Concerned	Road realignment. Shafts fenced off. Monitoring to enable farming to continue.
International/ Carrickfergus	Main mine, open partly flooded. W part, partially collapsed, partly flooded.	150	Intermediate (main) Very High (west)	Agriculture, Nursery, Road, Engineering Works	Main- Intermediate (0.03) West-High (0.1)	Concerned to Very Concerned Very Concerned	Monitoring Area of potential instability fenced off.
Duncrue	Substantially collapsed. Possible small area open.	250	Very low	Agriculture	Low (0.01)	Concerned	Limited Monitoring
Maiden Mount	Collapse migrated 140m into overlying strata, flooded	120	High to very high	Agriculture	Intermediate to High (0.1 to 0.03)	Concerned to Very Concerned	Monitoring Central area fenced off
Burligh Hill	Main mine open dry. Shafts partly infilled showing signs of movement	280	Intermediate to Low (main) High (shafts)	Agriculture	Low (0.01)	Concerned	Shafts treated. Limited monitoring.
Black Pit	Shafts part collapsed, flooded (Mine of very small dimension)	150	Very Low (main) Shafts (intermediate)	Derelict Engineering Works	Low to Intermediate (0.1 to 0.03)	Concerned to Very Concerned	Monitoring. Area fenced off.

mine being in private ownership was not investigated) revealed that a major factor leading to instability of the mineworkings, located within the halite beds of the Mercia Mudstone strata, was the seepage of fresh water into the mineworking on abandonment via the shafts. This resulted in erosion of the original mine pillars and roof strata leading to the breakdown of the overlying strata and surface subsidence. The nature of the mine collapse is such that there is likely to be an increase in the occurrence of such events with time since abandonment.

An appraisal of the record of collapses within the mines since abandonment revealed at least five collapse events, three of which had led to surface subsidence. Given that there are five mines remaining in an open or only partially collapsed condition an assessment of the risks posed by these mines and a cost benefit analysis of the options for them was required.

Based on the historical record of collapses within the mines, engineering judgement regarding their present condition based on site investigation and analogy with other mines within our experience an assessment of the relative Potential for Collapse of each mine was assessed. The Relative Risk was then evaluated taking into account the consequence of failure of the mine. This assessment was made on a mine wide basis and related to land use or importance. The area of land potentially affected took into account an assessment of the 'angle draw' likely to apply in each particular situation. A range of values for annual likelihood from High to Low was identified, see Figure 10. It should be noted that this assessment was made prior to the full development of the methods outlined in this paper and thus in the application of the case study there is a slight mis-match with them.

Much of the land use is agricultural with few structures within the predicted area of effect. However, there were two areas where the risk was assessed as High which would, according to Figure 5, give rise to a 'Very Concerned' attitude to reliability concerning involuntary exposure to potential impairments.

A range of options for each mine was presented to the Client including an NPV (nett present value) analysis. It should be noted that in general the size of the open voids remaining in the mine cavities is such that treatment by infilling would cost many millions of pounds. From the option presented the Client chose to close a road over the French Park Mine and construct a realigned section. At Burleigh Hill Mine the mine shafts were treated to prevent ingress of groundwater. At these and the other mines a system of interim monitoring has been established pending decisions on long term actions.

CONCLUSIONS

A strategy for evaluating risk has been described. The method is comprehensive yet simple, and is based upon a "10 times" array taking into account the subject at risk (life or property), the severity of the consequences (destruction and damage), the attitude of persons voluntarily or involuntarily involved, the importance of the ground at risk and the vulnerability of structures or of the materials from which they are made.

At all stages in the procedure; illustrated in the Flow Chart in Figure 6, the effect of alterations to the input on the outcome can be tested, and thus the method can be used in discussion between the client, engineer and checking authority.

ACKNOWLEDGEMENT

The authors wish to acknowledge the help and assistance given by Black Country Development Corporation and the Department of Economic Development, Northern Ireland in the preparation of this paper and their kind permission in allowing the data contained in the case studies to be used.

DEFINITIONS

Crown hole	A crater in the ground surface resulting from upwards roof migration (forming a "chimney" before the ground surface collapses).
General (areal) subsidence	Subsidence of the ground surface without the formation of craters (crownholes).
Mine entry	Shaft, adit, drift or level providing access into the mine from the surface.
Extraction (total or partial)	Amount of mineral removed from the plan area of the mined strata as a percent eg. 80% extraction. Effectively "total extraction" is greater than 95% and anything less is partial extraction.
Collapse ("open", "closed", "partial" or "full")	See Table 1 of Cole & Statham, 1992.

"Draw"	Ground beyond the mine working affected by subsidence. The angle of draw to the vertical above the mine edge marks the theoretical or actual limit of the draw.
Hazard	A set of conditions with potential for initiating an accident sequence where the accident may give rise to total, loss, impairment or inconvenience, following Blockley (1992).
Hazard event	The realisation of a hazard.
Likelihood (L) (related to Potential (P)).	The actual value of p and its relationship to L is discussed in the paper; see Table 1 and Figure 5.
Importance = (I)	The relative value of an area taking into accunt its use.
Vulnerability $[V \ (V_s, \ V_m)]$	Blockley (1993) calls this "proneness".

APPENDIX A

Calibration Examples

Destruction of Property (Structures, Services)

Example A1: Check risk for part of a mine where there is
- a High Likelihood (L) of collapse
- a Low Importance (I) of use of area (farmland)

Likelihood (L) from Figure 5 = 1 in 100 (N_L = 100)

Reliability ($1-1/N_L$) = 99%

Attitude to Reliability (concerning destruction)
Voluntary involvement - concerned (C)
Involuntary involvement - not acceptable (NA)

Importance (I) from Table 2, I = 0.3

Risk Number $N_{R(I)} = N_L \times \frac{1}{I} = 100 \times \frac{1}{0.3} = 300$ [$R_{(I)}$ = 1 in

From Figure 5
Degree of Risk = Risky to some risk

Risk description = Intermediate

23

Range of risk $(N_{R)(I)} = 170$ to $700)$ $R_{(I)} = 1$ in 170 to 1 in 700

Attitude to Risk
Voluntary involvement - concerned (C) to Circumspect (Circ)
Involuntary involvement - not acceptable (NA) to very concerned (VC)

Example A2: Check risk for part of a mine where there is
  - a Very Low Likelihood (L) of collapse
  - a High Importance (I) of use of area (Some essential
    services and a large petrol station)

Likelihood (L) from Figure 5 = 1 in 10,000 (N_L = 10,000)

Reliability $(1-1/N_L)$ = 99.99%

Attitude to Reliability (concerning destruction)
  Voluntary involvement - of little concern (LC)
  Involuntary involvement - concerned (C)

Importance (I) from Table 2, I = 15 (assessed value)

Risk Number $N_{R(I)} = N_L \times \frac{1}{I} = 10,000 \times \frac{1}{15} = 600$ $[R_{(I)} = 1$ i

From Figure 5,
  Degree of Risk = Risky to some risk
  Risk description = Intermediate to low
  Range of risk $N_{R(I)} = 300$ to $1000)$ $R_{(I)} = 1$ in 300 to 1 in 1000

Attitude to Risk
  Voluntary involvement - concerned to circumspect (C to Circ)
  Involuntary involvement - not acceptable to very concerned (NA to VC)

APPENDIX B

Calibration Examples

Damage to Property (structures, services)

Example B1: Check risk for part of mine where there is
  - a high likelihood (L) of collapse
  - an intermediate to low Importance (I) of use of area ("Suburbia")

Likelihood (L) from Figure 5 = 1 in 10 $[N_L = 10]$

Reliability $(1 - 1/N_L)$ = 90%

Attitude to Reliability (concerning damage):
      Voluntary involvement - concerned (C)
      Involuntary involvement - very concerned (VC)

Importance (I) (from Table 2) = 1
Risk Number $N_{R(I)} = N_L \times \frac{1}{I} = 10 \times 1 = 10$ [$R_{(I)}$ = 1 in 10]

From Figure 5
      Degree of Risk = Risky
      Risk description = High
      Range of risk ($N_{R(I)}$ = 7 to 17) $R_{(I)}$ = 1 in 7 to 1 in 17

Attitude To Risk
      Voluntary involvement - concerned (C)
      Involuntary involvement - very concerned (VC)

Example B2: Check risk for part of mine where there is
      - a Low Likelihood (L) of collapse
      - an Intermediate Importance (I) of use of area
      (small town
        centre)

Likelihood (L) from Figure 5 = 1 in 100 [N_L = 100]

Reliability (1 - 1/N_L) = 99%

Attitude to Reliability (concerning damage)
      Voluntary involvement - circumspect (Circ)
      Involuntary involvement - concerned (C)

Importance (I) from Table 2, I = 3
Risk Number $N_{R(I)} = N_L \times \frac{1}{I} = 100 \times \frac{1}{3} = 30$ [$R_{(I)}$ = 1 in 30]

From Figure 5
      Degree of Risk = Risky to some risk
      Risk description = Intermediate
      Range of risk ($N_{R(I)}$ = 17 to 70), R_I = 1 in 17 to 1 in 70

Attitude To Risk
      Voluntary involvement - concerned to circumspect
                    (C to Circ)
      Involuntary involvement - very concerned to
                     concerned (VC to C)

APPENDIX C

Calibration Examples

Cases involving areal risk with vulnerability of structure and structural materials also taken into account, for the severities of destruction and damage, are presented below.

$$R_{(I)(V)} = L.I. \frac{1}{V_s} \cdot \frac{1}{V_m} = \frac{1}{N_{R(I)(V)}}$$

The full range of V_s and V_m, from 0.7 to 3.0 see Tables 3 and 4 are covered in each example.

Example C1: Continuing Example A1 (Destruction). Areal risk $R_{(I)}$ = L.I = 1 in 300, range of $N_{R(I)}$ = 170 - 300 - 700

$N_{R(I)}$	V_s	V_m	$N_{R(I)(V)} = \dfrac{N_{R(I)}}{V_s \cdot V_m}$	Degree of Risk (from Figure 5)	Relative Risk (from Figure 5)
170-300-700	0.7	0.7	340-600-1400	Some risk	Intermediate to Low
170-300-700	1.4	1.4	85-150-350	Risky to some risk	High to Intermediate
					Very high
170-300-700	3.0	3.0	20-35-80	Very risky to risky	

Example C2: Continuing Example B2 (Damage): Areal risk $R_{(I)}$ = L.I. = 1 in 30, range of risk $N_{R(I)}$ = 17 - 30 - 70

$N_{R(I)}$	V_s	V_m	$N_{R(I)(V)} = \dfrac{N_{R(I)(V)}}{V_s \cdot V_m}$	Degree of Risk (from Figure 5)	Relative Risk (from Figure 5)
17-30-70	0.7	0.7	34-60-140	Some risk	Intermediate to low
17-30-70	1.4	1.4	9-15-35	Risky	High to intermediate
17-30-70	3.0	3.0	2-3-8	Very risky to risky	Very high

References

Ove Arup & Partners, 1983(a)   "Report on a study of Limestone Workings in the West Midlands". for the Department of the Environment, the Borough of Dudley Sandwell and Walsall and the West Midlands County Council.

Ove Arup & Partners, 1983(b)   Summary Report on above "Limestone Mines in the West Midlands: the legacy of mines long abandoned." HMSO.

DI Blockley, 1992,   "Engineering safety." McGraw Hill Book Co, Europe.

DI Blockley, 1993   Keynote address to this Conference.

K.W. Cole, 1987   "Building over abandoned shallow mines. A strategy for the engineering decisions on treatment" Ground Engineering May 1987 Vol 20 No 4.

K.W. Cole & I. Statham, 1992   "General (areal) subsidence above partial extraction mines "Ground Engineering March and April 1992 Vol 26 Nos. 2 and 3.

K.W. Cole, 1993   "Building over shallow mines. Paper 1: considerations of risk and reliability". Ground Engineering. January/February 1993, Vol. No. 1, Part 2 "Assessing risk" is in preparation.

H & SE, 1992   "The Tolerability of Risk from Nuclear Power Stations." Health and Safety Executive, London 1988; Revised 1992.

K.W. Cole, A.J. Turner and   "Limestone workings in the West Midlands".

N.J. O'Riordan, 1984   Proc. 2nd Conf. on Construction in Areas of Abandoned Mineworkings. Edinburgh.

27

N.J. O'Riordan, K.W. Cole
& D.J. Henkel, 1984

"Collapses of abandoned limestone mines in the West Midlands of England." Conf. on Design and Performance of underground excavations, BRM/BGS Cambridge.

N. J. O'Riordan, 1984

Internal communication concerning Importance Factors.

A.E. Griffith, 1991

"The collapse of the disused Tennat Salt Mine; Carrickfergus County Antrim, Northern Ireland" Ground Engineering November 1992, Vol. 24 No. 9.

Ove Arup & Partners,

1991 to 1993

Reports to Department of Economic Development (Department of Environment) of Northern Ireland. In particular Appendix D - "Risk assessment and probability" in Report on Site Investigation (Phase 1) of the French Park, International and Carrickfergus Mines in Carrickfergus County Antrim, Northern Ireland.

Arup Geotechnics 1992

Review of Mining Instability in Great Britain for the Department of the Environment. Volume 3/xi Case History, "Santon-Dragonby Ironstone Mine, Humberside".

C Starr

"Social benefit versus technological risk, what is our society willing to pay for safety", Science, Vol 165, 19, September 1969.

2. A question of judgement: expert or engineering?

B. O. SKIPP, Soil Mechanics Limited, UK, and G.WOO, EQI Limited, UK

SYNOPSIS. A distinction between expert and engineering judgement is identified and the attributes of both kinds of judgement are discussed with regard to two examples: a slope stbility analysis and fault modelling in seismic hazard analysis.

INTRODUCTION

During the past few decades, important changes have taken place affecting the way in which certain engineering safety decisions are made. These changes are associated with the development of risk-based methods for the design and assessment of engineering systems. A feature of these methods is the objective of quantifying the level of safety through estimating the likelihood of engineering failure. Because the tolerance of failures is usually low, failure likelihood cannot be inferred just from empirical frequency data, but must be gauged from a formal probabilistic analysis. The introduction of probabilistic concepts for treating uncertainty inevitably requires an engineer to exercise a form of judgement other than the professional engineering judgement which is developed during his or her career through training and practical experience. This other form of judgement is involved in all attempts at estimating probabilities, irrespective of application domain, and is generically termed expert judgement.

Engineering judgement is recognized as an essential tool of an engineer's trade, with much practical reliance being placed upon it, and professional kudos associated with it. However, an engineer's expert judgement, in the probabilistic sense of degree of belief, may not be honed through any specific training or previous experience; indeed, many engineers may be blissfully unaware of the very concept of an expert judgement distinct from the familiar engineering judgement. Faced with the task of expressing, in probabilistic terms, safety factors based on engineering judgement, many engineers find themselves ill-prepared and ill-equipped. One of the most

Risk and reliability in ground engineering. Thomas Telford, London, 1993

publicized and tragic case studies was the 1986 Challenger Shuttle disaster: NASA elected to rely on its engineering judgement that the rocket booster failure probability was 1 in 100,000, despite publication in 1983 of an estimate of 1 in 35, based on quantitative risk assessment, involving prior experience and Bayesian analysis (Cooke, 1991).

The distinction between expert and engineering judgement is more than of semantic interest. Engineers called upon to exercise probabilistic expert judgements may find themselves biasing their opinions in line with prior expectations; conversely, engineering judgements may be misconstrued as formally elicited expert judgements. Such terminological confusion can have serious potential consequences in all branches of engineering, not least in geotechnical engineering, where the ratio of speculation to observation is often high. Geotechnical engineers may have confidence in their choice of safety factors; but how many would have confidence in their estimates of equivalent failure likelihood?

Clarification of the distinction between expert judgement and engineering judgement is the primary purpose of this paper. To illustrate the underlying principles, a brief exposition of the basis for the distinction is given, followed by several actual examples drawn from the fields of slope stability and seismic hazard assessment.

WHAT IS EXPERT JUDGEMENT?

Uncertainty in decision-making exists in a multitude of forms, arising from a lack of information and knowledge; unreliability of data etc.. In as much as the study of uncertainty lies at the heart of probability theory, a decision made in the face of uncertainty is a probabilistic judgement, or, if made by a knowledgeable person, an expert judgement. Given that uncertainty pervades human existence at all times, and in almost all circumstances (de Finetti, 1970), expert judgement can be elicited over most issues of relevance to mankind, from trivia to the outbreak of thermonuclear war. Expert judgements of Think-Tanks are commonly sought in economic and political circles, but not in an engineering context, except within the narrow framework of a probabilistic risk assessment.

An assessment of risk is made quantitative through a probabilistic model which represents all the various processes and events which give rise to risk exposure. The choice of model and the parameterisation of a particular model are inevitably associated with uncertainty. According to the Bayesian paradigm, all entities whose values are unknown should have their uncertainties described by numbers that obey the rules of the probability calculus. In the limit of large datasets, these numbers would be obtainable using empirical frequency data alone, but, in practice, their resolution must involve some recourse to subjectivity. It is in enumerating subjective probabilities, which reflect degrees of belief, that expert judgement is elicited. The subjective element in assigning probabilities is often treated informally, or sometimes ignored to the extent that the very involvement of any expert judgement may be denied. But whatever attempts are made to slay the hydra of subjectivity in probability assignment, the myriad elusive forms of uncertainty ensure its survival in risk modelling.

It might be held that any judgement requiring expertise would count as an expert judgement (Bye et al., 1993). To the extent that judgements made by experts require their expertise, this is a true statement, but an expert judgement cannot be claimed by those lacking in experience or factual knowledge. It is an essential tenet of Bayesian theory that such experience and learning are vital factors in modifying subjective degrees of belief. The view that expert judgement is not so much a judgement made by experts, but rather a judgement requiring expertise, tends to encourage the notion that anyone's judgement is as good as any other's in expressing a degree of belief in a technical proposition. Such a devaluation of personal judgement neglects important differences in the informativeness and calibration of individuals, and the training they have received.

Expert judgements, properly elicited, are not arbitrary, but must satisfy various fundamental principles. In particular, they must be coherent with the axioms of probability theory, which provide systematic rules for the synthesis of subjective judgements. In particular, where expert judgements are elicited in respect of a multiplicity of values of a parameter, the numerical ranking of these values in itself serves as a logical restriction. To put it in mathematical terms: after revising beliefs to make them consistent, if and only if one believes that the state s is more likely than state s', then $P(s) > P(s')$. This consistency criterion is all too often neglected by those who suppose that subjective probabilities are arbitrary; in reality, the formulation of truly consistent judgements requires adoption of the structured Bayesian framework. In quantitative engineering risk assessment, where conservatism is liable to be spiral, the need to ensure consistency of all risk estimates serves as a constraint on individual excesses.

Recognizing the formal and mathematically rigorous definition of expert judgement within the context of probabilistic risk assessment, it is evidently unreasonable to expect elicitation to be successful without adequate training being provided in the measurement of uncertainty and the characterization of probability distributions. Experts in a specific engineering discipline may not be experts in measuring uncertainty: a task which seldom comes the way of engineers, except where frequencies may be enumerated. When asked to estimate probabilities, people tend to rely on informal rules-of-thumb. Examples of such heuristics are the tendency for estimates to be based on what can be most easily recalled by memory, and the tendency for upper and lower percentiles to be narrowly anchored to central values. Appreciation of the particular requirements of elicitation procedures, and awareness of the need for training, are starting points for engineers to come to terms with expert judgement as a complement to standard engineering judgement.

WHAT IS ENGINEERING JUDGEMENT?

By contrast with the mathematical formality of risk assessment, in standard civil engineering practice, judgement is much less tangible and less precisely defined, but rather is used in a holistic fashion. Thus engineering judgement is captured in colloquial statements of the form: 'To do it that way will lead you into difficulties', or, 'If you do it that way, you will be all right'. Such use of engineering judgement may well have set the initial conditions for the engineering project itself, and may be used to 'engineer a way out of trouble'.

Exercise of engineering judgement is required to compensate for a catalogue of possible shortcomings: uncertainty in soil characteristics, human errors, negligence, defects in materials, poor workmanship and construction practice, communications problems, not to mention weakness in making engineering judgements themselves. This recursive use of engineering judgement in estimating appropriate factors of safety defies quantification, except in the binary sense that inadequacy is ultimately exposed by failures, which have always provided valuable learning experience for honing engineering judgement.

From a traditional engineering perspective, diversity in the opinions of experts is hardly new; engineering judgements can be every bit as diverse and perverse. The consequence is that factors of safety will vary according to the engineer involved. Such differences are rarely analyzed systematically, because any investigation would transgress the boundaries of professional regulation. Outside the context of probabilistic risk assessment, judgements no longer need correspond with degrees of belief, and are free from the fundamental consistency requirements of the laws of probability. The relative merits of alternative engineering judgements are not bound by any rigorous mathematical structure, but then conventional deterministic engineering procedures do not have any such requirement.

TABLE I

Attributes of Engineering Judgement and Expert Judgement

Engineering Judgement	Expert Judgement
Not constrained by formal logic	Constrained by formal logic
Cannot be easily calibrated	Can be calibrated
May incorporate conservatisms	Must be true opinion
Tends to heuristic and holistic	Focuses on parameters

RISK ASSESSMENT OF SLOPE STABILITY

A prime geotechnical application of risk methodology is in
the study of slope stability. A systematic audit of
uncertainty in a risk-based analysis of slope stability
exposes the need to elicit expert judgement across a broad
range of topics. Included in this inventory are the
evaluation of geotechnical data; formulation of a general
geological model; definition of model elements;
characterisation of the strength of materials; and the
formulation of a slope failure model. A practical test case
for the risk assessment of slope stability is given by the
Stobswood opencast coal site details of which are given in
********** inthese proceedings.

In such a project many decisions have to be made, some fall
clearly within the definition of expert judgement, others
clearly can be regarded as engineering judgements. There are
also commercial judgements, management judgements and
judgements in the interpetation of regulatory requirements.
Many judgments which at first sight could be assigned to the
category of an engineering judgement can with examination and
perhaps decomposition are seen to be properly expert
judgements and are therfore reuired to fulfil the logical
canons. In Table II the suite of decisions which have had to
be made in the Stobswood case are listed and divided into the
two categories of judgement. It is clear that where the
parameters are concerned expert judgement has to be employed
and in order to assign ranges to these parameters for which
the number of tests on site does not permit a frequency
approach so Bayesian approaches are appropriate. In making
choices as to the failure model which is assumed the choice is
also amenable to the use of expert opinion in that
probabilities can be be assigned to one or other models and
logic tree formalism could then be employed.

FAULT MODELLING IN SEISMIC HAZARD ANALYSIS

Exposure to nearby active faults can sharply ratchet up the
level of seismic hazard at a site. Active faults which happen
to pass through a site constitute an even greater potential

33

TABLE II

Evaluation of principal components of opinion and judgement

Slope stability.

Determinstic approach for loosewall analysis	
Policy and setting up	
Decision to review previous analyses	1
Terms of reference for review	1
Decision to undertake literature review	1
Sufficiency or otherwise of existing data	1/2
Extent and type of further investigations	1/2
Evaluation of new geotechnical data	2*
Formulation of a general geological model	2*
Particularisation of model elements	2*
Definition of pavement composition	2*
Morphology of the pavement	2*
Persistence of weak layers in pavement	2*
Strength of pavement materials	2*
Assessment of operational field strength	2*
Characterisation of ground water regime	2
Classification and strength of fill	2*
Relative strengths of pavement and fill	2*
Formulation of slope failure model	2*
Choice of parameter bounds for sensitivity	2*
Choice of model	2*
Biplanar active-passive wedge	2*
Circular slip	2*
Selection of analysis procedure	1/2*
Sensitivity runs	1/2
Evaluation of earlier models	1/2
Evaluation of differences between results	1/2
Choice of alternative failure models	1/2
Parameterisation of alternatives	2*
Appropriateness of derived FOS	1
Effectiveness of methods to improve FOS	1
Definition of safe design slope	1
Probabilistic analysis	
Choice of software package	1/2
Choice of failure model (as above)	2
Identification of fixed elements	2
Identification of variable elements	2
(Strength, continuity of pavement materials)	2
Strength distribution of pavement materials	2
Truncation of distribution	2
Need for remedial action	1/2
Cost of remedial work	1/2
Cost of failure	1/2
Financial optimisation of slope design	1/2

Key:
- 1 : denotes engineering judgement or other judgement not expert judgement sensu stricto.
- 2 : denotes expert judgement sensu stricto.
- 2* : denotes technical judgements without explicit probabilism.
- 1/2 : denotes potential for expert judgement.

TABLE III

General Criteria for Active Faults

State	Evidence
Extinct	Fault does not displace materials or structures predating the current tectonic regime
	Fault does not displace material of age greater than the length of the longest seismic cycle of faults within the region.
	The mineralogy of mechanically continuous fault gouge is incompatible with the current stress / temperature regime
Unproven	Fault is a small secondary fracture
	Fault does not displace materials or structures younger than the average seismic cycle
	Fault style and orientation makes displacement unlikely in current tectonic regime
	Fault shows apparent geographical association with uncertainly located earthquake
	Fault has been active under a variety of different tectonic regimes
	Fault has a close analogue proved active
Active	Fault has appropriate dimensions and is uniquely implicated by well located large earthquake(s)
	Fault is the locus of well constrained earthquake hypocentre(s)
	fault displaces material younger than the duration of the current tectonic regime

engineering hazard, both in respect of higher levels of ground shaking, and also the possibility of ground displacement arising from fault rupture. Within a deterministic framework, as prevails for seismic design in many earthquake-prone areas of the world, resolution of the capability of a fault may alone decide the severity of the seismic design criteria, in terms of the size of the maximum credible event, if not the very viability of construction at the site.

With a deterministic approach adopted for dealing with faults, there is a significant element of engineering judgement in deciding how fault movement should be accommodated. Because there are no logical constraints on such judgements, and no formal procedure for their aggregation, partisan disputes are difficult to settle in a rational manner. A notorious example is the acrimonious controversy over the suspected faults underlying the nuclear test reactor at Vallecitos, California (Meehan, 1984).

From a probabilistic standpoint, there is no need to cut away the uncertainty surrounding a putative active fault so as to arrive at a simple 'yes-no' decision on fault capability. Tentative belief in the existence and active status of a local fault can be recognized within a systematic elicitation of expert judgement. Through the formal use of expert judgement, the probability of fault activity can be estimated, and used as logic-tree input into the probabilistic computation of seismic hazard. Thanks to the axiomatic foundations of probability theory, these probabilities constitute a logically consistent means to rank faults in perceived order of activity; the consistency of any alternative ranking procedure would have to be proved.

The need to rank faults for activity exists even in Britain, where probabilistic criteria are established for the safety of nuclear installations exposed to external hazards, including earthquakes. Geophysical, geological and seismological data contribute positive (and negative) evidence upon which probabilities of activity are assigned through the formal elicitation of expert judgement. An example of such an application is the assessment of seismic hazard at Hinkley Point C, in Somerset, where the potential activity of the Watchet-Cothelstone-Hatch Fault has been subject to expert scrutiny.

The decision to model that fault was made on the basis of a set of criteria developed by the Seismic Hazard Working Party of the CEGB (now Nuclear Electric plc) and listed in Table II. This decision was one of many which had to be made in the full hazard assessment and these have been listed in Table III. Again as with the example of loose wall stability, there are clearly those decisions which call for the use of expert opinion, usually those relating to parameterisation and those which fall outside that category.

TABLE IV

Evaluation of principal components of opinion and judgement

Seismic Hazard Assessment   (Sheet 1 of 2)

Policy and setting up	1
Formation of SHWP	1
Formulation of terms of reference for SHWP	1
Choice of ultimate deliverable	1
PGA (Max) at site	
PGA at specified exceedance probability	
Other hazard inputs:	
Site dependent RS, URS, surface rupture	1
Sufficiency of existing information	1/2
Development of data gathering strategy	1
Range and detail of search	1/2
Proactive data aquisition	1/2
Evaluation of gathered data:	
Quality rating of geological data	2
Level of knowledge of faults	2
Fault activity status	2
Quality rating of seismological data	2
Completeness	2
Locational accuracy	2
Ground motion hazard	
Choice of hazard modelling route - deterministic or probabilistic	1
Choice of hazard modelling software (PRISK)	1/2
Protocols for seismic source definition	2
Area source	2
Fault source	2
Protocols for fault source participation	2
Protocols of model boundary definition	2
Delineation of model boundaries	2
Delineation of area sources	2
Testing differentation of sources	2
Delineation of participating fault sources	2
Parameterisation of source seismicity .	2
Mmax (WDD)	2
Focal depth (WDD)	2
Activity rate (WDD)	2
b (WDD)	2
Choice of attenuation law	2
Scatter on attentation law (WDD)	2
Choice of sensitivity runs on basic model	2
Procedures for evaluating sensitivity runs	2
Evaluation of sensitivity runs	2
Characterisation of site: hard, intermediate, soft	2
Selection of site dependent RS	2
Decision to proceed to URS	1/2
Choice of frequency dependent attenuation relationship	2
Surface fault rupture hazard	
Protocols for candidate fault	
Activity status	2
Proximity to site	2
Size	2
Location on site	2
Extent on site	2
Protocols for clearance (ie sanitisation")	2
Activity status - extinct/active	2
Evaluation of status	2
Decision on candidacy	2

TABLE IV

Evaluation of principal components of opinion and judgement

Seismic Hazard Assessment   (Sheet 2 of 2)

Probabilistic assessment of rupture hazard	
Parmeterisation of candidate fault	
Fault geometry	
Length of segment	2
Hade of segment	2
Style of motion	2
M max(WDD) + constraints	2
b value(WDD)	2
Activity rate(WDD)	2
Focal depth (WDD)	2
Magnitude – displacement regression – scatter (WDD)	2
Geotechnical moderators	2

Key:
  1 : denotes engineering judgement or other judgement not
      expert judgement sensu stricto.
  2 : denotes expert judgement sensu stricto.
 2* : denotes technical judgements without explicit probabilism.
1/2 : denotes potential for expert judgement.

WDD : weighted discrete dsitribution used in PRISK
 RS : response spectrum
PGA : uniform risk spectrum
Mmax : peak ground acceleration
  b : slope of Gutenberg-Richter recurrence relation

CONCLUSIONS

The colloquial use of the word judgement is so pervasive, that
technical distinctions in meaning might seem a subtlety of
jargon only to be appreciated by a lexicographer. However, in
the context of engineering probabilistic risk assessment, the
differences between expert and engineering judgement are
sufficient to affect system safety in a tangible way. The
normal training and development of an engineer naturally
emphasizes the role of engineering judgement. However, an
engineer may not be aware of modern concepts of encoding
probabilities through the formal elicitation of expert
judgement. Ignorant of such techniques of risk analysis, such
an engineer would be poorly equipped for the task of
expressing engineering safety in probabilistic terms.

Differences of opinion over safety issues will always be
present; but terminological misconceptions are avoidable.
Where an engineering judgement is unwittingly offered in place
of an expert judgement, or vice versa, problems can be
expected. One area of potential importance is litigation. As
Bayesian methods become accepted as a means for weighing
evidence in courts of law (Kadane and Schum, 1992), there will
be a need to clarify the types of judgement offered by
professional engineers in this context.

The authors aknowledge the permission Nuclear Electric plc to
refer to Hinkley Point and the support of Soil Mechanics
Limited and EQEI Limited. This paper in number in the series
generated by the Seismic Hazard Working Party of Nuclear
Electric plc.

REFERENCES

Bye R.D., Inkester J.E., Patchett C.M. (1993) A Regulatory
View of Uncertainty and Conservatism in the Seismic Design of
Nuclear Power and Chemical Plant.

Cooke R.M. (1991) Experts in Uncertainty. Oxford University
Press.

de Finetti B. (1970) Teoria Delle Probabilità. Giulio
Einaudi, Torino.

Kadane J.B., Schum D.A. (1992) Opinions in Dispute: the
Sacco-Vanzetti Case, in Bayesian Statistics 4, Oxford
University Press.

Mallard D.J., Higginbottom, I.E., Muir-Wood, R. and B.O.Skipp,
(1991) Recent developments in the methodology of seismic
hazard assessment. Civil Engineering in the Nuclear Industry,
ed R. Dexter-Smith, Thomas Telford, London.

Meehan R.L. (1984) The Atom and the Fault. M.I.T.

3. Capturing engineering judgement in geotechnical design

J. OLIPHANT, Heriot-Watt University, UK

SYNOPSIS.   The purpose of this paper is to present a methodology for eliciting and interpreting expert knowledge from geotechnical engineers. The structured approach, labelled grounded theory, has been used in sociological research for analysing qualitative data and has been adapted here to analyse material from interviewing experienced retaining wall designers. The method provided a structure for developing a set of hierarchical organised and logically related propositions which modelled data and expert opinion for the design of retaining walls. The hierarchical model forms the knowledge base of a computer based advisory system for the selection of retaining walls.

INTRODUCTION

1.   Geotechnical engineers are primarily concerned with the design and construction of geotechnical structures which are either supported by or constructed from soil or rock.   Soil is used as a foundation to support buildings,highways,bridges and embankments as well as being used as a construction material. Geotechnical structures also retain soil from excavations and underground openings. The geotechnical engineer is required to design economical structures which are safe and serviceable. They will often have to provide an acceptable balance between risk of failure and cost which is appropriate to both the client and project.

2.   The geotechnical engineer will form part of a design team and work closely with: structural engineers on foundations and retaining structures; civil engineers on earthworks and foundations; and with planners on feasibility studies. The primary role of the geotechnical engineer will vary depending on the nature of the project. For example, on major road projects, the geotechnical engineer will provide significant input from desk study through preliminary and main ground investigation to detailed design of embankments, cuttings and bridge foundations. While, for small industrial units on prepared sites, the geotechnical engineer may only provide limited input such as a brief desk study, localised site investigation and foundation design advice.

3.   Engineering soil and rock are products of natural processes and, hence, are highly variable and display complex behaviour. Geotechnical engineers

Risk and reliability in ground engineering. Thomas Telford, London, 1993

will have to work with incomplete and imprecise data and to achieve a successful design will rely heavily on their judgement. A high degree of engineering judgement is a necessary requirement for the successful practice of geotechnical engineering. Few people in the profession would disagree with this statement, but few people would agree on the meaning of engineering judgement. Peck (1984) has outlined the essential character of judgement in geotechnical engineering. The main facets of judgement he outlined are :

(a) *A sense of proportion* ; obtaining a feel for the size of things and examining the results of a calculation against what is reasonable ; and

(b) *A sense of fitness* ; obtaining a feel for the appropriateness of the solution and, hence, avoid solving the wrong problem.

4. The successful design of a geotechnical structure will involve consideration of the components given in Figure 1 (adapted from Lambe & Whitman,1969). Using this figure, we can define geotechnical design as the overall design process, from inception to completion; while, geotechnical engineering would be a subset of design and relates to engineering aspects or components of the design e.g. problem solving, prediction of performance, interpreting information. The design will often require a sound knowledge of soil mechanics, a knowledge of engineering geology and site investigation procedures, an understanding of economics, experience and a high degree of engineering judgement. While the increased complexity of the problems geotechnical engineers are able to solve is almost entirely due to the growth of soil mechanics, the need for judgement has not reduced. A high level of judgement is usually the characteristic that one recognizes in an expert in geotechnical design.

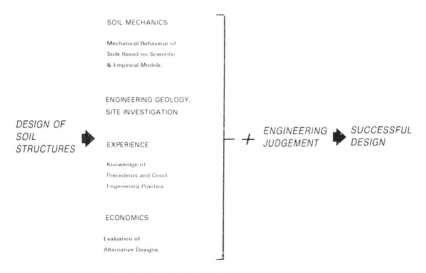

Fig.1. Geotechnical design process

5. The application of knowledge-based system technology to geotechnical design has the potential of providing an effective way of documenting and disseminating this expertise which is important when it is expensive and scarce. The objective of a knowledge-based system (KBS) is not to replace the experts in geotechnics but to make their knowledge more widely available and permanently stored on computer. The main purpose of this paper is to describe a methodology for eliciting and interpreting this form of expert geotechnical knowledge for the design of earth retaining walls. However, prior to this, it will prove useful for later discussion to describe the nature of geotechnical design at a deeper level.

NATURE OF GEOTECHNICAL DESIGN

6.   The assessment of safety of geotechnical structures is normally based on descriptions of behaviour using theoretical models. The performance of any model will attempt to be representative of the behaviour of the geotechnical structure. However, in view of the idealisations made for mathematical analysis, there will be some degree of mismatch between the predictions of the model and the behaviour of the completed structure. Clearly, some of the major judgements that a geotechnical engineer has to make are concerned with the uncertainties surrounding the nature and size of the parameters in a theoretical model (parameter uncertainty) as well as the quality of the model itself (system uncertainty).   The engineer must also consider gross uncertainty; the possible occurrence of external random hazards, such as fires, floods and explosions as well as the possibility of human error. The management of human based error is extremely difficult and is normally dealt with by ensuring proper professional competence and conduct.

7.   Whilst the science of soil mechanics may be strong, significant uncertainty does exist about the relationship between the theoretical models and actual behaviour of geotechnical structures. It is helpful to distinguish between comparisons in two sets of circumstances WIL and WOL (Blockley,1980). If theoretical predictions are compared with laboratory test results this has been done in the WIL (World Inside the Laboratory). If however the theory is compared with field experience this has been done in the WOL (World Outside the Laboratory).

8. A scientist will think that good performance in the WIL is necessary but not sufficient for a good performance in the WOL. The engineer, with the scientific approach, will argue that before progress can be made in the WOL, progress must be made in the WIL. The practical design engineer, working in a commercial environment, will argue that whilst it is agreeable if you have time and resources to work in the WIL, it is the WOL which is important. For example, the engineer will formulate empirical rules and judgements based on previous experience but will do this with knowledge of some of the techniques developed by scientists.

9.   Geotechnical design and soil mechanics have made good progress in both the WIL and WOL. Evidence for the former is the fact that there are many successful geotechnical structures. Critical state soil mechanics is one example of evidence of progress in the WIL. It provides a sound theoretical basis for the subject, but still requires interpretation when used in the WOL.

10.   System uncertainty is dominant in geotechnical design and has to be tackled by feedback from the WIL and WOL. Feedback from the WIL is an essential part of the development of a scientific theory. By contrast feedback from the WOL is difficult to organise in a significant theoretical manner; it rests in empirical rules and in the minds of experienced engineers. The use of knowledge-based systems provides a means of formally capturing this knowledge. A methodology is now presented for eliciting and interpreting this knowledge from geotechnical engineers.

KNOWLEDGE ACQUISITION

Background

11.   Knowledge acquisition can be defined as the process of obtaining knowledge from many sources (e.g. domain expert, text books, reports, codes of practice) to aid knowledge-based system development. It includes knowledge elicitation the process by which knowledge is obtained from the domain expert, and the interpretation technique used to analyse this knowledge. These two processes are interrelated and often overlap during system development. The elicitation process is often directed by the choice of interpretation model used to analyse the elicited knowledge.

12.   The knowledge engineer usually obtains the domain knowledge through direct interaction with the expert. In the majority of cases this interaction consists of a series of interviews to elicit the knowledge. This can often be arduous and time consuming and therefore requires great skill and patience on the part of the knowledge engineer. The problems that a knowledge engineer might face have been discussed by Hart (1986), and suggests that :

> *"Most of the problems are caused by the fact that the process of knowledge elicitation requires many hours of an expert who is already busy and has many demands on his time."*

Grounded theory analysis

13.   It is important in KBS development to adopt a structured approach when analysing elicited knowledge. A structured approach, labelled grounded theory, has been used in sociological research for analysing qualitative data. Grounded theory was developed by Glaser and Strauss (1968) to enable researchers to develop their own theories from qualitative data.   The developed theory is more than a conjecture of the problem, it is a systematic set of statements held as a precise explanation of facts or phenomena. The

adequacy or validity of the theory is then judged by how closely it fits the examined phenomena.

14.   The original methodology developed by Glaser and Strauss has been supplemented by practical methods of handling qualitative material for analysis. One such method is outlined in detail by Turner (1981) and illustrated by example (Turner, 1983).

15.   The theory provides a useful aid for the knowledge engineer when analysing interview data. Later discussion (para. 27) provides a detailed description of the use of an adapted version of grounded theory analysis to analyse material obtained from interviewing experienced retaining wall designers in the development of a knowledge base.

Development of a knowledge base

16.   Retaining wall design.

Earth retaining walls are commonly used to support soils to maintain a difference in elevation of the ground surface. A wide variety of different forms of retaining wall is available. Recent developments in wall construction techniques (e.g. reinforced soil) and the use of new materials (e.g. geosynthetics) has forced the engineer to look at these new developments. One view of how the design procedure progresses is shown in Figure 2.

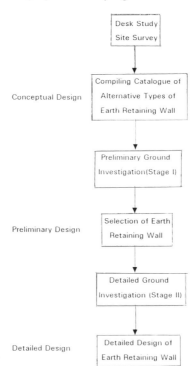

Fig. 2. Retaining wall design procedure

17. The preliminary site survey and desk study begin the design procedure. For the purpose of identifying the particular requirements of each wall, it is often convenient to carry out the site investigation in two stages. Stage I provides a broad picture of the sub-soil profile and the groundwater conditions across the site. Stage II provides a detailed picture of the sub-soil profile in terms of its variability and mechanical properties. The geotechnical engineer will be faced with the difficult task of planning the site investigation and interpreting the gathered information for design purposes.

18. Selection of an appropriate retaining wall is not straightforward, it requires considerable judgement and experience. The factors effecting wall selection cover the soil and groundwater conditions, environmental factors, construction requirements, the nature and size of the contract, and economic factors.

19. The final stage in the design procedure concerns the numerical calculations carried out to ensure the safety of the selected wall. At this stage, the engineer will have to outline the calculations to be done, and make sound judgements on what design parameters to adopt in these calculations.

20. At the preliminary design stage, the geotechnical engineer (designer) will often have to make decisions based on incomplete and imprecise information and will do so by using empirical rules that have been developed from experience. A knowledge-based system has been developed by the author to capture these rules and provide the engineer with a powerful decision aid. The paper concentrates on the development of the knowledge base for this system.

21.   Knowledge elicitation.
The process adopted by the author to elicit knowledge from experienced retaining wall designers can be described in four stages.
     1. Initial Contact
     2. Research Objectives and Requirements
     3. Recorded Interview
     4. Model Refinement.

22. Initial contact (Stage 1) with experienced retaining wall designers within a number of civil engineering organisations in central Scotland produced favourable responses. Follow-up meetings were arranged with the designers of three civil engineering consultants and two local authorities to discuss the research work. An assurance was given to all interviewees of complete confidentiality and, hence, no direct mention will be made of names or sources of information.

23. At the first meeting the research objectives and requirements were discussed with the designers (Stage 2). The objectives were to investigate in detail a number of recent case studies of different retaining wall types with a view to establishing the reasons, whether financial, constructional, aesthetic, or whatever, that a wall was chosen. A total of eleven case studies, covering six different types of wall, were made available by the designers. Time

constraints limited the number of case studies and availability limited the range of wall types.

24.　At the beginning of　Stage 3 a work schedule was planned for subsequent recorded interviews. A check-list was drawn up which was helpful in probing and prompting the designer into producing answers as fully as possible. Although specific questions were set out the interviews tended to be semi-structured　reflecting the responses of the interviewee i.e. the designer.

25.　The methodical recording and cross-referencing of interview data is a key factor in the success of elicitation and subsequent interpretation. For this reason the interviews with the designers were tape-recorded. The interview technique adopted was reclassification. Here the designer was asked, for each case study, to work back from the goal "select suitable wall type" to sub-goals which were reclassified into evidence for the goal. The sub-goals were successively reclassified until the evidence had been broken down into more specific facts. This allowed the production of reasoning chains between goals, sub-goals and facts.

26.　The interviews produced a recorded description of the designer's knowledge and the way in which it was manipulated to select a particular retaining wall.　Transcripts of the recordings were interpreted using an adapted version of grounded theory analysis, introduced earlier, and used to impose structure on the interview data.　This knowledge interpretation model is described next and includes a report on its refinement - Stage 4 given above.

27.　Knowledge interpretation

In order to use the adapted version of grounded theory as a knowledge interpretation model the following steps are carried out.
   1. Develop Categories
   2. Exhaust Categories
   3. Expand Categories
   4. Develop Connections Between Categories
   5. Model Refinement.

28.　Develop categories

The first step involves the development of labelled categories from the transcribed text of the tape-recordings which represent features of the information.　A method suggested by Turner (1981) involves taking each paragraph of the transcript in turn and noting the categories or labels needed to account for all the significant phenomena on separate file-cards. The categories describe the information as precisely as possible and form concise titles.　Figure 3 represents an example of a actual file-card showing a number of entries made relating to the wall selection category for the embedded wall case study.　The figure also illustrates a scheme for referencing and cross-referencing cards.

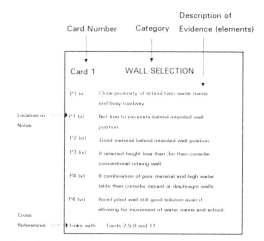

Fig. 3 Example of qualitative data category card

29. Exhaust categories

Examples of a given category are accumulated until no further examples from the data can be found. The exhaustive list of examples contained within the category label can be viewed as the elements necessary to validate the category. For example, in Figure 3, the category wall selection for the embedded wall case study is exhausted and validated for the given six elements. These elements will not necessarily occur at the same level in the hierarchical model but will be expanded into subordinate or superordinate propositions. This process of expanding categories is described in the next step.

30. Expand categories

The essence of this step is to expand the categories and elements for each case study to form a hierarchical model of the decision process for wall selection. The technique developed by the author is relatively straightforward but requires some practice.

31. The first stage in the development is to establish the top-most proposition (element or category) of the hierarchy ; the one most vague and imprecise. This proposition will represent the main objective of the study. For the preliminary design of retaining walls, the top-most proposition is "The choice of retaining wall is appropriate".

32. The next stage is to write down subordinate propositions which together are logically sufficient for the truth, validity or dependability of the first proposition at a level of detail which is only slightly less vague or more precise. However, we cannot ensure the sufficiency of these propositions for the first proposition, but can be happy with the fact that the most influential necessary conditions have been included. Thus at the preliminary design stage the top-level proposition can be developed as :

"The choice of retaining wall is appropriate if the construction process is appropriate and the design process is appropriate"

33.   Here the quality of choice has been modelled by the two most influential sub-concepts construction and safety which are both rather vague and imprecise.   Other concepts such as "environmental impact", "use of wall", "maintenance procedures" could be included for completeness. The task of developing subordinate propositions is termed a top-down analysis and can equally be applied at any level in the hierarchy and to either elements or categories.

34.   The third stage in the development is to carry out a bottom-up analysis on propositions and therefore establish superordinate propositions. This begins by   establishing the precisely defined or bottom-most propositions. These facts would correspond to many of the elements of categories.   The procedure is then to write down the proposition which is logically necessary for the truth, validity or dependability of the bottom-most proposition at a level of detail which is only slightly more vague or less precise.   Again the bottom-up analysis can be applied at any level in the hierarchy and to categories as well as to elements.

35.   The formulation of the hierarchical model for retaining wall selection can be seen as an exhaustive expansion of existing propositions by applying top-down and bottom-up analyses.

36.   Develop connections between categories

Once the general structure of the hierarchy has been produced, connections between categories or propositions need to be developed. It is important to be aware of three conditions : Duplication, Fragmentation and Negation.

37.   Valid duplication occurs when the same propositions have a different contextual meaning at different positions in the hierarchy. For example, the proposition   "ground conditions are suitable" would be relevant to both construction and excavation requirements and, hence, would appear under both these categories.

38.   Expansion of the propositions should provide for a uniform loss of vagueness or imprecision when travelling from top to bottom of the hierarchy.   If fragmented expansion does occur then this will normally be picked up at the model refinement stage.

39.   Retaining wall designers often selected a type of wall by adopting a process of elimination and, hence, gave reasons why a certain wall type was not chosen.   These negative reasons were incorporated directly into the hierarchy in order to ease both understanding of the hierarchy and logical inference.

40.   Each proposition in the development of the hierarchy is a rule of the form

$$X \text{ if } (Y1 * Y2 * Y3 * \ldots * Yn)$$

where (X and Y) are propositions and (if and *) are logical relations and (*) represents (and, or, not).   The proposition X is the consequence and Y the antecedent of the above rule, however each proposition will normally form the consequence of one rule and the antecedent of another within the hierarchy. The exception to this is when the antecedent proposition is a fact or base relation.

41. The propositions $(Y1 * Y2 * Y3 * \ldots * Yn)$ are considered to be logically sufficient for X. Thus $(Y1 * Y2 * Y3 * \ldots * Yn) \supset X$ where $\supset$ is the implication operator.

42. A very basic question now arises ; how can we ensure the sufficiency of $(Y1 * Y2 * Y3 * \ldots * Yn)$ for X ? The answer is of course that we cannot. However, in practical terms we can list as many of the necessary conditions we can think of and recognize the basic incompleteness of this or any other model.

43. The hierarchical model is therefore a deductive system of propositions which are conditions within the hierarchy. The nature of *modus ponens* implication is such that only information with true, valid or dependable characteristics will be transmitted up through the hierarchy.

44. Model refinement

This final and very important step of the collaborative process refers to the refinement of the draft hierarchical model previously produced. Here the experienced retaining wall designers were given the opportunity to criticize the model, and provide any missing information or correct any shortcomings they thought necessary. The author had to make certain refinements in the form of condensing or expanding certain propositions. Altogether, little alteration to the draft model was required.

45. Wall selection model

The propositions which make up the wall selection model are ordered according to their degree of generality. The higher propositions are the most general or vague propositions, whereas the lower propositions are well defined or precise propositions. The latter propositions constitute the facts of the problem.

46. The complete retaining wall selection model has been fully described by Oliphant (1988). However, for the purposes of this paper, the upper levels of the model will be discussed (Figures 4(a), (b), (c) and (d)). The layout of these figures is intended to clarify the hierarchical structure and should be read by inserting an "if" after each proposition. For example, the choice of retaining wall is appropriate if the series of necessary conditions is also appropriate (Figure 4(a)). The conditions are not sufficient because we cannot guarantee that every condition affecting wall selection has been included. A "catch-all" proposition is included to clarify this, shown as "other factors considered appropriate for choosing retaining wall".

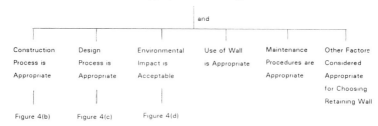

Fig. 4(a)   Upper levels of hierarchical model for wall selection

47.   The knowledge base can be categorized under three separate parts :

    1. Construction Process
    2. Design Process
    3. Environmental Impact & Miscellaneous Factors

and each is now briefly discussed.

48.   Construction process (Figure 4(b))

In order that the construction process is considered appropriate it is necessary that the following factors are satisfied :

(a) the contractor is capable of carrying out the wall construction work;

(b) the time for construction is easily available;

(c) the relationship between the design and construction processes is satisfactory; and

(d) the construction methods adopted are suitable.

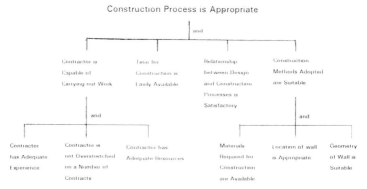

Fig. 4(b)   Upper levels of hierarchical model for construction process

49.   Factor (a) considers whether or not the contractor has the resources to construct the wall and the experience to carry out the construction work effectively. The contractor should be capable of executing the construction work as trouble free as possible and hence reduce the risk of construction error.

50.   Factor (b) is associated with any time constraint imposed on construction. This becomes important when the successful construction of a large project depends on the speedy construction of a retaining wall.

51.   Do the contractor's personnel, available for site work and supervision, appreciate the technical problems associated with the wall design ?   This is the question posed by factor (c).

52.   Factor (d) accounts for the suitability of the adopted construction method in terms of three necessary conditions : a suitable wall geometry ; the materials required for construction being easily available ; and an appropriate wall location.

53.   Design process   (Figure 4 (c))

The design process is appropriate if the relationship between the design and construction processes is satisfactory and it is expected that a safe wall can be designed.   The wall safety hierarchy allows the designer to assess the importance of gross errors and the dependability of the design model as well as carrying out the normal design procedures.

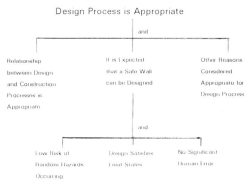

Fig. 4(c)   Upper levels of hierarchical model for design process

54.   Environmental impact & miscellaneous factors (Figure 4(d))

A retaining wall's impact on the environment is acceptable if it satisfies the criteria specified by the appropriate local authoritative body governing the general appearance of the wall, and if it is environmentally acceptable in the intended position. Figure 4 (d) shows some environmental factors relating to the choice of the wall with the surrounding area for certain types of wall.

55.   Two further necessary conditions for wall selection are the use and maintenance of the wall. The use of the wall is appropriate if it carries out the function or functions it was originally designed for. If a retaining wall is to be selected then any maintenance procedures carried out during its design life must be appropriate.

DISCUSSION

56.   The hierarchical model for wall selection was derived on the basis of a number of interviews with experienced retaining wall designers. The

interviews were structured around a number of case studies of different types of retaining wall. The adaptation of grounded theory analysis has provided a methodology for developing a set of hierarchical organised and logically related propositions which have modelled data and expert opinion for the problem of retaining wall selection. The structure of the knowledge allows for easy expansion as new knowledge emerges from the consideration of further case studies.

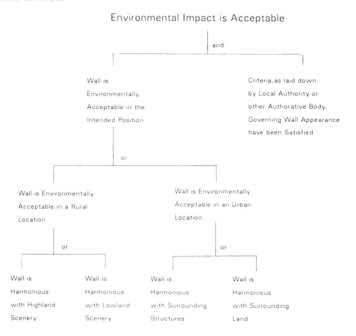

Fig. 4(d)   Upper levels of hierarchical model for environmental impact

57. The knowledge base hierarchy forms part of a knowledge-based system which has been set up to explore the wall selection process (Oliphant and Blockley,1991). The system has recently been developed to work on an IBM compatible PC under the Leonardo environment and is fully reported by Demetriou and Oliphant (1993). By using the facilities of Leonardo the user may consult the system for advice through interrogation of the knowledge base. Work is now being carried out to improve the quality of the knowledge base by extending the number and range of case studies examined.

SUMMARY AND CONCLUSIONS
58.   The mismatch between the predictions of the model and the behaviour of completed geotechnical structures involves three components of uncertainty; gross, system and parameter. Parameter and system uncertainty have been separately defined in order to set in context the role of feedback from the WIL and WOL. System uncertainty has to be tackled by feedback

both from the WIL and WOL. However, feedback from the WOL is difficult to organise in a theoretical manner because it rests in empirical rules and in the minds of experienced engineers. A methodology for organising and interpreting this knowledge from experienced retaining wall designers has been described.

59. The methodology was based on grounded theory analysis and used to analyse case study data obtained from interviewing experienced retaining wall designers. The steps necessary for using this methodology have been described. The outcome was a set of hierarchically organised and logically related propositions which modelled expert opinion for the preliminary design of retaining walls. The knowledge base hierarchy was discussed in terms of three main parts ; the construction process, the design process and environmental impact. It has been used in the development of a knowledge-based system for providing advice on the selection of retaining walls.

REFERENCES
1.   Blockley,D.I. (1980) *The nature of structural design and safety*, Ellis Horwood Ltd.
2.   Demetriou,I.& Oliphant,J. (1993) *Computer-based advisory system for the selection of earth retaining walls*, MSc thesis, Heriot-Watt University.
3.   Glaser,B. & Strauss,A. (1968) *The discovery of grounded theory: Strategies for Qualitative Research*, London: Weidenfeld and Nicolson.
4.   Hart,A. (1986) *Knowledge Acquisition for Expert Systems*, Kogan Page Ltd., London.
5.   Lambe,T.W. & Whitman,R.V. (1969) *Soil Mechanics*, John Wiley & Sons, NY.
6.   Oliphant,J. (1988) *Controlling safety and capturing engineering judgement in geotechnical design*, PhD thesis, University of Bristol.
7.   Oliphant,J. & Blockley,D.I. (1991) KBS: advisor on the selection of earth retaining structures, *Computers and Structures*, 40, 1, 173-183.
8.   Peck,R.B. (1984) *Judgment in Geotechnical Engineering, The Professional Legacy of Ralph B Peck*, J.Dunicliffe & D.U.Deere (Eds.), John Wiley and Sons, NY.
9.   Turner,B.A. (1981) Some practical aspects of qualitative data analysis: one way of organising the cognitive processes associated with the generation of grounded theory, *Quality and Quantity*, 15, 225-247.
10.   Turner,B.A. (1983) The use of grounded theory for the qualitative analysis of organizational behaviour, *Journal of Management Studies*, 20, 3, 333-348.

4. The impact of ground risks in construction on project finance

N. M. H. ALHALABY and I. L. WHYTE, UMIST, UK

SYNOPSIS: Construction projects of industrial, commercial and other buildings as well as roads, bridges and other civil engineering works are vulnerable to ground related problems from natural or man-made unforeseen conditions.   Clients, consultants and contractors expose themselves to high financial risk unless a good quality and adequate site investigation is commissioned in the early stages of a project. The benefits (in financial terms) of adequate site investigation can be demonstrated by risk modelling. This approach is described in the paper using data from a case study as the basis for the model.

INTRODUCTION

1. A statistical review of projects (1,2) revealed that 50% of commercial buildings and 37% of industrial buildings experienced delay due to unforeseen ground conditions. All developments on second-hand sites met unexpected ground during construction. Such events increase construction costs and may lead to disputes between the involved parties. Also the effect on the project's whole life financial performance can be significant, particularly if commissioning is delayed. Reports from NEDO (1,2) state that the most frequent origin of overruns and long delays (defined as being in excess of 10 weeks) are unforeseen obstacles in the ground.

2. The possible level of financial uncertainty from ground conditions has not been investigated in detail in the past. Research (3,4) has shown that this can be possible using financial risk management analysis. This indicated there to be significant reductions in the level of financial risks from improved site investigation planning, procedure and practice. The return to a client (ie – the amount of reduced financial uncertainty) was shown from these early studies to exceed by orders of magnitude the increased investigation/exploration costs. This paper reports on a continuation of this research in which data from a number of projects has

been used as input to the model analysis. The benefits and returns obtainable from an improved and adequate site investigation are quantified.

3. Quantification of the financial risks is of benefit since it leads to a better understanding of the geotechnical uncertainties and an appreciation of reliable site investigation. The benefit can be shown not only to those directly involved in construction (designers, contractors) but also to clients, financiers and insurers.

4. Data for model analysis has been obtained from a number of schemes, including specialist works (tunnels), commercial and industrial contracts. The results given in this paper are from an industrial development.

RISK ANALYSIS AND MANAGEMENT

5. In engineering and construction the most serious effects of risks are (5):
    (a) Failure to keep within the cost estimate
    (b) Failure to achieve the required completion date
    (c) Failure to meet the required quality and operational
        requirements.

6. Construction, as an industry, is susceptible to risk and uncertainty. These need to be managed and accounted for, most importantly in the early stages of a scheme. The systematic management of risk can be developed in three stages:

    (a) Identify the risks
    (b) Quantify their effect (risk analysis)
    (c) Respond to the risks (risk management)

7. Risk to projects originating from ground conditions can be often avoided by adequate and full site investigation. Ground uncertainty can be one of the most sensitive factors on the financial performance of a project. If the uncertainties are not recognised prior to start on site then serious delay and extra cost can occur.

Risk analysis

8. The simplest form of risk analysis, Deterministic Risk Analysis, handles each risk independently of others and no attempt is made to assess the probability of occurrence. Probabilistic Risk Analysis is more sophisticated and of more value in that the probabilities and independence of identified

risks are assessed. In such an analysis, risks are treated as variables having a specified probability distribution between upper and lower limits. Analysis as to how the risks can occur in combination is achieved by a random sampling approach (different values of each variable are selected and combined in a Monte Carlo simulation). Calculations are thus performed many times using the random values of each variable between the upper and lower bound limits. A number of uncertain variables can thus be combined to calculate an overall uncertainty for the project.

9. The effect of a change in a particular variable, or group of variables, can be investigated by means of a sensitivity study. In this, the values of variables are changed independently and the consequent effects are calculated. Thus the most critical (ie – the most sensitive) variables can be recognised, this is a valuable aid to the management strategy.

10. A computer program, CASPAR (Computer Aided Simulation for Project Appraisal and Review) has been developed (6). This models the interaction of time, resources, cost and revenue throughout the life of a project. It is based on a precedence network in which separate activities of work are linked together, with costs and revenues attached, to form a cost model. The cost (and time) implications of risks and uncertainties can be modelled and presented in terms of financial parameters such as NPV, IRR. Sensitivity and probabilistic risk analysis can also be performed.

Risk analysis modelling

11. The CASPAR program has been used to develop a risk analysis model to perform the following functions:

(a) to illustrate the sensitivity of various risk variables on a construction project.

(b) to calculate the effects of an uncertainty in ground conditions on the estimated cost and duration of a project.. This would normally be done during the planning stage.

(c) to quantify the effect of work arising from unforeseen ground conditions on the cost and completion date for a project, ie – to the end of construction.

12. The risk analysis model has been used on a series of case studies ranging from tunnels to commercial development and an industrial site.

Financial and contract data was used in the analysis. The results of a study from an industrial site are presented below:

CASE STUDY : AN INDUSTRIAL DEVELOPMENT

13. The development case study is on a brownfield site. The land had been previously occupied by industrial works and had been previously reclaimed for light industrial schemes. It was sold to a development company for the construction of a large industrial warehouse and offices. Before construction, agreement had been reached with the industrial client on rental terms and building specification. A fixed commissioning date was contracted for to meet commercial targets, delay would lead to heavy losses by the client and penalty to the developer.

Ground conditions

14. The site covered a large area which had previously consisted of several plots for light industrial use, all prior surveys having been planned for this purpose. The site was then purchased for a larger scheme which was planned to heavy industrial standards. It was known that the site contained underground obstructions from old foundations, etc.; these having been detected by desk study and exploration. The site purchase price contained an allowance for these obstructions and no additional pre-contract surveys were commissioned. Grid borings at 50 m centres across the site enabled the fill thickness to be determined with reasonable reliability, the fill being underlain by a thick layer of mixed Glacial Deposits.

Construction

15. Using the site information the structure was designed with driven steel pile foundations, their locations were chosen to avoid large obstructions. As piling started, many piles could not be driven through the fill due to obstructions that were not foreseen. As earthworks started, old foundations and structural remains were encountered which had not been previously recorded. Major earthworks (deep excavations) were then undertaken to clear the site, these additional works caused the planned site clearance period of 2 weeks to over-run by 8 weeks to 10 weeks total. More resources (plant and manpower) had to be brought to site in order to reduce the delay as much as possible. Subsequent activities had to be re-planned so as to meet the scheduled commissioning date, again this involved additional resource and cost. This resulted in a claim of 20% of the contract value and a dispute with the original site owner responsible for

57

TABLE 1
LIST OF MAIN PROJECT ACTIVITIES

Activity Number	Name	Duration	Start Date	Finish Date
1	Feasibility Study	8	01/01/92	23/02/92
2	Planning Permission	5	24/02/92	29/03/92
3	Land Purchase	5	30/03/92	03/05/92
4	Design	12	24/2/92	17/05/92
5	Set up Site, Preliminaries	2	04/05/92	17/05/92
6	Earthworks	2	18/05/92	31/05/92
7	Piling, Hardcore, Foundation	18	25/05/92	27/09/92
8	Steel Frame	6	27/07/92	06/09/92
9	Roofing & Cladding	11	17/08/92	01/11/92
10	Brickwork & Blockwork (Warehouse)	8	17/08/92	11/10/92
11	Drainage	2	24/08/92	06/09/92
12	Pre-cast Floors & Stairs	2	07/09/92	20/09/92
13	Floor Slab (Warehouse)	9	14/09/92	15/11/92
14	Floor Slab (Offices)	3	14/09/92	04/10/92
15	Brickwork & Blockwork (Offices)	7	21/09/92	08/11/92
16	Services (Warehouse)	10	12/10/92	20/12/92
17	Doors & Windows	6	12/10/92	22/11/92
18	Screed	3	19/10/92	08/11/92
19	Services & Lift (Offices)	11	09/11/92	31/01/93
20	Fire Protection	3	16/11/92	06/12/92
21	Joinery	11	16/11/92	07/02/93
22	Wall Finish	8	30/11/92	31/01/93
23	Commissioning (Warehouse)	2	04/01/93	17/01/93
24	Handover (Warehouse)		18/01/93	
25	Suspended Ceiling	3	18/01/93	07/02/93
26	Decoration	3	01/02/93	21/02/93
27	Commissioning	1	22/02/93	28/02/93
28	Floor Covering	2	01/03/93	14/03/93
29	External Work	2	01/03/93	14/03/93
30	Clean Out	1	15/03/93	21/03/93
31	Handover		21/03/93	

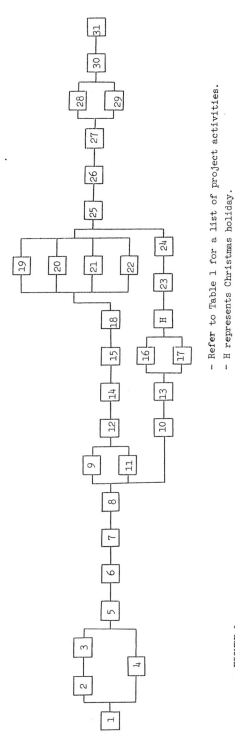

- Refer to Table 1 for a list of project activities.
- H represents Christmas holiday.

FIGURE 1
Precedence network for Industrial Development.

the surveys and reclamation. It is now reported (but not confirmed by the Authors of this paper) that desk study information may exist which could have indicated the full extent of the obstructions, these being the remains of industrial buildings on the site pre-dating the industrial works layout at the time of demolition.

16. Information from the site has been obtained and used for risk analysis modelling. 31 main activities were identified and cost information on these obtained. Table 1 lists the activities and a precedence network was then produced, as illustrated in figure 1. It is to be noted that the objective of the modelling is not to reproduce the site events but to quantify, at the planning stage, the financial uncertainties associated with ground conditions. The model and the results are therefore not of a real event but are a simulation using realistic inputs and schedules. The total planned cost (calculated before the start of construction) for the development was £4,321,762. This included civil, mechanical and electrical works.

Sensitivity analysis

17. The results of a sensitivity analysis are illustrated in figure 2. For reasons of clarity, the effect of variations in four activities, which occur relatively early in construction, are shown. The effect of a delay (as a % change in variable) is plotted against calculated construction cost. Examination of figure 2 shows that delay due to unforeseen ground has a significant effect on cost.

Ground uncertainty effects on estimates

18. All the uncertainties associated with ground conditions cannot be eliminated by even the best site investigation. The degree of uncertainty, however, is influenced by the extent and quality of the S.I., including desk studies and knowledge of the site. For the analysis, uncertainty levels were defined as shown in figure 2. The selection of these levels of uncertainty was made from subjective judgement, a direct proportional relationship was assumed to exist between the ground uncertainty and variance from best estimate levels of project duration and cost. Thus, a good quality S.I. designed to meet project criteria is assumed to provide reliable information on the ground such that major claims and delay from unforeseen conditions are avoided. Some variance, however, is possible but has a small effect (less than 10%) on cost and time. At the other end of the scale, an inadequate S.I. may lead to large claims and disruption with possible cost variances of up to 50% on estimates.

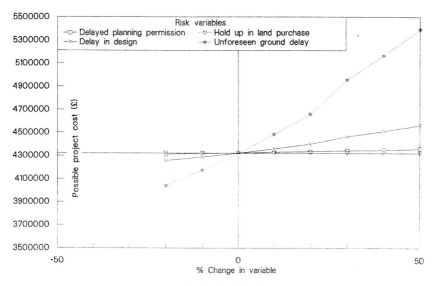

Fig. 2. Sensitivity diagram

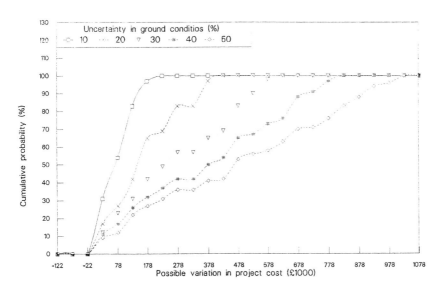

Fig. 3. Effect of uncertainty in ground conditions on project cost

61

19. Evidence to support the uncertainty levels selected is available in a survey of nearly 100 tunnel contracts by the US National Committee for Tunnel Technology (7). This showed a relationship to exist between the amount of site investigation undertaken and both the accuracy of cost estimates and the level and frequency of major claims. Where S.I. was of sufficient quantity (defined as at least 3% of project cost) then estimated project costs were reliable with final contract figures being less than 10% different. For tunnel projects where low levels of S.I. occurred (ie – less than about 0.5% of project cost) then cost estimates were variable and unreliable with final amounts extending up to 50% or more. In some cases, project costs more than doubled from the estimate with large claims for unforeseen ground causing disruption and delay.

20. Probabilistic risk analysis, incorporating the cumulative probability of ground uncertainty given in Table 2, produced figures for project cost variation and duration. These are plotted against cumulative probability in figures 3 and 4. The most probable value is associated with the mean (50% cumulative probability). The limits of 0% and 100% represent extreme conditions and a realistic degree of risk is better represented by the 15%–85% range, ie – extreme conditions are discounted. The data shown in figures 3 and 4 are summarised in Table 3.

21. The results confirm that the greater the uncertainty over ground conditions then the more likely there is to be cost escalation and delay. Whilst the investigation costs do increase to obtain reliable information, it is probable that for a project of this nature these costs would not exceed about 1% to 2% of the estimate, ie – in a range of £40,000 to £80,000. A S.I. that produces less reliable information (higher level of uncertainty) would cost much less, possibly less than £10,000. A comparison of these investigation costs to the range of financial uncertainty shows the benefit to be a large reduction in financial risk exposure by a client. The quality of a S.I. is a real factor that influences cost and time estimates. Such work should, therefore, be properly planned and executed with the necessary provision of finance and time resources. S.I. is a valuable tool in the development of reliable estimates during project planning.

Unforeseen ground conditions during construction

22. The modelling of the financial consequences of unforeseen ground conditions arising on a contract depends upon the quality of the investigation commissioned : an inadequate S.I. increases the chance of a serious error or omission. To develop a realistic model, information was

TABLE 2

UNCERTAINTY LEVELS USED IN THE MODEL

Uncertainty Level	Ground Uncertainty	Quality of SI Work
1	10%	Very Good
2	20%	Good
3	30%	Moderate
4	40%	Poor
5	50%	Very Poor

TABLE 3
EFFECT OF GROUND UNCERTAINTY ON PROJECT COST AND DURATION

Level of Uncertainty	Mean Estimated Variation in Cost (£1000)	Range of Estimated Variation in Cost (£1000)	Mean Estimated Project Delay (weeks)	Range of Estimated Project Delay (weeks)
1	65	10 - 135	1.5	0 - 2
2	140	25 - 345	2.5	0 - 5
3	235	40 - 485	4	1 - 8
4	380	60 - 675	6	1 - 11
5	465	95 - 855	8	2 - 14

TABLE 4
EFFECT OF UNFORESEEN GROUND DELAY ON PROJECT COST AND DURATION

Unforeseen Delay Due to Ground (weeks)	Mean Likely Variation in Cost (£1000)	Range of Likely Variation in Cost (£1000)	Mean Likely Project Delay (weeks)	Range of Likely Project Delay (weeks)
None	150	30 - 270	2.5	0 - 4.5
2	360	230 - 600	4.5	2 - 7.5
4	660	400 - 820	7.5	4 - 9.5
6	820	590 - 1030	9.5	6 - 11.5
8	1070	780 - 1370	11.5	8 - 14.5

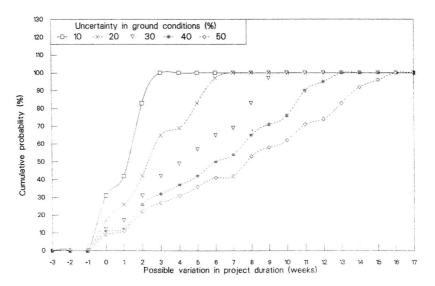

Fig. 4. Effect of uncertainty in ground conditions on project duration

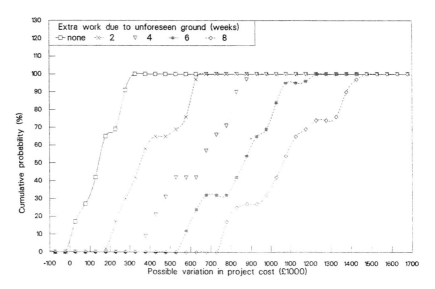

Fig. 5. Effect of unforeseen ground conditions on project cost

obtained on the site investigations carried out at this site (see para. 14 above). The investigations were properly conducted for light industrial development and were assessed as being of a generally 'good' quality. For model analysis, it has been assumed that this resulted in uncertainty level 2 with a 20% ground uncertainty. Since the obstructions encountered on site caused an 8 week delay to the earthworks, the model has been tested for five scenarios of 'unforeseen' ground which produce delays of 0, 2, 4, 6 and 8 weeks respectively.

23. It is to be noted that there is a residual financial risk to the project inherited from the 20% ground uncertainty assumed since unforeseen ground can influence activities other than the earthworks, eg: piling, hardcoring, foundation. Thus the simulation of no delay to the earthworks still results in a likely cost increase (50% probability) of about £150,000 and delay of about 2.5 weeks. The cost increase ranges from a low probability (15%) of £30,000 to an upper bound probability (85%) of £270,000.

25. The earthworks were planned to be for 2 weeks at a cost of £186,936. The analysis shows that each extra week caused by unforeseen events results in a probable increase in cost of £130,000 and a probable 1.5 week delay in commissioning. (These figures include other effects produced by the residual risk explained above.) It is to be noted that the probable effect of a week's delay in earthworks exceeds the cost of a site investigation which, if properly planned and executed, may have avoided the problem. It is probable, therefore, that the cost of a full, adequate S.I. can be recouped from cost savings arising from properly planned works.

Site events

26. The development was delayed in the earthworks and foundation activities by obstructions in the ground that were not foreseen. Additional costs of £900,000 have been claimed as a result, these represent about 20% of the original estimate.

27. The model analysis and the site events are not directly comparable since extra resources were employed and activities re-arranged such that the planned handover date of 21 March. 1993 was achieved. These adjustments to the programme are not modelled in the analyses reported in this paper. The calculations do, however, model events up to the discovery of the obstructions and then provide evidence as to what the cost overruns and delays could be under the original resource plans. It is shown in figure 5 and Table 4 that an 8 week delay in the earthworks produces a probable cost increase of between £780,000 and £1,370,000 with a most probable

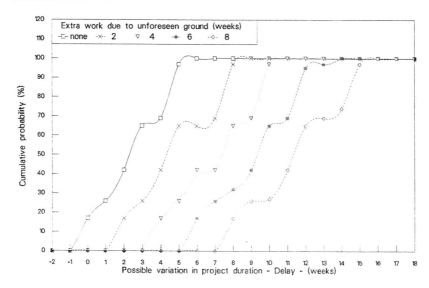

Fig. 6. Effect of unforeseen ground conditions on project duration

value of £1,070,000. The similarity with the claimed cost overrun gives support to the analysis and interpretation of the data.

CONCLUSIONS

28. The effect of ground conditions on project cost and time has been modelled using data from a recent industrial development. The following is to be noted:

(a) Sensitivity analysis confirms that delay due to ground conditions on site has a significant effect on project cost estimates.

(b) The proper planning and execution of a site investigation produces benefit by reducing the levels of financial risk to a client. An adequate S.I. aids not only the planning, design and construction of a scheme but also produces financial gain. Probabilistic risk analyses enables the risks to be quantified.

(c) Modelling the effects of delay in construction due to 'unforeseen obstructions produces cost data that relates to the site events. The analysis shows that a delay as short as one week in the earthworks activity brings costs in excess of a full S.I. Thus the cost of investigation (with full resourcing of time, technology and finance) produces benefit by avoidance of such delays.

ACKNOWLEDGEMENTS

The authors acknowledge the support of SERC in financing the research and give their thanks to those who provided the case study information.

REFERENCES

1. NEDO, Faster building for industry, National Economic Development Office, London, 1983.

2. NEDO, Faster building for commerce. National Economic Development Office, London, 1988.

3. PEACOCK, W.S., Site investigation procedures and risk analysis. PhD Thesis, UMIST, 1990.

4. PEACOCK, W.S., WHYTE, I.L. The reduction in financial risks from site investigations for construction projects. Proc.I.C.E., Civil Engineering, May, 1992, 74-82.

5. THOMPSON, P., PERRY, J., Engineering construction risks, Thomas Telford, London, 1992.

6. THOMPSON, P.A., WILMER, G., CASPAR – a programme for engineering project appraisal and management. Proc. 2nd Int. Conf. Civil and Struct. Comput., Vol 1, London, December, 1985.

7. US National Committee for Tunnelling Technology, Geotechnical Site Investigation for Underground Projects, Volumes 1 and 2, National Academy Press, Washington D C, 1984.

5. Reliability-based design using point estimate methods and capacity–demand models

A. McCRACKEN, Steffen, Robertson and Kirsten (UK) Ltd, UK

INTRODUCTION
1. Probabilistic and reliability based methods offer the geotechnical engineer the opportunity to use his or her experience and intuition when working with limited or incomplete data sets in design.

2. The objective of this paper is to make geotechnical and civil engineers more aware of the probabilistic design tools available and their relative ease of use.

3. The paper takes the reader through the logical steps of :
  - Defining parameter distributions for inherently variable geotechnical media via *Beta Distributions*
  - Through analysis of multiple variables using *Point Estimate Methods* (PEMs)
  - Assessment of *Capacity – Demand Models* (CD)
  - To obtaining measurements of *System Reliability* (R) and *Probability of Failure*, p(f)

4. The way along this route is made reasonably simple by way of computer programs and spreadsheets specifically developed for the task. These can be made available through the author. The methods can be applied to all branches of civil engineering and geotechnics.

5. Figure 1 presents a flowsheet which shows the logical steps taken from parameter analysis through to deiwing system reliability and is described below. Table 1 presents the forms of analyses employed and includes some of the computer programs used and the input required.

Risk and reliability in ground engineering. Thomas Telford, London, 1993

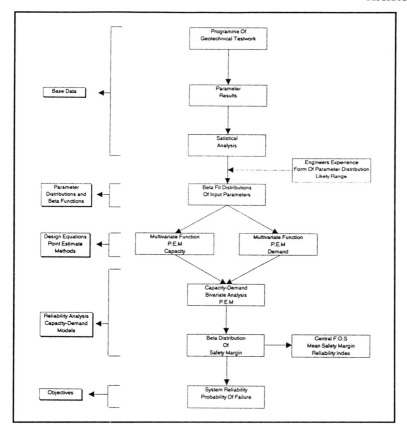

**Figure 1 : Logic For Deriving System Reliability
From Limited Data Sets**

6. It is not considered appropriate to present the detailed deviations of the functions in detail in the paper. Full details are provided in refs. 1 & 2.

Analysis	Progams	Parameter Input Required
BETA FUNCTION	**BETA. F**	**mean, coefficient of variation, min, max**
POINT ESTIMATE	**PEM 2PT** **PEM 4PT** **NPT**	**mean, standard deviation,** **correlation coefficients**
PROBABILITY OF **FAILURE** **(BIVARIATE** **C – D Point** **Estimate Method)**	**PEM** **PF.F**	**Safety Margin (S) of the** **Capacity (C)–Demand (D) model** **mean of C & D** **coefficient of variation of C & D** **min and max of C & D** **correlation co–efficient of C & D**

Table 1 Probabilistic Analysis Programs and Required Input.

PARAMETER VARIABILITY

7. Geotechnical site investigation programmes rarely identify the full distributions of engineering parameters which are required for design. This is generally a function of the inherent variability of naturally occurring materials such as soils and rocks as well as economics. A programme of testing will generally obtain a number of results, perhaps predetermined, before having an appreciation of variability. Statistical evaluation is then applied and design parameters chosen. The chosen design values may be related to the mean for the results obtained or more conservatively, ranging between the lowest value obtained and the mean less one or two standard deviations. Even where a large number of tests are carried out there often remains a lack of appreciation for the likely full range of values. This often results in the choice of overly conservative values being selected as input for design to obtain what is intuitively an acceptable level of risk. To select input parameters confidently an understanding of the general form of the distribution of the parameters in question and the likely position within that distribution of the test results obtained is required.

8. Techniques are available to assist in predicting parameter distributions using limited data sets given a knowledge of the general form.

9. Distributions of variables can take a number of forms. Some examples of geotechnical parameters which may conform to these general forms are presented below.

Distribution Types	Examples of Geotechnical Parameters
Uniform	Constant value conditions eg slope angle, height, span etc
Normal	Density, joint dip and dip direction, friction angel cohesion
Exponential	Joint continuity
Log–Normal	Joint length, joint spacing

Table 2   Types of distribution and representative geotechnical parameter

ESTIMATION OF PARAMETER DISTRIBUTION BY
BETA FUNCTIONS

10. The distribution of a random variable can be defined by a *beta distribution* if one has a reasonable estimate of the expected value (mean), the coefficient of variation (standard deviation) and the minimum and maximum value of the parameter. Experienced geotechnical engineers can generally develop a feel for parameter limits given a set of test data from which an expected value and standard deviation can be obtained. Even without feel for the range, the limits of 3 standard deviation (3 sigma units) either side of the mean generally provides a reasonable estimate (figure 2).

11. The tails of parameter distributions are particularly important. It is these which generally dictate the likelihood of failure of systems. If co–efficient of variation are not known, representative estimates can be obtained from published tables.

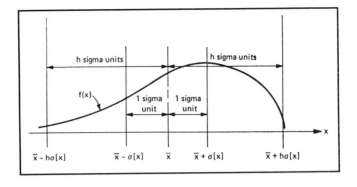

Figure 2 :   Sigma Units (after Harr)

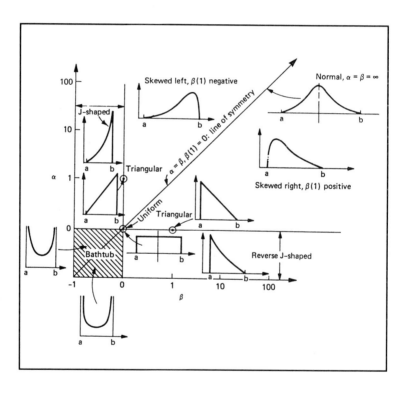

**Figure 3 :   Some Schematic Representaions Of
Probability Distributions (after Harr)**

12. Normal, uniform and exponential distribution are special cases of beta distributions. The shape of the distribution is described by the mean, standard deviation coefficients of skewness, $\beta(1)$, kurtoisis $\beta(2)$ and range (a, b). Figure 3 presents some diagrammatic examples of beta probability distributions defined as functions of α and β which are distribution shape factors (ref 1). Programs are freely available which describe the beta distribution for parameters given the mean, coefficient of variation and the minimum and maximum values.

POINT ESTIMATE METHODS (PEM)

13. PEMs can be used to estimate the distribution of single variables. They are more commonly used to solve or estimate a function of more than one variable parameter where there are correlation coefficients between the variables.

14. Previously the options to determine the probability distribution of such derivative conditions (eg. strength, stability) had disadvantages. Either it required the distribution of component variables to be known and plenty of computer time (eg Monte Carlo methods) or a knowledge of mathematics such Taylor Series expansion in first order second–moment (FOSM) methods, which often are not part of the geotechnical engineers armoury. PEMs offer a more simple approximating procedure, generally of sufficient accuracy, which takes account of conditionality of the input parameters.

15. In figure 4, p+ and p– are *two point estimates* of the mean and the distribution of f(x). The + and – denote the addition and subtraction of one standard deviation (sigma unit) to the mean. Given two points either side of the mean one is able to gain a good appreciation of the shape of a distribution. The expected value, x and the standard deviation, $\sigma[x]$ of a variable parameter, provide information regarding the central tendency and scatter of parameter values. Where y is a dependent variable, $y = y(x)$, estimates of the y variate can be obtained from the predicted distribution of x through the relationship between x and y(x). Deviations of PEMs are given on an example ref 1 is shown in figure 5 which represents this transfer of information from a parameter distribution through a relationship to obtain an estimate of the second variable..

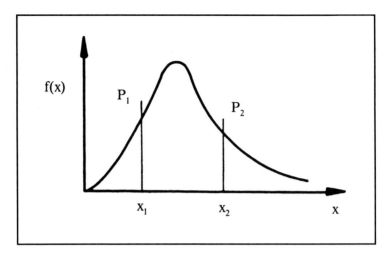

Figure 4 :   Two–point estimate (after Harr)

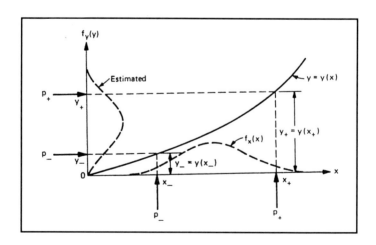

**Figure 5 :   Schematic Representaion Of
Transfer Of Information (after Harr)**

PEM FOR FUNCTIONS OF TWO VARIABLES (BIVARIATE)

16. When a condition is a function of two variables $y = y(x_1, x_2)$ then the probability distribution of the function is estimated by 4 points, p++, p+−, p−+, p−−. Fig. 6 presents the transfer of data for a function of two variables.

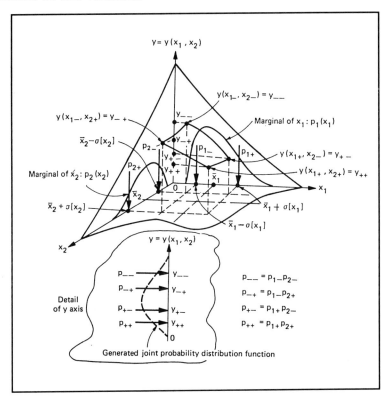

Figure 6 : Schematic Representation Of Transfer Of Information For Functions Of Two Random Variables (after Harr)

17. The importance of the correlation coefficient, ρ_{xy}, between variables can be significant. As the correlation coefficient increases to a high positive value, both parameters are high or low together. A high negative correlation coefficient means when one parameter is high the other is low and vice versa. If the correlation coefficient between two variables is not known care should be exercised to chose a value

which will not overstate reliability. For example, with shear strength (τ), described by cohesion (C) and friction angle (ϕ), a positive correlation coefficient would produce higher probabilities of failure

18. Straight forward spreadsheets have been developed for PEMs. Copies of these are available for up to 4 variables. In each case the input and output are as follows:

Input
- For each variable :
  - expected value
  - standard deviation
- Correlation Coefficients between variables
- The function/formula/equation when function is the calculation of Safety Margin

Output
- Expected value
- Variance
- Standard deviation
- Co–efficient of variation
- Range (mean + and − 3 sigma units)
- Reliability index (when function is the calculation of Safety Margin)

CAPACITY–DEMAND MODELS

19. *Safety margins*, as calculated from Capacity–Demand Models are logical replacements of *Factors of Safety* publications. Conventionally *Factors of Safety* are derived from the ratio of a chosen capacity and an anticipated demand. The chosen values may be either nominal, lower bound, or mean values depending on the confidence in input parameters and the consequences of failure. The calculated *Factor of Safety* is usually compared to an accepted minimum which is again usually a function of uncertainty in the input parameters and consequence of factors.

20. In Capacity–Demand Models there is however the opportunity to honour the distributions of all of the input parameters, of which the capacity and demand are a function, and the distributions of the resulting capacity and demand themselves. It is quite clear that factor of safety is in itself a variable. Similarly the *Safety Margin* has a distribution.

21. Fig 7a illustrates a Capacity–Demand Model. The area of overlap of the demand distribution over the capacity distribution indicates that a probability of failure exists.

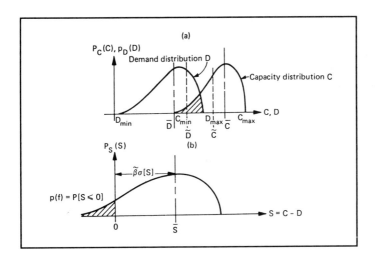

Figure 7 :   a) Capacity Demand Model
b) Safety Margin And Reliability Index

22. An alternative presentation of the Capacity–Demand Model is the Safety Margin (S) as seen in figure 7b. Here $S = C - D$ and the probability of failure p(f), where $S = C - D \leq 0$ is shown by the shaded position below the distribution of S. As the area under the curve is unity the probability of failure is the percentage shaded under the curve. The mean, and standard deviation of the distribution of the safety margin can clearly be determined.

23. As the capacity and demand are functions of variables, it follows that PEMs can be used to estimate the distribution of the safety margin. The safety margin is treated as a bivariate function of C and D, where $S = f (C,D)$, and can be estimated by way of point estimate methods as previously described.

SYSTEM RELIABILITY
24. Having obtained the expected values, coefficients of variation and correlation coefficients of the capacity and demand of the system the probability of failure can be devised. The probability distribution

of the Safety Margin can be sampled at various S values, such that the probabilities of failure is obtained. Alternatively the reliability of the system can be determined as :

Reliability R = 1 − p (f)

25. The *Reliability Index* β can also be determined. This is the number of times that the standard deviation of the Safety Margin can be divided into the mean safety margin ($\bar{S}$).

CONCLUSION

26. Probabilistic methods can be used to enhance incomplete data sets based on true data and engineers experience. This allows estimates of parameter distributions to be made which more accurately reflect the variable nature of the geotechnical conditions. Using the Beta Distribution, Point Estimate Method and Capacity−Demand methods described, probabilities of failure and system reliability can be quantified which are sufficiently accurate for engineering design and significantly improved over traditional factors of safety methods.

REFERENCES

1. HARR M.E. Reliability−Based design in Civil Engineering McGraw − Hill 1986.

2. HARR M.E. The Mechanics of Particulate Media − a Probabilistic Approach McGraw−Hill 1977.

3. HOEK E. and BRAY J.W. Rock Slope Engineering. Institution of Mining and Metallurgy 1977.

4. RUMPELT T.K. and O'CONNELL − JONES G. Probablistic Wedge Failure Analysis. The planning and Operation of Open−Pit and Strip Mines SAIMM Symposium Series S7, Pretoria 1986.

5. MCCRACKEN A, STEFFEN, O.K.H., HAINES A. Probabilistic Analysis of Discontinuity Data for Excavation Design Geotechnics No 10. 1988.

6. Application of an engineering system for the control of risk in ground engineering

R. D. BOYD, Sir William Halcrow & Partners, UK

SYNOPSIS.   The view is presented that one of the principal
sources of risk in ground engineering is lack of technical
awareness and that this may be minimised by application of an
appropriate engineering system. This should ensure continuity
of geotechnical thinking throughout ground investigation,
analysis, design and construction and provide documentation of
the process both for technical justification of decisions taken
and as a medium for communication of geotechnical issues to
others involved in the design process. An example is given of
the process employed on a major project.

SOURCES OF RISK
1.   There are three main sources of risk in geotechnical
engineering:

(a)   Geological uncertainty (variability of the ground)
(b)   Limitations of existing methods of analysis
(c)   Lack of awareness on the part of the persons
           involved.

2.   The first two may be grouped together as limitations on
knowledge and point to increased research and investigation as
ways of reducing risk. The third points to the development of
appropriate   engineering   systems   which   ensure   that   an
appropriate level of awareness is employed. The relationship
between knowledge and awareness is shown on Figure 1. What is
known is positive knowledge and what is yet to be discovered is
negative knowledge.   What the individual is aware of is
positive awareness while negative awareness represents the
awareness which the individual does not have but others do.
Muir-Wood (ref 1) has referred to awareness in a similar way
referring to different levels as "Aware", "Competent" and
"Expert". These represent increasing depth of area A (Fig 1).

3.   Problems seldom occur in area A, since by definition the
individual is knowledgeable, or in area B since awareness of
lack of knowledge normally results in a strategy of avoidance
or steps to increase knowledge. Area D by definition cannot be
dealt with.   There is a potential for problems arising in
area C but these may be minimised by the application of
appropriate engineering systems which reduce its size. These
should ensure the involvement of persons of adequate awareness,
provide continuity of geotechnical thinking and provide a
mechanism for communication within the project team.

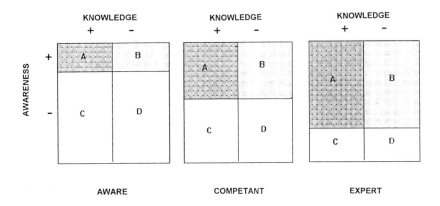

Fig 1 Relationship between knowledge and awareness

EXPERT AWARENESS
4. The expert requires experience, theoretical understanding and insight. The intuition or sense of fitness and proportion possessed by most experts may well be an ability to assimilate and process data subconsciously from all manner of sources, so as to develop a view. This may then be tested by some more transparent logical process and the arguments used to communicate the view to others. Understanding and modelling the intuitive process represents a significant challenge to those developing expert systems. It is important to recognise though that intuition can have a profound influence in the engineering process.

5. In Eurocode 7 (Draft) (ref 2) three categories of geotechnical complexity are identified. Clearly competency is required for categories 1 and 2 and expert awareness is necessary for category 3, and possibly 2 also depending upon the case in question. In the author's view simply by defining these categories and recognising the level of awareness necessary to address the issues properly, will go a very long way in the future to minimising geotechnical problems.

STANDARDS, QUALITY ASSURANCE AND TOTAL QUALITY MANAGEMENT
6. Traceability to national standards is essential for accurate communication between individuals, whether this be with regard to physical tests, soil descriptions or definitions of terminology. Quality assurance (QA) systems are intended to ensure that stated standards and procedures are employed.

7. Project management (PM) systems aim to optimise the application of resources to the accomplishment of the tasks required. For Total Quality Management (TQM) it is necessary to combine QA with PM and to superimpose on this a system of independent technical review which seeks to ensure fitness-for-purpose.

8.   In the author's view, the future will be toward TQM as a mechanism for ensuring that the appropriate level of awareness is employed.

CONTINUITY OF GEOTECHNICAL THINKING

9.   Another key element in the engineering process is ensuring continuity of geotechnical thinking. Muir-Wood has referred to the importance of a single controlling mind, using the metaphor of a "geotechnical conductor". Involving a single individual in this rôle throughout a long duration project may not be feasible. If replacement is necessary then it is important to ensure overlap and full documentation of information, so as to minimise the potential for loss of the intuitive understanding referred to above.

THE GEOTECHNICAL PROCESS

10.   The geotechnical process is about answering four basic questions:
- What have we got?   - ground investigation stage
- How does it behave?   - analysis stage
- What do we do?   - design stage
- Did we have what we thought we had and did it behave as we thought it would?   - construction stage

Ground Investigation

11.   The ground investigation stage should be geologically led. It should include a review of existing data including existing maps, air photos, historical records and existing ground investigation data as available and the site should be visited. The importance of the latter in relation to the intuitive process cannot be overstated. Ground investigations should be planned on the basis of knowledge of the intended development and an initial geological/ geomorphological understanding of the site. They should seek out information to allow a robust geological understanding to be developed and to gather specific quantitative information on spatial distribution of materials and material properties. Experience and precedent form the basis from which to develop an appropriate initial scope.

12.   In the author's view there should always be a formal contract for the ground investigation works, preferably using one of the standard formats for Conditions of Contract, Specification and Method of Measurement and the work should be directed and supervised by the "geotechnical conductor". The contract should allow flexibility to alter the scope within bounds, depending on conditions encountered. Both the contractor's site supervisory staff and the Engineer's site staff should be experienced in the methods to be employed and knowledge of the purpose of the investigation. Appropriate standards should be followed for field works, soil and rock descriptions and laboratory testing. Too tight a schedule should be avoided so as to allow the site staff time to review information as it is recovered and make any necessary changes to the scope. The factual report should be to an agreed format and should identify the standards and procedures employed.

13.   The Engineer responsible for the planning and direction of the investigation ("conductor") should prepare an interpretative report. This should describe the materials encountered, set this within the geological context, suggest

implications for design and construction and recommend values and ranges of parameters for the use in design.

Analysis

14.   The principal aim of analysis should be to understand potential behavioural mechanisms and their relative importance to alternative design options and may be simple or use highly complex numerical or physical models as appropriate to the problem.   It may be necessary to understand the influence of variations in ground parameters within credible ranges so as to identify those parameters which have most effect.   In most cases experience and precedent will indicate what these will be.   If necessary additional GI may be warranted to determine more accurate values for these parameters, whether they be geometrical values or material properties. Where quantifying parameters is difficult it may be appropriate (or necessary) to develop a design which envelops all credible possibilities. (This of course does not deal with area D in Figure 1.)   The purpose, information used and procedures employed in the analysis should be documented as well as the results.

Design

15.   This is the art of devising appropriate solutions.   It is driven by precedent, experience and imagination.   Often there will be many possible alternatives.   Good design in geomechanics is that which delivers good performance for money and is illustrated on Figure 2.

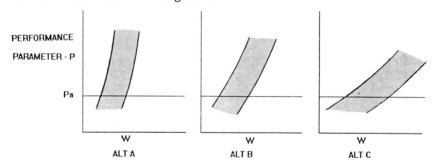

Fig 2 Performance   factor   versus   physical   or   dimensional property for various alternatives

16.   The vertical axis is a performance factor (P) (eg factor of safety, settlement, etc).   The horizontal axis is a physical or dimensional property of the design (W) (eg footing width, pile embedment, etc) and the shaded areas represent possible values dependent upon the parameters and methods of analysis used.   W can be related to cost.   At the acceptability limit, P_a, alternatives can be compared directly. However, P_a may not be prescribed (open to judgement), in which case where costs are similar, the choice between options should reflect best performance for money.   Option A is the best alternative since only a small increase in W gives the largest increase in P, thus minimising risk.

17.   Until recently such judgement has often been subjective (intuitive).   However   with   ready   access   to   computers, increasingly it is becoming possible to undertake realistic comparisons and thus better justify designs.

18.   Once developed, the design needs to be communicated to the contractor by way of drawings, specification and possibly also by way of reports and technical notes which explain the technical thinking embodied in the design.   In particular such notes are necessary where an observational approach is proposed and where specific testing or instrumentation is to be installed.

Construction
19.   The geotechnical process up to this point hopefully has been one of problem identification and avoidance, either directly or by design provision.   However, it must always be accepted that unforeseen problems may still arise due to lack of knowledge or lack of awareness, and continued diligence in geotechnical matters is essential throughout construction and sometimes into operation.   In effect the observational method (ref 3) applies to a greater or lesser extent in all cases.   It is necessary for a responsibility chain to be established to confirm that what was found was indeed as designed for or if not then issues should be referred back to the designer and the situation re-assessed.   If necessary alternative action may need to be instructed.

20.   The above process applies whatever form of contract is adopted for the construction.   Also, the requirements for appropriate level of awareness, use of relevant standards, technical review and ensuring continuity of geotechnical thinking need to be embodied in the engineering systems employed.

EXAMPLE
21.   Figure 3 shows an example of the geotechnical process employed on a major civil engineering project in Scotland for which initial construction phases ran in parallel with final design and for which it would eventually be necessary to submit a detailed nuclear safety case statement to regulating authorities.   All works were undertaken in accordance with project specific quality assurance procedures complying with BS 5882. (ref 4)

22.   Key elements of the process were as follows:

(a) Considerable emphasis was placed on understanding the geology of the site.   This included borehole investigations together with seismic refraction and reflection investigations.   These indicated stratification in both drift and bedrock, local faulting in the bedrock and other features such as pockets of methane gas concentrated in granular soils in places. Results from boreholes and geophysical data were used to build a three dimensional computer model of the site geology.   This allowed a robust and compatible understanding to be developed of the quantitative data.

(b) Because of the several years' duration of the project it was necessary for the "geotechnical conductor" rôle to be started by one individual then handed on to a second. The first engineer's responsibility extended from concept initiation through to start of preparation of the

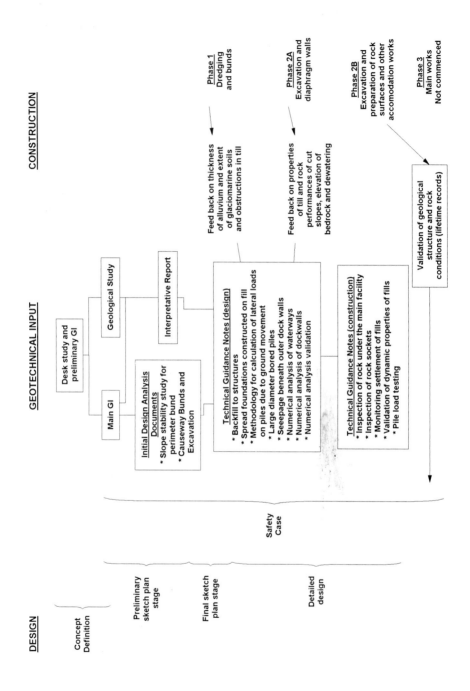

Fig 3 Example of Geotechnical input to a major project

interpretative report and much of the essential technical thinking was done at this stage. The second's responsibility commenced with preparation of the interpretative report (there being a significant overlap at this stage) and extended throughout the remainder of the project. Additional to this, a technical audit was provided by an engineer external to the design team whose involvement extended throughout the project. Thus the benefits of continuity of geotechnical thinking were established.

(c) A particular element of the interpretative report was the inclusion of a detailed discussion of the overall performance requirements for the structures, and the basis for selecting design parameters and setting performance limits, compatible with the nuclear safety requirements of the project. This included overall safety factors on the ultimate limit state and serviceability requirements at the design load condition, which predominantly was the seismic load case. Dealing with these difficult issues at this stage and setting out the geotechnical design philosophy was of considerable benefit as detailed design progressed. The interpretative report became a corner-stone of the safety case.

(d) A series of detailed technical guidance notes (TGNs) were prepared to extend the recommendations of the interpretative report into the design and to document various sets of analysis which were undertaken. The subjects covered are shown on Figure 3. The TGNs both helped in justification of the design and acted as a method for ensuring compatibility of approach between different parts of the design team. They were all written in a common format.

(e) Technical guidance notes were prepared also to extend the requirements of the design into construction. In particular, it was considered necessary to validate that rock conditions under the massive foundations were as anticipated in the design. A detailed procedure was written to cover inspection of prepared rock surfaces and measurement and testing of rock properties. Observations were combined within a project specific calculation and the derived values compared with pre-determined acceptance criteria. The objective was to minimise the subjectivity in the evaluation process by providing a system with perceived high reproducibility and repeatability. The observation and testing was undertaken by one team with 10% independent validation by a separate team. The data gathered forms part of the lifetime records for the facility. Certain aspects of the original procedure did not cover all observations and with some combinations the derived parameters did not accord with sensible judgement. Consequently, it was necessary to modify the procedure and review each apparent non-compliance on its merits. Notwithstanding this, the essential elements of providing a mechanism for documentation of observations and minimising subjectivity was achieved.

CONCLUSION
23. The principal conclusion of this paper is that the risk of technical errors or omissions and their associated cost implications may be minimised by the application of an appropriate engineering system which ensures utilisation of geotechnical personnel of adequate awareness and provides continuity of geotechnical thinking.

ACKNOWLEDGEMENTS
24. The form of illustration used in Figure 1 was first made known to the author as a contribution from the floor during discussion at the conference on 'Uncertainty and Conservatism in the Seismic Design of Nuclear Plant' organised by the British Nuclear Energy Society at Risley in April 1993. The originator is unknown to the author but is to be commended for the succinctness of the idea.

REFERENCES
1. Muir-Wood, AM: "Control of Uncertainty in Geotechnical Engineering".   Special Publication in advance of XIII ICSMFE New Delhi 1994.   Oxford and IBH Publishing Ltd (In press).

2. Commission of the European Communities "Eurocode 7 Geotechnics", Draft, March 1993.

3. Pack, RB "The observational method in applied soil mechanics" Geotechnique Vol 19, No 2 171-187 (1969).

4. British Standards Institute "BS 5882, Specification for Total Quality Assurance Programme for Nuclear Installations". BSI, 1982.

7. Dissolution features in the chalk: from hazard to risk

J. RIGBY-JONES, C. R. I. CLAYTON and M. C. MATTHEWS,
University of Surrey, UK

SYNOPSIS. Dissolution in the chalk leaves the rock head uneven and sometimes with "pipes" which may contain voids or be infilled with soft material. Such features are a hazard to construction, and can be extremely difficult to detect using conventional ground investigation methods. This hazard, when related to the cost of development and the possible consequences of failure, can be translated into a degree of risk. This paper describes the hazard caused to construction by Chalk dissolution, and suggests suitable strategies for dealing with the resultant risk.

THE NATURE OF THE HAZARD

Factors influencing formation

1. Wherever ground water flows through soluble rocks dissolution of the rock fabric will take place. All carbonate rocks are susceptible to dissolution and in the U.K. the two rocks most commonly affected are the Carboniferous limestones and the Cretaceous chalk. In limestones the results of dissolution are often quite vivid, with swallow holes and cave systems being commonplace. In the Chalk the results of dissolution are often more subtle and less dramatic, but are still of great importance to the civil engineer considering construction.

2. There are several factors which influence the rate of dissolution, some chemical and some physical. Dissolution of chalk takes place slowly in pure water, but acidity increases the rate. Acidity of the ground water can be increased in several natural ways. Normally the partial pressure of carbon dioxide (CO_2) in the air has the most significant effect in increasing the acidity of the ground water. 0.03% of the atmosphere (by volume) is CO_2. Up to 74 mg l^{-1} of carbonate can be dissolved by water under normal atmospheric pressure. Dissolved CO_2 then reacts with the water to form carbonic acid.

3. An increase in acidity of ground water is also associated with its passage through overlying ground. The concentration of CO_2 in soil air is higher than that in atmospheric air and there may also be the presence of organic soil acids. The importance of organic material in increasing acidity is shown by Sperling et al (ref. 1) who found that the average pH of groundwater in granular superficial deposits overlying Chalk was 3.8-4.0, whilst being a relatively neutral 7.8-8.0 on chalk with no superficial cover. The acidic pH associated with granular Eocene and Pleistocene deposits is postulated as being due to its characteristic acid heath vegetation.

4. Temperature is also thought to have had an important bearing on the rate of dissolution. At low temperatures more CO_2 can be dissolved in water; for example twice as much CO_2 can be dissolved at 0° C as at 30° C. As a result of this it would be expected that in colder environments (for example during periglacial conditions) dissolution would have occurred at a higher rate than at the present. But the effect of temperature may be more than compensated

for by a greater availability of CO_2 and higher rainfall.

5. Physical factors relating to the rate of dissolution are connected with the supply of ground water and the ease of dissolution of the chalk. Softer chalks of higher porosity appear more susceptible to dissolution than more dense chalks. This is demonstrated by a correlation between Edmonds's map of solution feature density (ref. 2) and Clayton's map showing chalk densities for England (ref. 3). More recently, in contrast with this hypothesis, Veni (ref. 4) found from a study of 300 caves and sinkholes in Texas that dissolution features tended to occur more commonly in limestones of low to medium porosity.

6. The factors which affect the flow of ground water are; the mass structure of the chalk, groundwater levels, and the surface geology and topography. Groundwater will flow preferentially along the natural joints and fractures in the chalk. Areas of high permeability tend to drain water downwards more efficiently and lead to the enlargement of vertical joints into pipes which have relatively little surface expression. Areas of lower permeability tend to pond water and lead to more lateral dissolution. Much work has been carried out in the U.S.A. on the relationship between fracture patterns and the occurrence of dissolution features and both Price (ref. 5) and Hubbard (ref. 6) agree that dissolution tends to follow natural macroscopic fracture and jointing systems.

7. Dissolution of the chalk is generally restricted to above the water table, where the level of dissolved calcium carbonate is still below saturation. Previously lower ground water levels may have lead to the formation of cavities below the present ground water level. Cavities should be particularly suspected at ground water level, where chemical erosion is supplemented by mechanical erosion. Dissolution rate is also related to the velocity and volume of flow through the chalk. Rates of dissolution are therefore higher after periods of rainfall.

8. Unless the chalk extends to the surface the ground water must flow through a layer of superficial cover. The nature of this cover will not only affect the acidity of the water but also the flow rate and spatial variations in flow. Non-cohesive permeable cover tends to supply an even distribution of relatively-acidic water to the chalk rock head, whereas cohesive impermeable cover focuses flow at specific positions. In addition the surface topography will influence the distribution of ground water flow onto the chalk, with more inflow occurring in hollows and valleys than on hilltops.

Types of dissolution feature

9. Aggressive dissolution of the chalk leads to the development of a number of different dissolution features. These various types of feature have been given three descriptive terms;

    (i) **Dolines**, which are conical or bowl shaped depressions at ground surface. This is purely a surface morphological descriptive term with no mode of genesis (eg dissolutioning) inferred.

    (ii) **Swallowholes**, which are points where water is partially or totally seen to flow or be absorbed into the ground.

    (iii) **Solution pipes** are roughly cylindrical cavities, partially or fully infilled with unconsolidated superficial soils, normally only a few metres in diameter and extending to depths of up to 30m.

These descriptive terms are ambiguous and confusing. Swallowholes are relatively rare on the chalk outcrop and when they do occur they are readily visible. They will not therefore be discussed further.

10. The term solution pipe describes the subsurface form of a vertically linear feature formed by preferential dissolution along a vertical joint. These features are often invisible from the surface due to their small surface area. Their small diameter means that arching can occur at depth, allowing cavities to be bridged over and preventing noticeable subsidence at the surface.

11. The term doline (now often referred to as a sinkhole) generally relates to an area which has undergone localised surface subsidence or collapse. This ground movement can be related to a variety of subsurface forms and modes of genesis which can be described by the terms;

      (i)   Dissolution sinkhole
      (ii) Subsidence sinkhole
      (iii) Collapse sinkhole.
      (iv) Buried sinkhole.

These four features are illustrated in figure 1.

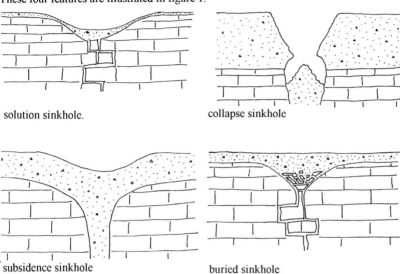

solution sinkhole.   collapse sinkhole

subsidence sinkhole   buried sinkhole

Fig. 1 Principal types of dissolution feature.

12. **Dissolution sinkholes** occur over a point of ground drainage which is usually an existing fracture or fault. They are commonest where the ground surface is being subjected to a high precipitation load due to the location of adjacent impermeable areas (these areas can either be impermeable superficial cover or areas of manmade development). The water dissolves the chalk as it travels downwards leaving the characteristic conical depression. Dissolution sinkholes generally occur in areas of thin superficial cover.

13. **Subsidence sinkholes** occur in covers of unconsolidated sediment approximately 1-10m thick. They form due to the overlying material being washed down into the fissures in the Chalk which are being opened up by dissolution. Subsidence occurs over a long period of time.

14. **Collapse sinkholes** occur when underground cavities migrate to the surface due to repeated roof collapse. They are rarely more than a few metres in diameter. Large air-filled cavities in Upper Chalk are relatively rare due to the low strength of the host rock, and cavities are usually infilled with soft Tertiary deposits. Collapse sinkholes are recognised by their steep sides.

15. **Buried sinkholes** are the most common dissolution feature to be found in English Chalk. They form when sinkholes are filled with superficial deposits either concurrently with their genesis or at a later date. They are usually relatively small (by international standards). Diameters of 1-20m are common and depths rarely exceed 10m. Most are wide and shallow. It is not uncommon for buried features to form with no surface expression, or for dolines to be ploughed out. Some sinkholes can be infilled to great depth especially where the underlying solution feature has formed as a pipe structure.

Areas and frequency of occurrence

16. Wherever soluble carbonate rocks outcrop or occur under less than 50m of cover there is the potential for dissolution features to develop. The chalk outcrop accounts for 35% of the U.K. land area (figure 2). The distribution of dissolution features on this outcrop is far from uniform. We have already discussed the factors which are likely to control frequency when considering influences on feature formation, and spatial distribution is a function of a combination of these factors.

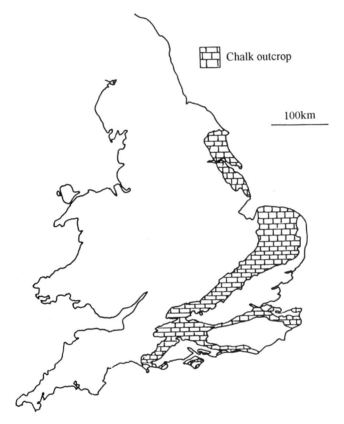

Fig. 2 Map showing extent of the Chalk outcrop in England.

17. The most important factor in dissolution feature development is the supply of ground water, especially in situations where it is focused onto small areas of chalk rock head. This can occur commonly at the feathering edge of impermeable Tertiary beds, at points of natural land drainage (eg dry valleys), and where man has changed the ground water regime (eg soakaways).

18. In past studies of dissolution feature spatial distribution much emphasis has been put on the presence of superficial cover, and close proximity to its feathering edges (refs. 7-9.) Whilst there is a good correlation between the density of identified features and this geological location it must be remembered that this relationship is based on features which have been positively identified, and upon geological boundaries which have often been assumed. The situations in which dissolution features are less readily identifiable has not been considered. Although features close to feathering edges may be younger and more readily visible there will still be a considerable number of other features which are not now associated with superficial cover, but are relevant to civil engineering development.

19. The frequency with which dissolution features occur in the English Chalk is, perhaps rather surprisingly, still a matter of some uncertainty. Edmonds (ref.2) found that the frequency varied from <5 to 90 dissolution features per 100 km^2 (equivalent to a maximum of 0.9 dissolution features per square kilometre). This figure is very much less than that quoted by Sperling et al. (ref. 1), who give a figure of 157 dissolution features per square kilometre for certain areas of the Dorset heathland. Our preliminary research, based upon examination of air photographs in the Dorset area, has indicated that frequencies can be at least as great as Sperling et al. have suggested.

THE RISK TO CIVIL ENGINEERING CONSTRUCTION

Problems associated with dissolution features
20. Risk results both from the combination of a hazard and a vulnerability to that hazard. In the case of dissolution features it is low-rise construction which is often considered to be the most vulnerable, and this will be discussed below. But general civil engineering construction is also at risk; earthworks can be seriously disrupted, sheeted excavations can be threatened (ref.10), and piling may also be affected (ref.11).
21. The ongoing genesis of a dissolution feature involves either slow subsidence as soft infill material migrates downwards, or sudden collapse when arching over an air-filled void fails. Fortunately the latter is less common in Chalk (due both to the low strength of the Chalk and of the infill). Situations where arching will occur are in narrow dissolution pipes, where the distance to be arched by the infill is small, or below harder bands in the chalk.
22. In the majority of cases where dissolution features exist beneath granular cover engineers are faced with areas of loose ground, formed when the superficial soil over dissolution features expands to fill the dissolved chalk rock head (ref. 12). Where they exist in areas without cover the infill will be considerably more compressible than the host rock. The uniform loading of an area of ground containing such conditions would result in differential settlement and this needs to be taken into account during design.
23. In many situations dissolution features will have been inactive for many thousands of years and the infill might be considered stable, yet these features can still be problematic if reactivated. Indeed it is as the result of triggering both old and more recent features that many cases of subsidence occur. Natural triggers include heavy rainstorms or longer term changes in groundwater levels. More relevant to civil engineers are the triggering factors for which they are responsible. These can be divided into two types;
    (i) Factors which change the soil stress levels such as static or dynamic loading
    (ii) Factors which change the groundwater flow regime such as leaking water services, surface water soakaways or drainage off the edges of areas of impermeable surfacing (eg hardstandings).

Case Histories
24. Fontwell. During November 1985 a 24" plastic water main burst adjacent to a country lane in Fontwell, Hampshire. As a result an area of land on which there was no history of ground movement suffered considerable subsidence. This subsidence led to claims against the responsible water company by four separate parties.
25. The site is located on the feathering edge of valley gravel deposits overlying Upper Chalk. In many areas the Chalk is overlain by a thin layer of sand which lies beneath the head gravel. This layer is very easily washed down into fissures in the Chalk, allowing voids to form underneath the gravel. In this case what was remarkable was the speed with which the leaking water main triggered collapse. The water main burst at approximately 5.00am and the water supply was turned off by 7.30am. By lunchtime about eighty circular collapses had occurred (see Plate 1). These collapses were witnessed by a local resident. She recalls the majority of

the holes forming in a wave motion within the space of minutes.

26. The resultant surface depressions had near-vertical sides, and were typically two to three metres in diameter and up to three metres deep. Of four properties affected one suffered serious structural damage. The highway pavement was destroyed in several places and one motorist's car was damaged when a collapse took place beneath it, as he was driving along the road.

27. For collapses to have occurred in such a short space of time the voids which collapsed must have already been present. The cavities were stable enough, prior to the burst, to allow agricultural machinery and road traffic to pass overhead, yet within two hours of water being allowed to pass through them collapses took place. This case study demonstrates the dramatic triggering effect induced ground water flow can have on metastable dissolution features.

Plate 1 Dissolution feature collapses at Fontwell, West Sussex

28. North Chichester. The geology north of Chichester comprises Reading Beds overlying Upper Chalk with a few metres cover of drift valley gravel. In addition, as at Fontwell, the remnants of a raised beach lie directly over the chalk in many areas. The feathering edge of the Reading beds runs approximately east-west and it is along this line that there is a history of ground subsidence and collapse.

29. To the northwest of Chichester is Brandy Hole Lane, famous locally for its abundance of dolines and associated subsidence. There are also some swallowholes and caves. Local properties are subject to subsidence and occasionally collapse on a regular basis. At one property subsidence of ground in the back garden occurs every two years or so, and is used to dispose of garden refuse.

30. Surprisingly these regular subsidences have led to minimal structural damage of the adjacent properties. One possible explanation is that when originally constructed the houses were sited on the flattest ground available and consequently have avoided the majority of dissolution activity.

31. Further east, in Tregarth Road, houses have been subjected to minor structural damage, resulting in underpinning being used to secure the properties against further damage. Whilst the ground investigation for the underpinning was underway further subsidence took place under the road. This caused further damage to an adjacent property, but since then no further movement has been recorded.

32. Close by, in Summersdale Road, a local water main burst during 1976, causing a 3m diameter crater in the road, about 1m deep. The subsidence caused considerable damage to three adjacent properties, one of which was declared unsafe to be inhabited. There was also damage caused to a gas main. It is possible in cases where a leaking water main triggers collapse that small naturally occurring movement initially causes the burst. A sudden discharge of water then goes on to accelerate the subsidence process.

33. In the years following the collapse referred to in paragraph 32 a large new housing development was constructed just to the east of Summersdale road. As a result of the local history of subsidence additional measures were taken to avoid reoccurrences. These measures were based upon a detailed ground investigation utilising boreholes, trial pits, geophysics and dynamic probing. As a result of the site investigation expensive vibrocompaction and gravel placement techniques were employed to improve the bearing capacity of the ground. Some of the houses were resited away from unstable ground and the groundwater soakaways were carefully positioned. In addition raft foundations able to span 1m unsupported were specified. Since construction ten years ago there have been no reports of any ground movement.

34. Identifying the presence of dissolution features. As has been noted, dissolution features are likely beneath any site where the Chalk is at or near to the ground surface. A risk to construction is present when there is uncertainty over the location of dissolution features, but this can be designed out once the locations are known. But even on a site where features are likely to be present there is no positive way of identifying all the features short of excavating the whole site to chalk rock head. There will always therefore be a risk of some magnitude when the conditions for dissolution feature development, discussed in paragraph 16, are present.

35. Routine ground investigation typically involves the drilling and sampling of boreholes, and the excavation of exploratory pits. These methods will probably sample less than 1 part in 1,000,000 of the ground that may subsequently affect construction. The use of such 'direct' methods of investigation alone can have several consequences;

    (i) Some features are found during a ground investigation, and additional cost is incurred in redesign or ground improvement. But doubt remains that additional, unidentified, dissolution features are present.

    (ii) No features are identified, despite considerable expenditure on ground investigation in an attempt to locate the hazard. Doubt remains as to the acceptability of the design, but construction is successfully completed.

    (iii) No features are identified during ground investigation, but features are unearthed during construction, and further costs are incurred as a result of disruption to the contract, redesign, temporary works and ground improvement measures

    (iv) No features are identified during ground investigation, but subsidence and consequent structural damage occurs after construction due to movements of a previously unidentified dissolution feature.

This is a slightly negative view of the situation, but illustrates the difficulties facing an engineer who is confronted with a site where there is the possibility of dissolution features being present. Cost is incurred when dissolution features are identified but this is preferable to the possible danger and higher costs of remedial works on a site where these features remain unidentified.

36. The cost of housing subsidence claims in 1992 is thought to have been of the order of £550 million. From this, the area of the Chalk in southern England, and an estimate of the percentage of subsidence claims which result from construction on or near dissolution features we have conservatively estimated the annual cost resulting from this hazard at between £1m and £5m. We currently have no information regarding the cost of dissolution features to civil engineering construction; subsidence insurance cover is not available for this type of work, and the quantum of a contractual claim is rarely made public. However, the annual cost must be considerable.

37. What is required in avoiding this type of problem is a strategy which can form the basis for the decisions which must be made. For this to be achieved it is necessary to assess not only what level of hazard is involved, but also what combination of methods are best suited to locating any dissolution features on a given site, and what the various cost implications might be for design and construction. Only on the basis of this information can informed decisions be made.

38. Attempts in the past have been made to assess the level of hazard associated with dissolution features for various sites (refs. 7-9.) What these hazard assessments actually do is to predict areas of high feature density. Little attempt has been made to assess the risk, which is a function of the nature of the features and the proposed use to which the ground is to be used (eg the vulnerability of a particular type of structure). Risk assessments are useful in the planning stage of a project and will be discussed, along with cost implications, later in the paper.

Relevance to various types of construction

39. Low rise construction, such as housing and industrial units, apply relatively low loads to the ground. Because pad or strip foundations are typically used the depth of stressing of the ground is relatively shallow. Site investigations are often brief and generalised, a situation in which dissolution features may be overlooked or unidentified. In addition such sites generally have a very high percentage of land area which is impermeable, which leads to high groundwater loading on the remaining permeable land and possible activation of existing features. It can be seen that in this situation, where the budget for ground investigation is small, a detailed deskstudy and assessment of hazard is essential. The existence of dissolution features may not be noticed until after construction when subsidence takes place.

40. Where sites are to be subject to loadings from large scale structures the scale of ground investigations is often more detailed than for low rise structures, and foundations will probably be deeper. This not only increases the likely-hood of detecting any major dissolution features, but also means that minor features will pose less of a risk to construction. If the features are not detected during the ground investigation stage then there is a good chance of them being discovered during construction due to the deeper depth of excavation required for foundations. This situation, whilst preferable to discovery after construction, still leads to delays and expense.

41. Where road schemes cross the Chalk outcrop, allowance must be made not only for remedial works to any dissolution features encountered, but also for the possibility that the mixing of cohesive infill with the Chalk will make the entire fill untrafficable. Due to the large area of most sites it cannot be expected that all features will be identified before construction, except perhaps around the sites of structures such as bridge abutments, where the ground investigation can be intensified.

42. A hazard which must be considered in road schemes and all other schemes where polluted run off is produced, is pollution of the chalk aquifer. If any dissolution features are present then surface run off will quickly be passed into the aquifer. As many areas utilise the chalk aquifer as a source of drinking water pollutants must be prevented from reaching the aquifer.

APPROACHES TO THE ASSESSMENT AND CONTROL OF RISK

The Risk

43. The potential risk in constructing on a site where dissolution features may be present has now been discussed. It is important that this risk is quantified at an early stage in order to enable rational decisions concerning the construction program to be made.

44. Hazard Assessment. An assessment of the expected density of dissolution features should be carried out as part of the ground investigation desk study. This study will draw upon data from several sources and has been discussed in detail by Edmonds (ref. 7), Culshaw and Waltham (ref. 13), Holliday (ref. 9) and West (ref. 14.) In summary these sources are; geological maps, memoirs, remote sensing, geological field slips, and other literature sources. From these sources some dissolution features may be identifiable, but more probably there will be little hard information on the actual site to be developed.

45. Information will also be available relating to the conditions suitable for dissolution feature development as discussed in paragraphs 1-7 which will help in density prediction. Attempts have been made to relate these genetic factors to density in a formalised model (paragraph 18). The authors of references 7-9 claim some success for these models, which enable predicted density maps to be produced. From the predicted density the probability of a dissolution feature being located under the proposed construction can be calculated and expressed as an integer between 0 and 1.

46. A strategy is then required to allow logical decisions to be made during the ground investigation of the site. Given the typical plan area of dissolution features, the use of direct methods of investigation (ie drilling and trial pitting) cannot be regarded as an economical way of determining whether or not such features are present, and where they may be located, even when very significant expenditure on such techniques is possible.

47. Location of dissolution features. If an attempt is to be made to delineate any existing dissolution features then it must be realised that success very much depends on the physical size of the features and the depth of cover. A well-designed ground investigation will involve a combination of indirect methods of investigation (air photo interpretation, geophysics), and direct methods (drilling, probing and trial pitting).

48. A direct investigation on its own is of little value as the quality of ground truth will only be a function of the number of boreholes or probes. This gives even a very thorough and consequently expensive site investigation a low chance of detecting many features. Conversely indirect methods such as geophysics will enable data to be obtained for the whole site at a much lower cost but with ambiguity and a lack of clarity.

49. With a combination of direct and indirect techniques, air photo interpretation and geophysics could be used as a precursor to drilling and trial pitting, focusing attention on suspicious anomalies. But at the present time no definitive study has been carried out to determine which of the available indirect methods of investigation are likely to be successful, and under what conditions.

50. Risk to development. The amount of expenditure on ground investigation (whether direct or indirect) should clearly be related to the financial risks associated with development of a particular site. The financial loss would be different depending upon whether a dissolution feature was found during construction or whether subsidence took place after construction. This loss would also be influenced by the type of foundation being proposed, the intended use of the building, the type of contract being used and the expected damage if subsidence took

place. These matters are therefore not only inter-related, but also difficult to determine with any accuracy, particularly in the light of the large variation in the expected density of dissolution features, and the high levels of loss which are associated with dissolution features.

51.   Perhaps for this reason, and because currently available ground investigation techniques are not seen to be particularly well-suited for the purpose, it is common for the sums of money available for expenditure on ground investigation to be small, and unrelated to the variations in risk which occur. Clearly further research is needed to determine the efficacy of indirect methods, but until this is completed it is suggested that other (design) strategies are available. These are described below.

Unacceptable Risk
52. If the risk to development is considered unacceptable then two courses of action are open. The first is to design the structure to cope with the localised settlements associated with the unknown dissolution features. The second is to decide on the location(s) of structures on the site, and then carry out a detailed direct and indirect investigation to determine whether features exist in this specific area. If dissolution features are found then the construction must either be resited, or redesigned to accommodate the expected settlement, or the features must be stabilised by ground improvement. The decision between the two courses of action would be made on the basis of time and cost. The two options will now be considered in further detail.

53. Unidentified dissolution features. The risk of subsidence due to dissolution features which have not been located can be reduced in two ways. The first is to minimise any triggering factors and the second is to produce a construction which can cope with the expected differential settlement.

54.   For example, the careful siting of groundwater soakaways and the use of raft foundations would considerably reduce the risk of subsidence for a housing development. Such a case is cited by Edmonds (ref. 12) for a housing development in Henley-on-Thames, and this example demonstrates the triggering factor of the construction process itself.

55. It is important to not only reduce the risk of subsidence after construction but during construction. The major causes of failure during construction are overstressing of the ground and increased input of water into the ground.

56. For larger structures being constructed on a site with unidentified dissolution features an alternative foundation solution is to pile into proven bedrock. Other strategies for the reduction of risk by design relate to general ground improvement. The intended sites of structures can be preloaded, dynamically compacted or jet grouted in an attempt to reduce the possible differential settlement connected with unidentified dissolution features.

57. Reducing the risk for identified features. There are two strategies for reducing the risk of subsidence once the location of existing dissolution features is known. The first is to undertake ground improvement and the second is to carry out redesign of the construction. The decision between the two will be made as a result of a careful comparison of all the possible alternatives and the reduction in risk each affords.

58. As discussed in paragraph 56 there are several methods available for general ground improvement. In situations where the location of dissolution features is known these efforts can be concentrated. The technique of pressure grouting has been described by Ryan (ref. 15) and Sowers (ref. 16). The injection of grout is preceded by the installation of grout tubes to a specified depth which makes the technique expensive. It is a technique thought mainly suitable where voids, as opposed to loose ground conditions, exist.

59. The use of dynamic compaction has been described by Guyot (ref. 17) both as a method of ground improvement and as a means of locating features. Voids and loose zones can be compacted down to depths of 9 metres and the resultant depression can then be topped up with compacted granular fill.

60. A solution applicable only in cases where the exact location of the feature is known is to excavate and replace the loose infill with compacted material. A generalised scheme for repair is demonstrated by Sowers (ref. 16) which includes the use of geotextile reinforcement and a low permeability capping layer.

61. Differential movement can be reduced by using piled foundations founded in sound rock. Another solution is to produce a foundation grid spanning between proven areas of chalk rockhead. Where the spanning distances are too great for an economical solution and the depth too great for excavation an alternative solution has been suggested by Wagener and Day (ref. 18). The solution uses a mattress of improved material to reduce foundation stresses and consequent differential settlements. This solution has not been included under ground improvement as it forms an integral part of the foundation system dispersing stresses to acceptable levels.

62. The complete strategy suggested above for dealing with the risk inherent in constructing on a site where dissolution features are suspected is summarised in a flow diagram in figure 3.

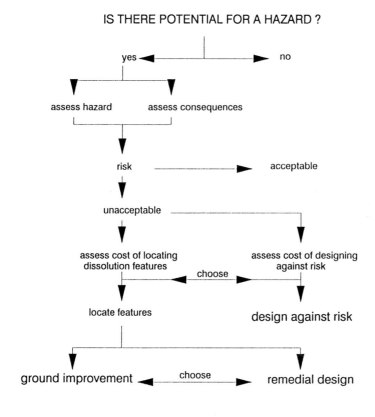

Fig. 3 Flow diagram summarising the straegy for dealing with dissolution feature risk.

CONCLUSIONS

63. Dissolution features pose a real hazard for civil engineers contemplating construction on a site underlain by chalk. These features are generally difficult and expensive to locate using direct ground investigation techniques. Indirect methods of ground investigation appear attractive, but their efficacy is uncertain.

64. At present, then, the most effective method of allowing for the presence of dissolution features is during design. A design strategy has been illustrated in the form of a flow diagram. Although subjective it is aimed at the civil engineer who has the responsibility of choosing between alternative sites and construction techniques. If used in a comparative way logical decisions can be made.

65. Work is currently being undertaken at the University of Surrey attempting to make a comparative evaluation, both in terms of cost and success, of the various indirect methods available for locating dissolution features. This work is being based on a detailed examination of the shape and form which features typically take. It is hoped that the results from this research will help further improve the assessment of risk due to dissolution features.

ACKNOWLEDGEMENTS

This work forms part of a research project funded by SERC. Photograph (Plate 1) reproduced by kind permission of Sealand Aerial Photography.

REFERENCES

1. SPERLING, C.B.H., GOUDIE, A.S., STODDARD, D.R. and POOLE, G.G. (1977) Dolines in the Dorset Chalklands and other areas in southern Britain. Trans. Inst. Brit. Geogr. NS 2, pp.205-23.
2. EDMONDS, C.N. (1983) Towards the prediction of subsidence risk upon the Chalk outcrop. Q.J.Eng.Geol. Vol.16. pp.261-66.
3. CLAYTON, C.R.I. (1983) The influence of diagenesis on some index properties of chalk in England. Geotechnique. 33,3. pp.225-241.
4. VENI, G. (1987) Fracture permeability: Implications on cave and sinkhole development and their environmental assessments. From Karst Hydrogeology. Beck B.F. (Ed.) Florida Sinkhole Research Institute, Orlando, Florida.
5. PRICE, D.J. (1984) Karst progression. From Sinkholes: Their geology, engineering and environmental impact. Beck B.F. (Ed.) Florida Sinkhole Research Institute, Orlando, Florida.
6. HUBBARD, D.A. (1984) Sinkhole distribution in the central and northern valley and ridge province, Virginia. From Sinkholes: Their geology, engineering and environmental impact. Beck B.F. (Ed.) Florida Sinkhole Research Institute, Orlando, Florida.
7. EDMONDS, C.N. (1987) The engineering geomorphology of Karst development and the prediction of subsidence risk upon the chalk outcrop of England. PhD Thesis. Royal Holloway and Bedford New College.
8. HIGGINBOTTOM, I.E. (1979) Pipes and swallow holes on chalk. Presentation to Eng. Group of the Geol. Soc. of London. Unpublished.
9. HOLLIDAY, J.K. (1992) The genesis, occurrence and engineering significance of solution features in the chalk of Kent. M.Sc. Dissertation. University of Surrey.
10. LORD, J.A. (1990) Foundations in Chalk. Proc. Int. Chalk Symposium, Brighton, pp.301-327. Thomas Telford Limited, London
11. BRACEGIRDLE, A., MAIR, R.J., DAYNES, D.J. (1990) Construction problems associated with an excavation in chalk at Costessy, Norfolk. Proc. Int. Chalk Symposium, Brighton, pp.385-393. Thomas Telford Limited, London.
12. EDMONDS, C.N. 1988. Induced subsurface movements assosciated with the presence of natural and artificial openings in areas underlain by Cretaceous Chalk. Geological Society Engineering Special Publication. No.5, pp. 205-214.

13.   CULSHAW, M.G., WALTHAM, A.C. (1987) Natural and artificial cavities as ground engineering hazards. Q.J.E.G. V.20. pp. 139-150.

14.   WEST, G. (1986) Desk studies, air photograph interpretation and reconnaissance for site investigation. Proc. Engineering Group Conference, Guildford. Geol.Soc., Eng.Geol. Special Publication No.2.

15.   RYAN, R.R. (1984) High volume grouting to control sinkhole subsidence. From Sinkholes: Their geology, engineering and environmental impact. Beck B.F. (Ed.) Florida Sinkhole Research Institute, Orlando, Florida, pp.413-417.

16.   SOWERS, G.F. (1984) Correction and protection in limestone terrane. From Sinkholes: Their geology, engineering and environmental impact. Beck B.F. (Ed.) Florida Sinkhole Research Institute, Orlando, Florida, pp.373-378.

17.   GUYOT, C.A. (1984) Collapse and compaction of sinkholes by dynamic compaction. From Sinkholes: Their geology, engineering and environmental impact. Beck B.F. (Ed.) Florida Sinkhole Research Institute, Orlando, Florida, pp.419-422.

18.   WAGENER, F. von M., DAY, P.W. (1984) Construction on dolomite in South Africa. From Sinkholes: Their geology, engineering and environmental impact. Beck B.F. (Ed.) Florida Sinkhole Research Institute, Orlando, Florida, pp.403-411.

8. Project risks and site investigation strategy

I. L. WHYTE, UMIST, UK, and D. M. TONKS, Manstock Geotechnical
Consultancy Services Ltd, UK

SYNOPSIS. A significant cause of inadequate site investigation is
the lack of proper strategic planning and provision of time and
money resource.   The paper outlines four levels of site
investigation which are then combined with reliability, risk and
complexity to form a strategic matrix. A flow-chart of actions
is given.   These form the basis for a strategy such that
investigations can be adequately planned and resourced.   The
reliability and risk levels proposed have to be reviewed to
stricter criteria for life-threatening situations and can be
relaxed when considering the financial uncertainties of a
construction project.

CONSTRUCTION RISKS AND GROUND CONDITIONS

1.   All construction projects are subject to risk from many
sources that originate from engineering, materials, management,
finance and politics.   Some risks offer gains (for example a
reduction in loan interest rates) but most have an adverse effect
leading to losses.   These can include structural collapse,
bankruptcy,   strikes,   flood   damage,   war   etc.;   they   may
individually have a high or low probability of recurrence and may
have a high or low impact.   In engineering terms ground
conditions are known to carry potentially high risks and
uncertainty. They can have a significant impact on both cost and
time resources, though it is only relatively recently that the
effects have been explicitly quantified.

2.   A 1984 study of 87 tunnelling and shaft projects in America
(1) concluded that improvement was needed in the management of
site investigations and in the levels and amount of work done.
The median cost for S.I. was 0.44% of the Engineers' estimate for
the works (range from 0.01% to as high as 24.4%).   A detailed
analysis of the projects showed a direct correlation between the
accuracy of the estimated cost (in relation to completed costs)
and the amount of investigation. In addition, claims were found
to be a significant part of tunnel costs with 49 of the 84 mined
tunnels experiencing geotechnical claims, about 60% of the total.
95% of the claims were for large amounts. For 32 projects with
sufficient data, construction costs were $1364.8M and the total
claims submitted came to 18.5%. The amount paid on the claims

came to 12%. It was suspected that these figures may be low due to unresolved claims and litigation in process on some contracts. The level and number of claims was found to relate inversely to the extent of site investigation, high levels of investigation moderated both the occurrence of claims and their severity. It was recommended that for future tunnel works the expenditure for site investigation should be increased to an average of 3% of estimated project cost. This would result in improved management and financial control of the works.

3.   A more recent American study (2) of 500 geotechnical failures has revealed that 88% of the failures were produced by human shortcomings. Most failures originated in the design process (approximately 75%). The number of incidents can be reduced by improving both communications and design and construction strategies.

4.   In the UK, a report by the ICE Ground Engineering Board (3) stated that in civil engineering and building projects the largest element of technical and financial risk lies normally in the ground. With building projects, two representative studies showed 37% and 50% suffered delays due to ground problems. Similar problems were reported for road and bridge schemes. More recently, a Government report (4) of October 1992 showed the average final outurn cost increase above tender values for completed highway contracts rose from 15% in 1986–87 to 28% in 1990–91. Analysis of 17 contracts showed 44% of the cost increase to be attributable to unforeseen ground conditions and earthworks: an earlier analysis of 42 contracts completed in 1988–89 showed the geotechnical cost increase to be 40% of the total overrun (again 28% of contract value for 1988–89).

5.   In 1990–91 the value of highway contracts awarded was £880 million, an amount which represented about 17% of all civil engineering works for that year. If it is assumed that these contracts increased in cost by 28%, and that 40% of this figure (about 0.4 x 28% = 11%) was attributable to geotechnical problems, then the annual cost of ground uncertainties on highways was about £100 million. If it is further assumed that these figures can be extrapolated to all civil works, then the cost of geotechnical uncertainty in 1990–91 can be estimated to have been of the order

$$£\frac{880}{0.17} \times 0.11 = £570 \text{ million} \tag{1}$$

Whilst this figure may not be reliable, it does indicate a possible order of cost to the country of the failure to foresee ground conditions.

6.   Figures on the cost of site investigations in the UK are not reported but published data (5,6) suggest an average value of 0.5% of contract cost, a figure of similar order to that reported from the American tunnel study. The cost of site investigation for highways in 1990–91 in the UK could therefore have been

around £4.4 million. It is likely that a relatively modest increase in investigative/planning costs would have produced a significant reduction in "unforeseen" geotechnical claims. The American tunnel study reports, for example, that an average 3% spend on investigations would be sufficient to avoid major claims and for contracts to complete on cost. It is of interest to note that the UK approach for highways (4) has been to recommend a transfer of the risk from the client to contractor rather than to invest more on the technology to avoid the uncertainty.

SITE INVESTIGATIONS

7.   The development and practice of site investigations have been reported (5,6). Routine investigatory work evolved as a contractual service commissioned by competitive tender, though formal conditions of contract were rarely used. Over the years, standards deteriorated and the industry suffered severe financial problems in the 1980's. A report by BRE/CIRIA in 1986 (7) confirmed the problems inherent with site investigations. This produced a response in the industry and has led to the publication of reports such as that by the ICE Ground Engineering Board (3). Research also started into quantifying the risks associated with ground conditions (8).

8.   A call for change was made by Rowe in his 1972 Rankine lecture (9). In this, three classes of investigation appropriate to the proposed work, ground conditions and available finance were proposed. These are summarised below:

Class	Projects	Notes
A	Major works: dams, retaining walls, heavy/deep foundations in difficult ground.	Large quality sampling, modelling. Flexible procedure.
B	More limited projects where difficult ground occurs	A few large samples may be desirable.
C	Building work, factories, housing, sewers, highways at or close to ground level	Sample examination, a few index tests

Rowe adapted and recommended a quality classification system for sampling procedures, this was later used in the 1982 Code of Practice BS 5930.

9.   A more detailed assessment of site investigation requirements was presented in 1987 in a draft model for Eurocode 7 (10):

Geotechnical category	Structure	Ground conditions
1	Small Simple Straightforward	Uniform Adequate Characteristics
2	Conventional	Varied
3	Large Unusual	Complex Problematic Poor Characteristics

Detailed comment was made on the various features of each geotechnical classification. The Eurocode recommendation is more detailed than that given by Rowe. No guidance is offered however as to how to deal with a small, simple structure on complex and problematic ground.

10. Considerations as to how to deal with risk and reliability have been developed for specific geotechnical problems, for example Cole (11,12) reported a strategy for building in areas of abandoned shallow mineworkings.

RISK, RELIABILITY AND COMPLEXITY
11. Risks relate to hazards and the chances of suffering adverse consequences and losses. Analysis of the hazards may lead to a quantification of the probability of a risk occurring, for example the chance of death in a year from all causes is 1 in 84. Other death risks per annum are:

Cause	Risk per annum
	Risky
All causes (mainly natural)	1:84
Rock climbing (200 hrs/year)	1:125
Deep sea fishing (employees)	1:1140
	Some risk
Road accidents	1:10,000
Construction (employees)	1:10,870
Fire or flame	1:66,700
	Not likely
Excessive cold	1:125,000
Gas incident	1:555,000
Lightning	1:10 million
(Source HSE, 1989 (13))	

12. It is possible to relate the probability to the degree of risk (11,12) and a simple system is adopted in this paper. Thus events having a 1:100, or less, probability are termed 'risky', up to 1:10,000 represent some risk whilst at 1:1 million events are unlikely to occur.

13. In many management situations reliable data on risks are not available or are non-existent. Risk events are then uncertain and any estimate is bound to be partly subjective. Estimated failure probabilities are : more of an indication of a belief in the system reliability. It may be more valuable to convert 'risks' to 'reliability' as a better expression of an engineer's belief in his designs and estimates. This may aid the communication of the concepts to others involved in the process, particularly clients.

14. Reliability is related to failure probability, risk, (14) as follows:

$$R = 1.0 - P_F$$

where R = Reliability
       P_F = Probability of Failure (<1)

Thus a 1:100 risky event is 99% reliable, can give cause for concern and may not even be acceptable. A 1:10,000 event is 99.99% reliable and may be of little concern. Caution in design would be warranted.

15. A 1:1 million risk would not normally cause any concern. (Major exceptions are life-threatening and catastrophic risks such as those associated with nuclear safety, for example).

16. Table 1 summarises the above classifications. In addition, complexity is considered since construction and development is variable. Complex situations can be power stations, dams, etc. Routine construction would be most highway systems, building development, sewage works etc. whilst simple structures would include houses, industrial sheds, low-rise buildings etc.

Table 1(a)   CLASSIFICATIONS FOR RISKS

	HIGH	MODERATE	LOW
RISKS	10^{-2}	10^{-4}	10^{-6}
	Risky	Some Risk	Unlikely

Table 1(b)   CLASSIFICATIONS FOR RELIABILITY

	LOW	MODERATE	HIGH
RELIABILITY	99%	99.99%	100%
	Concerned	Cautious	Unconcerned

Table 1(c)   CLASSIFICATIONS FOR COMPLEXITY

COMPLEXITY	HIGH	MODERATE	LOW
	Complex	Routine	Simple

17.   Examples of some risk and reliability factors and their degrees are reported in Table 2.   Factors that comprise complexity are also considered. Other items can be considered as necessary on an individual project basis, eg., political uncertainty, terrorism,

Table 2:
EXAMPLES for RISKS/RELIABILITY and COMPLEXITY

Risks/Reliability:			
▪ Life ▪ Environment ▪ Money ▪ Property ▪ Contractual	Death Major/Extensive gamble structural claim probable	Injury some/local commercial cosmetic claim possible	Normal Natural secure stable claims unlikely
Complexity:			
Structural Geotechnical Hydrology Hazards Remedial measures	Complicated Complex Variable Hazardous Complex	routine varied simple toxins routine	simple non-problematical not relevant phytotoxins straightforward

18.   Estimating the levels of risk/reliability and complexity has to be subjective in most circumstances. It is possible, however, for example:

Property risk/reliability
19.   Clients would be concerned if there was a high risk of structural instability and damage (ie. low reliability of performance).   They would, however, be less concerned about cosmetic damage to surface finishes provided these are readily repaired by routine maintenance. Absolute stability may not be necessary, but may be required for particularly sensitive structures such as nuclear plant and dams where 100% effective reliability is demanded.

Geotechnical Complexity
20.   Ground conditions can be difficult and problematical, such as a recent alluvial sequence of deposits that vary laterally and vertically.   These represent complex conditions.   In glacial areas, however, varied conditions can also exist but the ground

may have adequate strength and stiffness such that it is less difficult to engineer. Where deposits are known, relatively uniform and exhibit good characteristics then the conditions can be considered to be non-problematical.

Level of Investigation

21. Four levels of investigation are outlined in table 3:

Table 3

	LEVEL			
	A	B	C	D
Operation	Simple	Routine	Special	Excellent
Preliminary/ Desk study	General	Detailed	Extensive	Complete
Trial pits/ probes	Some	Possible	Special	Special
Boreholes	---	Standard	Specific	Special
Sampling/ Testing	Identification	Routine	Special	Particular
Monitoring	---	Possible	Some	Extensive
Report	Confirmatory	Skilful	Authoritative	Specialised

22. Level A: Investigations that are most simple and take account of empiricism and engineering experience. Detailed specification of site works is not warranted and costs can be expected to be low. Skill is necessary to confirm, by exception, from the criteria that a simple investigation is adequate and sufficient.

23. Level B: Investigations that have evolved as a general good practice within the construction industry. Works can be properly let according to standard specifications and guidelines, within the UK this would consist normally of cable-percussion borings with U100 and SPT sampling. Some engineering analysis is warranted, but information may not be wholly reliable and skilful interpretation is necessary from geotechnical engineers.

24. Level C: An investigation of greater depth and scope that the more routine (level B) studies. Desk Studies are extensive and thorough. Specifications would be written to suit the site conditions for the exploratory works. For example, special drilling methods may be required with water balance maintained in the borings. Large diameter boreholes with piston sampling may be specified, U100 sampling can not be of adequate quality. Special in-situ

tests may be commissioned, eg. self—boring pressuremeters, along with piezometer instrumentation. Authoritative reports would be given.

25. Level D: Investigations are to the highest standards and specifications. Desk studies are exhaustive with all available information from any possible source consulted. State—of—the—art technology would be employed in drilling, sampling and testing, possibly including research levels of work. Reports could be from specialists of national and international reputation. Work would be to the highest level of specification and the necessary cost and time resources to undertake the work has to be made available. It is not likely that work of this quality would be commissioned at the start of a project (except for particularly complicated schemes where the highest levels of reliability are required). It is to be expected that earlier studies at levels B or C would identify the problematical conditions that justify a study of this intensity.

STRATEGY MODEL

26. Previous strategies for investigation have been reviewed. Whilst these are helpful, they are not sufficiently complete to account for the various risks/reliability levels and complexity of engineering works. Positive guidance is needed if the expensive experiences reported for ground conditions from both the UK and USA are to be avoided. A tentative strategy model incorporating the considerations given above is shown in Table 4.

Table 4:

		GROUND RELIABILITY		
		High "unconcerned"	Moderate "cautious"	Low "concerned"
COMPLEXITY	LOW "Straightforward"	A	(A)→B→(C)	B→C
	MODERATE "Routine"	B	B→C	B→C→(D)
	HIGH "Complex"	B→C	B→C→(D)	C→D
		LOW "not likely"	Moderate "some risk"	High "risky"
		GROUND RISK		

Investigation levels (A,B,C,D) in relation to ground reliability, risk and complexity.

27.   Examples of possible combinations include:

(i)   <u>A simple portal-framed factory (a structure of low complexity).</u>

28.   Such a building on a greenfield site in a known area of good ground can be designed and built with high reliability and low risk: a simple investigation is necessary to confirm the conditions.

29.   A factory on a "brownfield" site (which may be detected from the simple investigation) needs to be treated more cautiously because of the increased risk of instability and more difficult foundation conditions.   Generally a "routine" investigation of good practice would suffice, but on occasion a more extensive study of a particular problem that has been identified may be necessary (eg. methane gas).

30.   A factory to be built on polluted land containing "highly toxic" contaminants could represent a straightforward structure on a high risk site where there are concerns over safety to people. It is likely that a "routine" investigation may identify the high risk elements with special investigations then into these areas.

(ii)   <u>Routine structures</u>

31.   More routine works include bridges, highways, tunnels and high rise structures. A sewer tunnel through competent, uniform clay could represent a job of "moderate" complexity with "high" reliability, i.e. low risk. A similar tunnel in variable water-bearing ground would require a more cautious approach. Should the ground become hazardous (a danger to the workman or public) with, perhaps, listed buildings overhead then this would cause concern due to the risky nature. A "routine" exploration can be used to help define the risks, but this would be backed up with special surveys(C) and, if warranted, levels of excellence (D).

(iii) <u>Complex projects</u>
32.   Projects of high complexity can be of large scale, eg a major motorway commissioned under BOOT conditions, of structural nature, eg a major process plant development or nuclear power station, of environmental concern, eg. waste disposal, etc. The ground reliability would relate not only to specific site geotechnical operations (eg.deep excavations, heavy foundations) but may also involve wider considerations such as regional seismicity, ground water regime etc.

33.   It is to be noted that the selection of an investigation

level and strategy can be conditioned by the nature of the
uncertainty. Thus factors which offer financial reward/gain may
be accepted with relatively higher risks (ie. lower investigation
levels) than factors which offer life risks. The latter demand
higher levels of investigation for a particular risk category.
For example, a developer may be prepared to gamble on the ground
conditions for a fast track development but such gambles are not
acceptable for life-threatening structures such as flood
defences, dams, radio-active facilities. What is important is
planning, designing and building with "eyes open" to the risks.

34. An outline flow-chart giving the iterative procedure is
shown in figure 5. This has been derived from general
considerations and should perhaps be modified to suit the
particular conditions of any development. For example, different
approaches are possible for conventional design and contract
works relative to turnkey contracts and BOT or BOOT projects.

DISCUSSION
35. A strategy for selecting the level of site investigation to
the degree of risk or reliability required has been presented.
Further development will occur, both in terms of debate over
levels of risk and reliability and in terms of specifications for
the various stages of an investigation. Care is also needed in
adjusting attitudes to differing uncertainties − it is necessary
to differentiate between hazards to life and those to structures
and finance. This paper has concentrated on the latter two
factors. Other research, for example into risk ranking and risk
analysis, will find application in strategic thinking for
construction.

36. Construction is a business with an inherent uncertainty,
particularly in financial terms. It will never be possible to
eliminate the financial risk, but control over the degree can be
exercised. At present, financial uncertainty of the order of 10-
15% may be acceptable to clients in their quest for value for
money (see ref.4 for example) but much higher levels have been
reported (reference 3). It may be necessary, therefore, to adapt
the risk classifications in this paper when considering financial
uncertainty.

37. The adoption of a risk strategy for S.I. is likely to
result in additional cost due to the increase in resources
compared to a more traditional approach. Benefit will result,
however, in improved planning and estimating, a reduction in the
level and number of claims and disputes and, perhaps most
importantly, a major reduction in the level of financial risk to
clients.

Table 5:

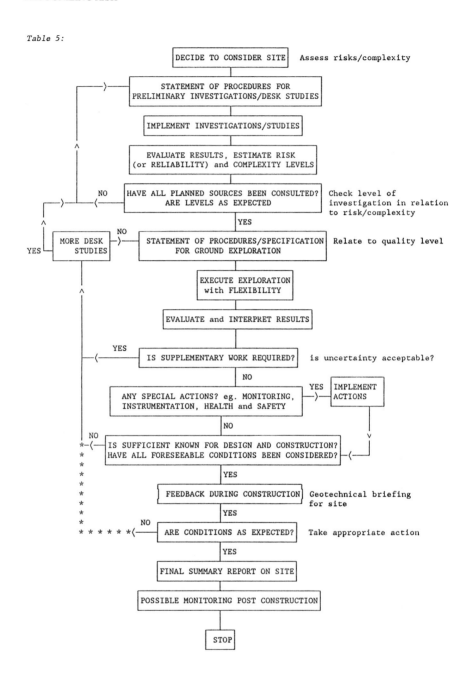

REFERENCES

1. NATIONAL RESEARCH COUNCIL. "Geotechnical Site Investigations for Underground Projects" vol.1 National Academic Press. Washington DC 1984, 182pp.

2. SOWERS G.F. "Human Factors in Civil and Geotechnical Engineering Failures". ASCE Journal. Geot.Eng. Vol 199. No.2 Feb.1993. 238-256

3. INSTITUTION OF CIVIL ENGINEERS "Inadequate Site Investigation". Thomas Telford Ltd., 1991, 26pp.

4. NATIONAL AUDIT OFFICE "Department of Transport: Contracting for Roads" HMSO, October 1992, 39pp.

5. WHYTE I.L. "The Development of Site Investigation" Ground Engng. 1976, Oct. 35-38.

6. WHYTE I.L., PEACOCK W.S. "Site Investigation Practice". Mun.Eng.Vol 5. 1988, Oct. 235-245.

7. UFF J.F., CLAYTON C.R.I. "Recommendations for the procurement of ground investigations" CIRIA, London. 1986 Special Publication 45.

8. WHYTE I.L., PEACOCK W.S. "Site Investigation and Risk Analysis" Proc.I.C.E. Civil Engineering May 1992, 74-82.

9. ROWE P.W. "The Relevance of Soil Fabric to Site Investigation Practice" Geotechnique, XXII No.2 June 1972, 193-301.

10. COMMISSION OF THE EUROPEAN COMMUNITIES COMMON UNIFIED RULES FOR GEOTECHNICS DESIGN. Draft Model for Eurocode 7, December 1987.

11. COLE K. "Building over Abandoned Shallow Mines. A Strategy for the Engineering Decisions on Treatment". Ground Engng., May 1987, Vol 20. NO.4, 14-30

12. COLE K. "Building over Abandoned Shallow Mines. Paper 1: Considerations of risk and reliability. Ground Engng. Jan/Feb. 1993 Vol 26 No.1, 34-37

13. HSE "Risk Criteria for Land Use Planning in the vicinity of Major Industrial Hazards" HMSO, 1989, London

14. COX S.J., Tait N.R.S. "Reliability, Safety and Risk Management". Butterworth-Heinemann, Oxford 1991, 289pp.

9. A new approach to safety factors for shallow foundations: load combination factors as a basis for risk assessment

R. BUTTERFIELD, University of Southampton, UK

SYNOPSIS. The paper presents a summary of both the form of, and experimental data in support of, a 3 dimensional failure envelope for shallow, sand-supported footings. This is followed by a new development of the concept of Safety Factor for such foundations under all possible planar-load increments and demonstrated that it is unlikely to exceed 1.25. The consequences of this and the significance of more-restricted load-paths are discussed, comparable results for shallowly embedded footings are presented and conclusions drawn about the practical implications of the work. Related analytical developments are presented in an appendix.

INTRODUCTION
Two-dimensional failure envelopes
1. It is well established (refs. 1-7) that, for surface, or very shallow, sand-supported, model footings (breadth = B, ranging from 50 mm to 100 mm) the envelope relating the vertical and horizontal loads (V and H) at failure, when plotted in the V - H plane, can be represented very well indeed by a simple parabolic curve. The vertical load versus moment-ratio (M/B) failure envelope can also be represented by a similar curve in the V - M/B plane as shown in Fig. 1. The tips of both parabolas lie at $V = V_{max}$ on the V axis where V_{max} is the, assumed known, centre-line, ultimate-load capacity of the footing.
2. The two parabolas are not identical but their respective maximum ordinates can be approximated closely by $H_{max} \approx V_{max}/8$ and $(M/B)_{max} \approx V_{max}/10$, Fig. 1 (ref. 3).

Three-dimensional failure envelopes
3. The full 3D failure envelope (F) in (V,H,M/B) space has now also been determined Fig. 2 from a series of extremely precise experiments in which rigid steel footings were loaded to failure using a variety of 2D and 3D loading and load-unload paths. Some of the key experiments were carried out at the University of Southampton (refs. 4,5) and others at the University of Padova (refs. 6,7). All of them used dense sands

Risk and reliability in ground engineering. Thomas Telford, London, 1993

with relative densities ranging from 75% to 85% in order to ensure that failure loads could be unambiguously identified.

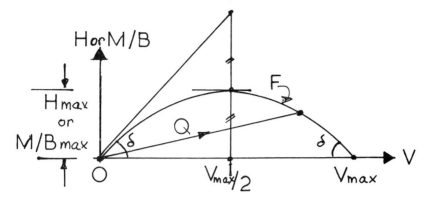

Fig. 1 Parabolic 2D failure envelopes

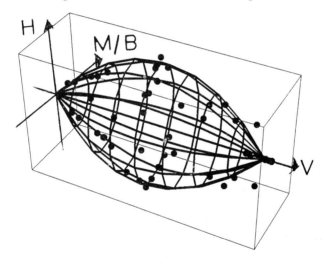

Fig. 2 A general 3D failure envelope for model footings on dense sand

4. The last of these, ref. 7, presented, for the first time, the precisely defined form of the failure envelope in H versus M/B planes (i.e. V constant sections of F). Fig. 3 shows this plotted as (H/V_{max}) versus (M/BV_{max}), with all the failure-load points, measured at different V values, scaled (parabolically) to lie in the $V = V_{max}/2$ plane. The failure envelope is clearly an inclined ellipse with, in this case, its major axis at $14°$ to (H/V_{max}) and an axis ratio of 1.60.

5. This envelope confirms the well-known result (ref. 8) that when H and M act in 'conjunction' on such a footing (Fig. 4a) its horizontal load capacity (for specific values of V and M/B) is less than when H and M

113

act in 'opposition' as in Fig. 4b. The latter situation is therefore a desirable design objective.

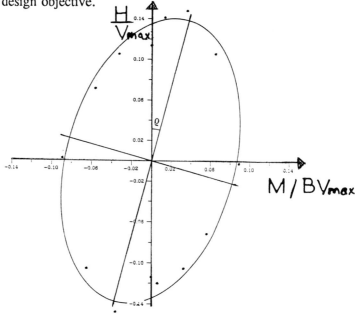

Fig. 3 Cross-section of the 3D failure envelope in the
H/V_{max} - M/BV_{max} plane

6. Fig. 3 also serves to reinforce the point that, once full planar (V,H,M/B) loading conditions arise, there is no longer a single unambiguous definition of failure load. For example, it can be seen from Figs. 1 to 3 that, for a specified value of H, two values of M/B, each of them combined with two values of V, can cause the footing to fail (i.e. there are, in all, four different (V, M/B) load pairs which will cause failure for any value of H. Therefore the general situation is far more complex than that of a conventional bearing capacity analysis).

EQUATIONS OF THE 3D FAILURE ENVELOPE
7. The complete failure envelope (F), illustrated in Figs. 1 to 3, has parabolic boundaries in planes passing through the V axis and inclined elliptical boundaries in V = constant planes. By definition, all possible (V,H,M/B) load combinations causing failure of the footing lie on F which can be described by the equation (ref. 9),

$$F = (m/t_M)^2 + (n/t_H)^2 - 2C(m/t_M)(n/t_H) - \{r(1-r)\}^2 = 0 \qquad (1)$$

where m = $M/(B.V_{max})$; n = H/V_{max} ; r = V/V_{max} and, if δ_H is the footing-sand friction angle for horizontal sliding, t_H = $\tan(\delta_H)$.

114

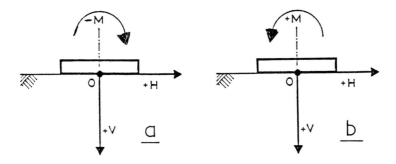

Fig. 4 Definition of load combinations

8. Therefore δ_H is also the end slope of the V - H parabola (Fig. 1). δ_M (usually less than δ_H) is the corresponding parameter for the V - M/B parabola and $t_M = \tan(\delta_M)$. As noted above the axis ratio for the experimentally determined elliptical section in ref. 9 is R = 1.60 and the inclination angle $\rho = 14°$, corresponding to $t_H = 0.52$, $\delta_H = 27.5°$ and $t_M = 0.35$, $\delta_M = 19.3°$ for the roughened, steel model-footings used.

9. From the basic geometrical properties of parabolas and inclined ellipses R, ρ, δ_H, δ_M and C are inter-related, R has therefore to satisfy,

$$R^2 = \{1 - (\tan\rho.t_M/t_H)^2\} / \{(t_M/t_H)^2 - \tan^2\rho\}$$

and C in eq.(1) is determined by the requirement that,

$$C = \tan 2\rho \ (t_H - t_M)(t_H + t_M) / 2.t_H.t_H \ = 0.22, \text{ in our case.} \qquad (2)$$

(i.e. knowledge of V_{max}, δ_H, δ_M and R or ρ fully define F and thereby ALL possible combinations of (V,H,M/B) which will cause failure of the footing). The simplest possible, rotationally symmetrical failure-envelope is defined by R=1, ρ=0, and $\delta_M = \delta_H = \delta$.

SAFETY FACTORS

10. Throughout the following development the term Safety Factor (S) will be used to designate the ratio of, the sum of the magnitudes of the initial load on a foundation (Q) and the load-increment magnitude (ΔQ), causing a bearing capacity failure, to the initial load magnitude (i.e. S = (Q + ΔQ)/Q). It is also an implicit assumption in the following that some form of failure envelope, generally similar to F, will exist for prototype foundations.

Failure under arbitrary loading regimes

11. In general, the initial load on a foundation can be plotted at P_1, say, in Fig. 5 representing a loading state $(V_1, H_1, M_1/B)$ below failure. A very important practical question is then - **what is the 'Safety Factor' of such a footing if it might be loaded subsequently by arbitrary combinations of $\pm(\Delta V, \Delta H, \Delta M/B)$ increments?**

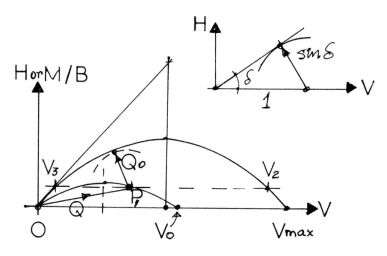

Fig. 5 Failure from a general load point

12. A possible approach would be to scale eq. (1) to pass through the load point, which means that the V axis apex of the new figure (F_o), geometrically similar to F, would lie at V_o, say, in Fig. 5, such that,

$$V_o = r_o \cdot V_{max}$$

r_o can be determined from eq. (1), by requiring F_o to pass through P_1, whence,

$$\{r_o(1-r_o)\}^2 = (n_1/t_H)^2 + (m_1/t_M)^2 - 2C(m_1/t_M)(n_1/t_H) \qquad (3)$$

a cubic equation in r_o in which $n_1 = V_1/V_{max}$ and $m_1 = H_1/V_{max}$.

13. The simplest possible definition of a Safety Factor (S_o) might then be,

$$S_o = 1/r_o = V_{max} / V_o \qquad (4)$$

which clearly includes the conventional definition of S for simple vertical, centreline loading as a special case and always becomes unity for load points on F.

14. If, however, general non-radial load increments, and/or load

decrements have to be catered for, this definition can lead to overestimates of the reserve load capacity. In particular it fails to indicate that such a footing can be brought to failure by the addition of a modest load 'increment' Q_o at P_1 in Fig. 5 (i.e. a ΔH increase together with a small ΔV decrease). Even though S_o might have an arbitrarily high value!

15. To overcome this we could require Q_o to be the **minimum distance** between the two surfaces F and F_o (i.e. between F and any P_1), Fig. 5, and the **minimum** Safety Factor **for any subsequent load increments or decrements**, might then be defined as,

$$S_{min} = (Q + Q_o)/Q = 1 + Q_o/Q \tag{5}$$

Q being the magnitude of the initial load point vector, OP_1.

$$Q = \sqrt{\{V_1{}^2 + H_1{}^2 + (M_1/B)^2\}} \tag{6}$$

Q_o is therefore the radius of the smallest **sphere**, centred on P_1, which touches the failure envelope.

16. If we consider an unpiled gravity oil platform as an example of a structure most likely to undergo extremes of combined H and M/B loading and realise that, in this case, H is also the source of M (i.e. M increases monotonically with H, $M = \alpha H$, say) and therefore all possible loading states will lie in an inclined, planar section of F passing through the V axis. Q_o will then be the radius of the smallest **circle in this plane**, centred on P_1, which touches F. An algebraic expression for the radius of this circle is developed in the Appendix and numerical examples are provided below.

17. If the tangent point on F, at the end of Q_o, is (V,H,M/B), Fig. 5, and we define $n' = \sqrt{\{(H/V_{max})^2 + (M/BV_{max})^2\}}$, and, correspondingly, $n_1' = \sqrt{\{(H_1/V_{max})^2 + (M_1/BV_{max})^2\}}$, then the analysis in the Appendix establishes the following cubic equation (eq. 19), for $r = V/V_{max}$ at failure,

$$2t^2r^3 - 3t^2r^2 + r(1 + 2tn_1' + t^2) - (r_1 + tn_1') = 0 \tag{7}$$

with $t = \tan(\delta)$ an assumed known friction coefficient. n' can then be calculated from (eq. 20),

$$n' = t.r(1 - r) \tag{8}$$

Hence the vector components of $\{Q_o/V_{max}\}$ are $\{(r -r_1),(n'-n_1'\}$ and S_{min} can be found from eqs. 5 and 6.

18. These equations generate the following results if we use $t = 0.5$

(δ = 26.6°) and define a' = Q_o/V_{max} , which is therefore the radius of the circle in the loading plane tangent to F expressed as a fraction of V_{max}.

Table 1.   Safety Factors for different initial loading states, t = 0.5

r_1'	n_1'	a'	S_{min}
0.75	0.05	0.042	1.06
0.75	0.025	0.067	1.09
0.50	0.05	0.079	1.16
0.50	0.00	0.125	1.25
0.25	0.05	0.042	1.17
0.25	0.025	0.067	1.27
0.25	0.00	0.091	1.36

19. The striking thing about the S_{min} values in the table is that they are all substantially less than 2. Reflecting on this and inspecting Fig. 5 it becomes apparent that the **maximum possible, limiting, value of S_{min}** arises when P_1 lies on the V axis at (V ,0,0) and V -> 0 (i.e. when the initial load is vertical and very small) from which,

$$(S_{min})_{max} \nrightarrow 1 + \sin(\delta) \tag{9}$$

Alternatively, **if P_1 is at ($V_{max}/2,0,0$)** halfway along the V axis then, from the geometry of a simple parabola, such as eq. (8), it follows that,

$$(S_{min})_{max} = 1 + \tan(\delta)/2 \tag{10}$$

20. Thus $(S_{min})_{max}$, as defined by eq. (5) will always be less than 1.5 unless δ > 30°. Even if δ = 35°, tan(δ) = 0.7 - an optimistic expectation for general use - $(S_{min})_{max}$ = 1.57, subject again to P_1 lying on the V axis close to the coordinate origin. A similar conclusion can be drawn for loading in any plane passing through the V axis.
21. **We have therefore established two new, practically important results, that, for S defined as in eq. (5),**

(i)   A SHALLOW FOUNDATION INTENDED TO RESIST ANY, OR ALL, ±(ΔV,ΔH,ΔM/B) LOAD INCREMENTS CANNOT, IN ANY CIRCUMSTANCES, HAVE A FACTOR OF SAFETY SIGNIFICANTLY GREATER THAN 1.5 (S $\nrightarrow$

1 + sin(δ)) AND, IN GENERAL IT WILL BE VERY MUCH
SMALLER (Table 1).

(ii)   IF SUCH A FOUNDATION IS INITIALLY LOADED
       VERTICALLY TO ONE HALF ITS LOAD CAPACITY AND
       THEN, LOADED SUBSEQUENTLY AS IN (i), IT WILL
       NOT HAVE A SAFETY FACTOR SIGNIFICANTLY
       GREATER THAN 1.25 (S = 1 + tan(δ)/2).

Failure under restricted loading regimes

22. From the previous analysis it is apparent that, even in the long
term, significant and acceptable Safety Factors can only be achieved for
such a foundation if subsequent load increments either increase the initial
loading components monotonically or decrease the inclination of the
final load vector to the V axis.

23. It is a much simpler matter to determine individual $\pm\Delta V$, or
$\pm\Delta H$, or $\pm\Delta M/B$ load increments which will lead to failure from any
initial loading point P_1. For example, the solution of eq.(1) for V_2 and
V_3, say (Fig. 5), after substituting H_1 and M_1/B, will provide the two
vertical failure-loads which are relevant if only V is allowed to change.
Then $\Delta V_2 = (V_2 - V)$ etc. and

$$S_2 = 1 + \Delta V_2/V_1 \qquad (11)$$

24. Equation (5) is useful in so far as it emphasises the inherent
vulnerability of very shallow footings, especially to horizontal load
increments, and reminds a foundation designer to consider carefully
what possible load increments and decrements are to be catered for.

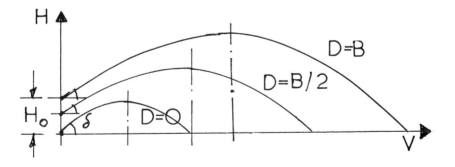

Fig. 6 Effect of embedment depth on 2D failure envelopes

Deeper footings

25. A less exhaustive set of experiments on model footings, buried at depths of B/2 and B (ref. 10), defined an (H -V) failure surface essentially similar in shape to Fig. 2 augmented by a passive (Rankine) contribution to H = H_o, say, causing increases in the H_{max}/V_{max} ratio to 1/6 and 1/4, respectively, as shown in Fig. 6. Therefore, for such cases, the value of $(S_{min})_{max}$ will be increased, with a limiting value (for very small V) easily shown to be,

$$(S_{min})_{max} = 1 + (V .\sin(\delta).\cos(\delta) + H_o) / V .\cos(\delta) \qquad (12)$$

Eq. (12) generates S = ∞ for V = 0 but substituting, as an example, V = H_o in eq. (12) we obtain, as an upper bound,

$$(S_{min})_{max} = 1 + (\sin(\delta).\cos(\delta) + 1) / \cos(\delta) \qquad (13)$$

26. For $\tan(\delta)$ = 0.5 eq. (13) produces $(S_{min})_{max}$ = 2.57. Which demonstrates that slightly deeper foundations can achieve satisfactory Safety Factors against completely random ±load increments when their initial vertical loads are well away from their ultimate vertical load capacity.

An offshore-platform example

27. In 1975 a model, offshore platform was erected in Christchurch Bay. It had been designed jointly by BRE and NPL (ref. 11) to have a modest Safety Factor of about 1.5 against wave loading so that it would undergo measurable oscillations and displacements under service-load conditions. The rigid, circular platform base had a diameter of 10.5 m founded on the surface of a medium-dense sand bed ($\phi \approx 35° - 38°$). V_{max} can be calculated conventionally to be about 40 MN. The design service-loads were V_1 = 1.25 MN, H_1 = 0.49 MN, M_1 = 3.23 MN.m and therefore $M_1/B \approx 0.34$ MN.

28. Hence Q = $\sqrt{\{(V_1)^2 + (H_1)^2 + (M_1/B)^2\}}$ = 1.38 MN and the 'equivalent' H' (see Appendix) in the loading plane will be H' = $\sqrt{\{(0.49)^2 + (0.34)^2\}}$ = 0.60. In the loading plane r_1 = V_1/V_{max} = 0.031 and n' = H'/V_{max}' = 0.015.

29. Fig. 7 shows a section of the failure envelope for the platform drawn in the loading plane of $M_1 B$ = 0.69 H_1 and, by definition, all possible load states Q will lie in this plane. In this case eq. (1) simplifies again to the simple planar parabola of eq. (8), see Appendix eq. (20).

30. It is immediately apparent that V_{max}/V_1 = 32 is a quite irrelevant quantity! Alternatively S_1 (eq. (5)) will provide the value of $(S_{min})_{max}$ using eqs. (7,8) with the above values of r = 0.031, and n' = 0.015. Using the maximum plausible value of t = 0.70, δ = 35° leads to a

predicted value of $(S_{min})_{max} = 1.15$. This would not be acceptable which suggests that the structure was **not** designed with completely general load increments in mind. (Note also that $V_o = 3.91$ in this case, hence S_o (eq. 4) comes out to be ≈ 10 - a gross overestimate!).

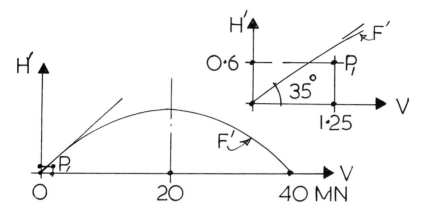

Fig. 7 Failure envelope in the plane of loading for the Christchurch Bay model platform

31. In fact, the designers **knew** that ΔV would not be negative and may, in practice, have a small positive value. It is easily checked that, at the 'failure state' in para. 30, V has decreased from 1.25 MN to 1.05 MN and H' increased from 0.60 MN to 0.71 MN. (i.e. ΔV is negative, whereas, merely from a visual inspection of Fig. 7, the whole structure could be made very much more stable by drastically **increasing** V.)

32. It would therefore be legitimate for the designers to have assumed a restricted loading regime in which failure could occur solely by an increase in n' (i.e. only an increase in H and a consequent increase in M/B, $\Delta M/B = 0.70 \Delta H$). We can find this value of n' simply by inserting r into eq. (13) which generates n' = 0.021 and therefore, at failure, H' = 0.84 MN. The value of the Safety Factor for this situation is then S = .84/.6 = 1.4 which is essentially identical to the planned design value.

33. Nevertheless it is worth observing that H and M will always act in 'conjunction' on such a platform which will locate the (H, M/B) load combination in the 'lower value' quadrant in Fig. 3. S = 1.4 may therefore be an overestimate. The platform failed following heavy storms a few weeks after installation.

CONCLUDING REMARKS
34. The critical observation made so far is that, **IF** the Safety Factor (S) of a shallow foundation is defined, conservatively, as the ratio

$(Q + \Delta Q) / Q$, where Q is an initial load magnitude and ΔQ a load increment magnitude which will bring the foundation to a failure condition, **AND** ΔQ can be any, or all, of $\pm (\Delta V, \Delta H, \Delta M)$, **THEN S $\not>$ 1 + sin(δ) and is very unlikely to exceed S = 1 + tan(δ)/2.**

35. IF the load increment path can be reliably specified, or is naturally restricted, then, depending on the path involved (paras. 30-32), the value of S might be increased substantially.

36. Nevertheless this still leaves us with the unrestricted load-increment problem. The value of δ is, in principle, independent of B and therefore increasing B produces an expansion of F without changing its intrinsic geometry near either $V = 0$ or $V = V_{max}$. Consequently both the value of M_1/BV_{max} and V_1/V_{max} can be reduced at will by increasing B, thereby enhancing the ΔV and ΔM load-increment capacity of the foundation.

37. However, the value of ΔH, acting alone, and causing failure can never exceed that necessary to produce ground-surface sliding when $\Delta H = V_1.\tan(\delta)$, whence S $\not>$ 1 + tan(δ) and we note that the value of δ is crucial in such estimates.

38. One might remark that, if the initial load point is either at, or closely adjacent to, the centroid of F (Fig. 2) (i.e. P_1 is very near $(V_{max}/2,0,0)$), then the footing will have S = 2 against (ΔV) vertical load increments, S = 1 + tan(δ_H)/2 against (ΔH) horizontal load increments and S = 1 + tan(δ_M)/2 against $\Delta(M/B)$ loading increments (the admissible value of ΔM can always be increased arbitrarily by a sufficient increase in B).

39. All of this is quite evident merely by plotting P_1 and considering loading data on diagrams like Figs. (1,2) which is, perhaps, one of the most useful outcomes of this study. It is also worth noting from Table 1 that the circle radii (a') indicate the actual **magnitudes** of the minimum load increments which will cause failure of the footing and these may be more useful in many cases than the value of S.

40. The symmetry of a' for values of r and (1-r), at a specified n_1', is evident from Fig. 3 (and Table 1) and serves to emphasise that, whereas ΔQ will be identical in both cases, the value of S will be higher for the lower value of r.

41. It is important to note the major improvement in Safety Factor which can be achieved, against all ΔQ load increments, and horizontal load increments in particular, by modest depths of burial, (Fig. 8, paras. (25,26)).

APPENDIX
Minimum Factors of Safety for general 2D loading systems
42. Fig. 8 shows a loading point P_1 (V_1, H_1') and a section F' of the failure envelope in a general loading plane (V, H'). The load vector from the origin O to P_1 = **Q.** The load increment vector $\mathbf{Q_o}$ = **a** is a

radius (a) of a circle, centre P_1, touching F' and is therefore the minimum load increment which will bring the footing to failure.

43. The equations to the parabola F' and the circle C' in Fig. 8 are,

F' $H'/t - V(V_{max} - V)/V_{max} = 0$ (15)

C' $(V - V_{max})^2 + (H' - H_1')^2 - a^2 = 0$ (16)

in which $t = \tan(\delta)$ is the relevant friction coefficient.

The components of the normal gradient vectors ∇f and ∇c to F' and C' are,

$$\{\nabla f\} = \{(2V/V_{max} - 1), 1/t, 0\} \quad \text{and}$$

$$\{\nabla c\} = \{(V - V_1), (H' - H_1'), 0\} \quad (17)$$

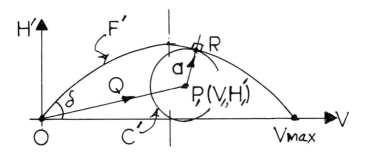

Fig. 8   A planar footing-failure envelope with a minimum critical load increment P_1R

44. We seek the common tangent point to F' and C'. This will be identified by the condition that the cross-product, $\nabla f \times \nabla c = 0$, which is necessary for the two vectors to be co-linear and leads to,

$$(2V/V_{max} - 1)(H' - H_1') - (1/t)(V - V_1) = 0 \quad (18)$$

Eliminating H' between eqs (17,18), writing $r = V/V_{max}$,

$n' = H'/V_{max}$, $r_1 = V_1/V_{max}$, $n_1' = H_1'/V_{max}$,
and re-arranging to solve for r, produces the cubic equation,

$$2t^2r^3 - 3t^2r^2 + r(1 + 2tn_1' + t^2) - (r_1 + tn_1') = 0 \quad (19)$$

From eq. (15), $n' = tr(1 - r)$ (20)

123

The circle radius $a^2 = (H' - H_1')^2 + (V - V_1)^2$, and if $a' = a/V_{max}$

$$a' = \sqrt{\{(r - r_1)^2 + (n' - n_1')^2\}} \tag{21}$$

By definition $Q = \sqrt{\{(V_1)^2 + (H_1)^2\}}$, and if $Q' = Q/V_{max}$

then

$$Q' = \sqrt{\{(r_1)^2 + (n_1')^2\}} \tag{22}$$

Whence,

$$S = (Q + Q_o)/Q = 1 + a'/Q' \tag{23}$$

Equivalent t values for general planar loading

45. The magnitude of t in the above development is not arbitrary if the loading plane is a specific section of a failure envelope (F) which incorporates known values of t_H and t_M. This section determines the value of t for this case when the plane of section, passing through the V axis, is inclined at an angle β, $\tan(\beta) = \alpha$, to the H - V plane (Fig. 3).

46. Since, by definition, $\alpha = (M_1/BH_1) = m_1/n_1$ for any specified loading point P_1 and all loading increments are to occur in this plane, then $m/n = \alpha$. The relevant parabolic failure envelope F' can therefore be determined from F (eq. 1) by substituting $m = n\alpha$. Whence,

$$(n\alpha/t_M)^2 + (n/t_H)^2 - 2C\alpha n^2/(t_M t_H) = \{r(1 - r)\}^2 \tag{24}$$

this equation can be written in the standard form $n/t = r(1-r)$ if t, which we require, has the value,

$$(1/t) = \sqrt{\{(\alpha/t_M)^2 + (1/t_M)^2 - (2C\alpha/t_M t_H)\}} \tag{25}$$

Eq. (25) therefore generates the t value relevant to a parabolic failure envelope, lying in a plane determined by P_1, and cutting a known 3D envelope itself defined by the values of t_H, t_M and C.

REFERENCES
1. BUTTERFIELD R. and TICOF J. The use of physical models in design. Discussion, Proc. VII European Conf. SMFE, Brighton, 1979, Vol.4, 259-261.
2. NOVA R. and MONTRASIO L. Settlements of shallow foundations on sand. Géotechnique, ICE, London, 1991, Vol. 41, 243-256.
3. BUTTERFIELD R. Another look at gravity platform foundations. Conf. SMFE in offshore foundations, CISM, Udine, Italy, 1981.
4. TICOF J. Surface footings on sand under general planar loads. University of Southampton, 1977, PhD thesis.

5. GEORGIADIS M. and BUTTERFIELD R. Displacements of footings on sand under eccentric and inclined loads. Can. Geotech. Journal, 1988, Vol. 25, 199-212.

6. GOTTARDI G. Modellazione del comportamento di fondazioni superficiali su sabbia suggette a diversi condizioni di carico. Universita di Padova, 1992, PhD thesis.

7. GOTTARDI G. and BUTTERFIELD R. On the bearing capacity of surface footings on sand under general planar loads. Soils and Foundations, Japan, 1993, Vol. 33, No.3.

8. ZAHARESCU E. Sur la stabilité des fondations rigides. Proc. V Int. Conf. SMFE, Paris, 1961, Vol. 1, 867-871.

9. BUTTERFIELD R. and GOTTARDI G. A complete 3D failure envelope for shallow footings on sand. Géotechnique, ICE London, 1993, accepted for publication.

10. TSUI Y.C. On the safe design of rigid foundations in granular materials. University of Southampton, 1978, MSc dissertation.

11. PENMAN A.D.M and GALLAGHER K.A. Preliminary study of a gravity foundation failure. Ground Engineering, ICE London, 1976, Vol. 9, No.4, 15-20.

10. Probabilistic characterization of Irish till properties

T. L. L. ORR, University of Dublin, Republic of Ireland

SYNOPSIS. The difficulties in determining the values of the
properties of Irish tills for use in design are considered.
Standard Penetration Test results on Dublin Boulder Clay are
examined using a probabilistic approach to assess the characteristic value. The use of this approach is compared with the
results of the traditional approach for assessing design
values and it is found that the characteristic value is the
same as the lower bound value currently used in design.

INTRODUCTION

1. Eurocode 7(ref. 1), the new European code of practice
for geotechnical design is based on the limit state design
method and the use of partial safety factors. This method
requires that calculations are carried out to check that no
limit states will occur. These calculations use design values
for the ground properties obtained by dividing characteristic
values by appropriate partial safety factor values. The
values of the partial safety factors for ground properties
given in Eurocode 7 are constant. Therefore the reliability
of any structure designed according to Eurocode 7 depends
crucially on the characteristic values selected for the
ground properties. However, the selection of soil property
values for use in geotechnical design is often the part of
the design process involving the greatest uncertainty and
relies on local experience and engineering judgement as well
as the results of field and laboratory tests.

CHARACTERISTIC VALUES

2. Eurocode 7 states that the characteristic value of a
ground property "shall be based on the results of field and
laboratory tests" and "selected as a cautious estimate of the
value affecting the occurrence of the limit state". An application rule providing an explanation to this principle states
that "the governing parameter is often a mean value over a
certain surface or volume" and that "the characteristic value
is often a cautious estimate of this mean value".

3. Probabilistic concepts are implicit in the limit state
method. In the Eurocodes, the characteristic value of a
material property is defined to be a particular fractile in

Risk and reliability in ground engineering. Thomas Telford, London, 1993

the assumed statistical distribution of the particular property. In the case of manufactured materials, such as steel or concrete, this fractile value is normally the 5% fractile from a large number of tests on different samples. Eurocode 7 states that if statistical methods are used to determine the characteristic value of a ground property "the characteristic value should be derived such that the calculated probability of a worse value governing the occurrence of the limit state is not greater than 5%". Therefore, in the case of a soil deposit, the characteristic value is the 5% fractile in the distribution of the mean values for the relevant volume of soil and not the 5% fractile of the individual test results as in the case of steel and concrete.

4. The codes of practice currently used Ireland do not specify precisely how the values of ground properties for use in geotechnical designs shall be selected. When designing according to these codes, lower bound values of ground properties are normally selected and these values yield satisfactory designs when used in conjunction with the specified lumped factors of safety. Thus the selection of the ground property values used in present designs is based on experience with the existing design codes. With the introduction of the limit state design method, involving the use of characteristic values of ground properties, it is appropriate to examine how the characteristic value as defined in Eurocode 7 compares with the value currently selected for use in design.

IRISH TILLS

5. Many soils in Ireland consist of glacial tills. These soils often contain a large number of cobbles and boulders which cause them to be difficult to sample. Another feature of these soils is that, besides containing cobbles and boulders, they often contain weaker zones such as silt and sand lenses. The granular nature of these glacial soils and presence of the large particles mean that it is often very difficult, if not impossible, to obtain undisturbed samples of these soils for testing in the laboratory. In addition, the presence of the large particles means that the results of field tests can be very variable, depending on whether the test is carried out in sand or silt lenses or in the vicinity of a larger particle. The most commonly used in-situ test in Ireland is the Standard Penetration Test(SPT). Because of the predominance of the SPT, the use of this test to assess the characteristic values of the properties of Irish till is examined in this paper.

CASE HISTORY

6. In order to examine the use of the SPT to assess the characteristic values of the properties of Irish till, a particular case history involving a site investigation for a shopping centre at Tallaght, to the west of Dublin, has been chosen. The ground conditions at the Tallaght site, as in much of the greater Dublin area, consist of a deep deposit of

of a stiff to very stiff lodgement till, known as the Dublin
Boulder Clay, overlying limestone bedrock. This deposit is
described as a silty, sandy, gravelly clay with cobbles and
boulders. The upper part of this deposit, generally at depths
less than 3m, is brown and is known as the Dublin Brown
Boulder Clay. The deeper part of this deposit, below 3m, is
much darker and also stiffer and is known as the Dublin Black
Boulder Clay. The gradings and plasticity indices of these
two soils are same and it has been shown(ref. 2) that the
Brown Boulder Clay is in fact weathered Black Boulder Clay.

7.   The site investigation at Tallaght consisted of 50
trial pit excavations and 18 cable tool borings, mostly 200mm
diameter. In general, because of the granular nature of the
soils and the presence of the cobbles and boulders, it was
not possible to obtain undisturbed samples using this boring
method but disturbed samples were obtained for identification
and grading purposes. Tests carried out on the portion of the
Black Boulder Clay passing the 425μm sieve gave liquid limit
values ranging from 19% to 31% and liquidity index values
ranging from 5% to 14% but generally about 10%.

8.   A total of 102 SPTs were carried out in the boreholes
at depth intervals of approximately 1.5m. Of these tests, 26
were carried out in the Brown Boulder Clay and 76 in the
Black Boulder Clay. The N values recorded at the different
depths are plotted in Figure 1. None of the SPTs in the Brown
Boulder Clay reached refusal while, in the Black Boulder
Clay, 18(24%) did reach refusal, probably through encountering cobbles or boulders, and these tests are represented by
the values of 100 in Figure 1.

9.   The N-values plotted in Figure 1 clearly show the great
scatter in the test results which is a reflection of both the
soil type and the particular test. In view of the presence of
so many stones in these soils causing the scatter in the N
values and in order to obtain more complete information about
their overall properties, there is a strong case for examining the SPT blowcounts over shorter depths of penetration
than just over the standard 300mm intervals used to determine
the N value.

ANALYSIS OF TEST RESULTS
10.   The N values for the Brown and the Black Boulder Clays
have been plotted in the form of histograms in Figures 2 and
3. These histograms show the N values grouped in ranges of 10
and the number of extreme values obtained for both soils. In
carrying out regression analyses on these data in order to
assess the characteristic values of the properties of these
soils, it was assumed, on the basis of engineering judgement
and experience, that the extreme N values were not representative of the overall behaviour of these soils. All the N
values less than 10 were ignored as being probably due to
testing problems. Similarly all the N values greater than 60
in the case of the Brown Boulder Clay and greater than 70 in
the case of the Black Boulder Clay were assumed to be due to

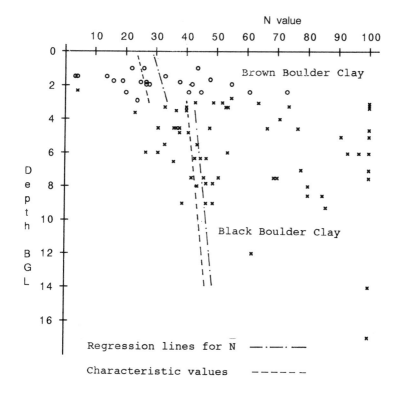

Fig. 1. Variations of N value with depth, regression
          lines and characteristic values

encounters with cobbles or boulders and so were also ignored.
Thus the analyses and results presented below relate to the
assumed over-all behaviour of these soils ignoring the
presence of the larger particles and do not take account of
the effects of these larger particles.

11. The selection process described above resulted in 23
(almost 90%) of the 26 N values being selected for the analysis of the Brown Boulder Clay but only 42(55%) of the 76 N
values for the Black Boulder Clay being selected. Using the
selected sets of N values, the following regression lines for
the variation with depth in the estimated mean N values, $\bar{N}$ of
the Brown and the Black Boulder Clays, were obtained:

Brown BC: $\bar{N}$ = 28.5 + 1.65d   (1)

Black BC: $\bar{N}$ = 40.7 + 0.57d   (2)

where d is the depth below ground level.

12. The regression lines given by Equations 1 and 2 are
plotted in Figure 1. These graphs show that the rate of
increase in the mean N value with depth is small in both
soils, being 1.65N/m in the case of the Brown Boulder Clay

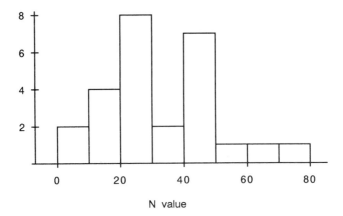

Figure 2. Histogram of N values for the Brown Boulder
Clay

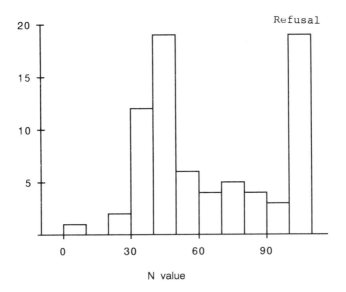

Figure 3. Histogram of N values for the Black Boulder
Clay

and only 0.57N/m in the case of the Black Boulder Clay.
Considering the inherent uncertainty in the N value, it is
therefore reasonable in design to assume constant N values
with depth for both of these soils.

13. Using the selected set of N values, without the extreme values, estimates of the mean($\overline{N}(e)$), standard devia-
tion($\sigma(e)$) and coefficient of variation($COV(e)$) of N for the
Brown and the Black Boulder Clays were calculated and these
are given in Table 1.

14. The values in Table 1 show that, using all the selected test results and ignoring the variation with depth, the estimated mean N value of the Brown Boulder Clay is 32 while that of the Black Boulder Clay is 44. Also the COV(e) of the Brown Boulder Clay is much greater than the value for the Black Boulder Clay which probably reflects the weathering of this soil.

Table 1. Estimated mean values, standard deviations and coefficients of variation of the N values for the Brown and Black Boulder Clays

	$\overline{N}(e)$	$\sigma(e)$	COV(e)
Brown B. Clay	31.5	12.0	0.38
Black B. Clay	43.9	9.4	0.21

15. Having estimated the mean N value and the standard deviation of N in a volume of soil from a set of test results, the characteristic mean N value, $\overline{N}_k$, calculated such that the probability of a worse mean value occurring is not greater than 5%, is given by:

$$\overline{N}_k = \overline{N}(e) - \frac{t \times \sigma(e)}{\sqrt{n}} \qquad (3)$$

where t is Student's value and n is the number of test results. This equation shows that for more variable soils (larger $\sigma(e)$ values) and a smaller number of test results (lower n values), the characteristic value is smaller, i.e. a more cautious estimate of the mean value is obtained.

16. Using the $\overline{N}(e)$ and $\sigma(e)$ values given in Table 1 and the appropriate t values corresponding to the number of test results, the characteristic mean N values, based on all the selected test results are as follows:

Brown Boulder Clay $\quad \overline{N}_k = 31.5 - \dfrac{2.07 \times 12.0}{\sqrt{23}} \quad = \quad 26.3$

Black Boulder Clay $\quad \overline{N}_k = 43.8 - \dfrac{2.02 \times 9.4}{\sqrt{42}} \quad = \quad 40.9$

17. Assuming that the COV value for the soils is constant, the variation in $\overline{N}_k$ with depth, d is given by the following equations, which are effectively 5% confidence bounds on the mean N value:

Brown BC: $\quad \overline{N}_k = 23.8 + 1.40d \qquad (4)$

Black BC: $\quad \overline{N}_k = 38.1 + 0.53d \qquad (5)$

These equations are plotted in Figure 1 and indicate how the characteristic mean N values compare with the estimated mean values shown by the regression lines.

DISCUSSION

18. When selecting the properties of tills for use in design in Ireland, the normal practice is to take account of in situ test results such as N values, laboratory results when these are available, previous experience of the behaviour of these soils and engineering judgement and to select reasonable lower bounds(ref. 3) to the experimental data. In the case of the data from the Tallaght site investigation, Farrell(ref.4) selected a reasonable lower bound of "about 40" for the Black Boulder Clay. This value, determined without the use of statistics, is the same as the characteristic value determined above for a depth of 4m and indicates that the characteristic values of soil properties as defined in Eurocode 7 are the same as the reasonable lower bound values used in current designs.

19. When field or laboratory tests are not available to determine directly the strength and deformation properties of soil, published correlations between, for example, N values and various soil properties for the particular type of soil may be used. As such correlations have not yet been published for the Dublin Boulder Clays, use is often made of the correlations such as those published by Stroud and Butler(ref. 5) from tests on various soils in the UK. The correlation factor between N and c_u given by Stroud and Butler for soils with a the plasticity index of 10%, such as the Dublin Boulder Clays, is about 6 and this provides characteristic c_u values of about $150kN/m^2$ and $250kN/m^2$ for the Brown and the Black Boulder Clays.

20. Preferably the values of soil properties should be derived directly from in situ measurements and not through using N values and correlations. The use of correlations to determine the values of soil properties introduces another source of uncertainty to be considered in the assessment of characteristic values. If , however, N values are used, then in order to minimise this uncertainty and improve the relia- bility of geotechnical designs, it is important that appro- priate correlations are used in the determination of the values of soil properties.

CONCLUSIONS

21. The statistical analysis of Standard Penetration Tests carried in the Dublin Boulder Clays has provided valuable in- formation about the properties of these soils, their varia- bility and variations with depth. Using a probabilistic approach and following the Eurocode 7 definition of the characteristic value, the cautious estimate of the mean, the calculated characteristic mean N value is found to be the

same as the reasonable lower bound value currently selected in Ireland for use in design.

22. It must be noted, however, that the use of a probabilistic approach on its own cannot provide the characteristic value of a soil property. It is just one tool in the process to select the characteristic value. The other tools must include experience and engineering judgement to take account of the field situation in assessing the raw data for use in a probabilistic analysis and to evaluate the characteristic value calculated by such an analysis. Also uncertainty in any correlations between test results and soil properties must be taken into account.

ACKNOWLEDGEMENTS
The author would like to thank Irish Geotechnical Services Ltd. for kindly providing the results of the ground investigation.

REFERENCES
1. EUROCODE 7, Part 1: Geotechnical Design, General Rules. Comité Européen de Normalisation, 1993, February.
2. FARRELL E.R., DOSS D., COXON P. and PRIEDHOMME L. The genesis of the Brown Boulder Clay in South Dublin (to be published)
3. ORR T.L.L. Limit State Design and Geotechnical Engineering in Ireland, Proc. Int. Symp. Limit state design in geotechnical engineering, Copenhagen, 1993, vol. 2, 551-559.
4   FARRELL E.R, BUNNI N.G. and MULLIGAN J. The bearing capacity of Dublin Black Boulder Clay, Trans. IEI, 1988, vol. 112,77-104.
5. STROUD M.A. and BUTLER F.G. The Standard Penetration Test and the Engineering Properties of Glacial Materials, Proc. Conf. The Engineering Behaviour of Glacial Materials, Birmingham, 1975, 124-135.

11. An expert system for assessment of surface structural damage in mining areas

D. J. REDDISH, R. K. DUNHAM and X. L. YAO, University of Nottingham, UK

ABSTRACT:

The assessment of damage to surface structures from mining is a difficult process requiring significant human judgement. This process is complicated by the fact that the information needed to make a damage assessment with high confidence is incomplete and involves uncertainty.

This paper presents the potential application of a knowledge - based expert system in the assessment of surface structural damage from mining disturbance. The system takes into consideration of the three main contributing factors leading to structural damage, i.e. mining, geological and structure factors. The statistical results from analyses of historical structural damage cases are incorporated into the system to represent the degree of structure damage. By using certainty factor risk assessment techniques, the system indicates the final level of damage for a particular surface structure, the contributing factors leading to the damage, a description of likely damage and possible measures to be taken to reduce the damage to the particular structure.

INTRODUCTION

1   Mining subsidence is major problem to both the mining industry and the people it directly effects. From the mining industries point of view it is an additional cost affecting the industries competitiveness in an already difficult market , it is also a source of bad publicity and resentment from the public. From the general point of view it is an annoying disruption to peoples way of life in terms of the damage it causes to their homes or businesses, even if ample financial compensation follows. Therefore, from all points of view the minimisation of damage has major benefits for all concerned. This problem is not limited to the UK but also effects mining operations world-wide.

2   There is already an extensive range of subsidence modelling and prediction techniques developed and in use. However none of these models evaluates subsidence in the form of risk or in the three vital contributing components of mining factors, site factors and structural factors.

3   Mining factors are essentially the geometry of the mining method, its relative location, depth, extent, and thickness. These factors are easily

determined and most subsidence models have concentrated on relating damage directly to them.

4   Site factors are closely related to the geology of the location with particular emphasis on the very near surface properties of the overburden.

These factors are more difficult to obtain and are largely ignored by most models. However some 25% of subsidence cases in the UK are significantly effected by site factors and they should be addressed.

5   Structural factors concern the physical construction and use of a particular building or structure, and therefore is susceptibility to damage.

6   All three factors are important in terms of the overall damage risk. A comprehensive and effective evaluation of surface structural damage due to mining subsidence should incorporate all three. In practice many field engineers use computer models to evaluate the mining factors and then use their judgement or experience to evaluate site or structural factors. Many simply ignore structural or site factors as they present too many difficulties.

7   Based on a number of building damage case histories from the UK coal fields and literature studies, the authors have carried out an intensive statistical analysis to determine the certainty factors affecting surface building damage from the above three factors. These statistical results have been incorporated into the expert system shell, Expertch Xi plus, to evaluate the structural damage degrees in terms of the classification of severe, appreciable and slight. This paper outlines the development of this trial expert system for assessment of surface structure damage in mining areas. The future expansion of the trial expert system is also discussed in the paper.

METHODOLOGY

8   Expert systems have been defined as intelligent computer programs that use knowledge and inference procedures to solve problems that are complex and normally require significant human expertise for their solution (Kaufmann(1981)). The expert system environment basically consists of a knowledge base and an inference engine. A knowledge base is a storage in which useful knowledge is stored in a stylised form recognised by the inference. An inference engine is a control process which deduces an answer from a given problem, and performs the reasoning tasks and seeks specific goals.

9   There are many different tools available for developing expert systems. An expert system shell is one of these tools, which contains both a ready - made inference engine and some form of knowledge representation scheme. For this research, a shell Expertech Xi Plus has been chosen to develop the system to assess structure damage in mining areas. Details of this shell have been described by Ren et al (1991).

10   The production system approach (Davis et al, 1977) provides a convenient way to express a piece of knowledge in engineering application.

The general form of rules in Xi Plus is as follows:

> Rule: if <condition>
>
> [and <condition>]
>
> then <consequence>
>
> [and <consequence>]

An example of a rule that might be used in this expert system has been indicated in Table 1. It can be seen that uncertain information can be expressed in rules, and certainty factors can be assigned in these uncertain rules. A scale for representing the degree of certainty concluded is illustrated in Fig.1. This technique of certainty factors has been successfully used by Shortliffe (1976). Details of this risk assessment technique will be discussed in the following section.

Table 1 - An example of a rule in the system

if fault existence is yes
and fault is normal fault
and building location is on outcropping point
then the evidence leading to severe damage due to fault = 0.95
and the evidence leading to appreciable damage due to fault = 0.60
and the evidence leading to slight damage due to fault = - 0.80

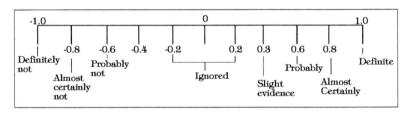

Fig.1 The degree of certainty expressed as certainty factors

PRODUCTION SYSTEM WITH CERTAINTY FACTOR

11   In the certainty factor technique, all the assertions have associated with them a measure of belief (MB) and a measure of disbelief (MD). A certainty factor can be calculated by the following formula:

$$CF[h,e] = MB[h,e] - MD[h,e]$$

A particular piece of evidence either increases the probability of hypothesis 'h', in which case $MB[h,e] > 0$ and $MD[h,e] = 0$, or it decreases the probability of hypothesis 'h', in which case $MD[h,e] > 0$ and $MB[h,e] = 0$. Several pieces of evidence can be combined to determine the CF of one hypothesis. The combining function of certainty factor plays an important role in the production system to keep knowledge modularity. The combined CF can be determined according to the following formula:

$$CF = CF1 + CF2 * (1 - CF1)$$

Where CF1 = first certainty factor, and CF2 = second certainty factor. Fig.2 illustrates this in a graphical way. By using these technique, the final damage

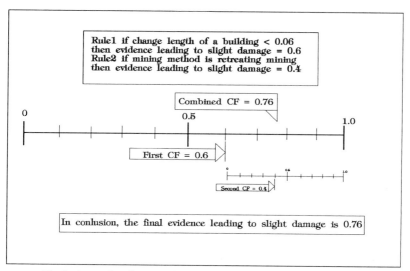

Fig.2 A graphical view of the combination of certainty factors

degree can be evaluated by the propagation and combination of all certainty factors from the three main factors: mining, site and structure factors.

ESDAS - EXPERT STRUCTURE DAMAGE ASSESSMENT SYSTEM

12   ESDAS is a rule - based damage assessment system of surface structures subjected to underground mining. This application has been designed based on case histories of damage in the UK coal fields and previous researchers' results. Fig.3 shows the method used to determine the Certainty Factor by statistical analyses from the database containing the case histories.

13   As described before, the structure damage degree is mainly controlled by three factors: mining factors, site factors and structure factors. Therefore, this system is designed to have three main knowledge bases, namely mining, site and structure factors. Fig.4 illustrates the general structure of the three knowledge bases of this system. In each of these three knowledge bases, a number of sub - parameters have been taken into consideration. By using the rules described earlier, the final damage risk level can be evaluated by the calculation and combination of all the certainty factors from each of these sub - parameters.

Development of the three main knowledge bases

14   The sub - parameters for structural damage arising from mining factors are considered to be horizontal strains, tilt, radius of curvature, deflection ratio, mining method and face advance. Table 2 indicates the criteria used to determine limit values of each sub - parameters for damage classification in mining factors knowledge base.

15   The main causes of surface structural damage due to site factors are considered to be faulting, fissures (surface rock condition), jointing, and

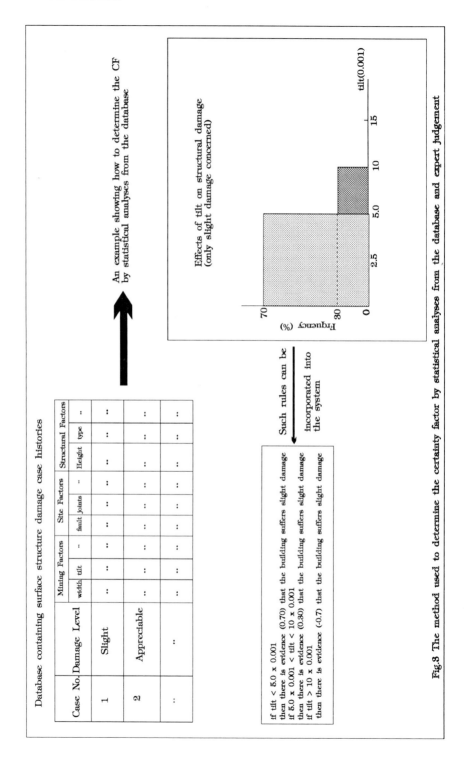

Fig.3 The method used to determine the certainty factor by statistical analyses from the database and expert judgement

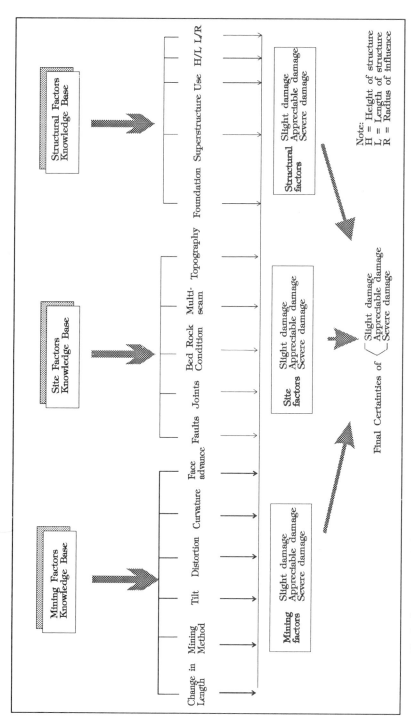

Fig.4 Structure of three main knowledge bases for Expert Structure Damage Assessment System

Table 2 Components of Mining Factors Knowledge Base

Sub-parameters	Factor Based for Damage Classification	Empirical Models Used for Sub-parameters Determination	Criteria Defined by Authors for Damage Classification	Comments
Main Parameters:	Mining width, Mining depth, Extraction thickness, Dip of seam, etc.			
Horizontal Strains	Change Length of Structure	Models from Yao et al (1991) are used to determine: Position of inflection points; Position of maximum strain points; Position of subsidence limit.	Change Length of Structure — Damage Class: <0.06 m — Slight; 0.06 - 0.12m — Appreciable; >0.12m — Severe	This criterion is based on S.E.H (NCB,1975) with authors' re-definition.
Tilt	Tilt	Graph 15 in S.E.H.(NCB,1975)	Tilt 10^{-3} — Damage Class: <5.0 — Slight; 5.0 - 10.0 — Appreciable; >10.0 — Severe	This criterion is modified from Brauner.
Radius of Curvature	Radius of Curvature	$R = A\,\dfrac{h^2}{ma\cos\alpha}$	Radius (km) — Damage Class: >12 — Slight; 4 - 6 — Appreciable; <4 — Severe	This criterion is modified from Yu. Note: A = 0.075 for UK condition; h = mining depth; m = seam thickness; α = seam inclination; a = subsidence factor.
Deflection Ratio	Visible Cracking	$\varepsilon_b = \dfrac{ma\cos\alpha}{0.075*h^2*[1.33\frac{1}{H}+5.2\frac{H}{L^2}]}$ $\varepsilon_d = \dfrac{L*ma\cos\alpha}{0.075*h^2*[2\frac{L^2}{H^2}+8]}$	Limit values of ε_b and ε_d (After Arioglu et al, 1984): Building Material — ε_b — ε_d; Brickwork — 0.05-0.1% — 0.05-0.1%; Reinforced concrete — 0.035% — 0.03-0.05%	ε_b = limiting direct tensile strain, ε_d = diagonal tensile strain; H = height of the structure; L = length of the structure. If one of these two parameters (ε_b, ε_d) exceeds its limit value, visible cracking will appear in the structure.
Mining Method	Mining Method			Bruhn (1982) reported that subsidence damage from advance mining, retreat mining with pillars split, longwall mining above a barrier pillar is more severe than from full extraction retreat mining. Rare subsidence occurs when partial mining is practised.
Face Advance	Face Advance			Rapid face advance has the effect of increasing the damage to buildings.(Kratzsch(1983)). This aspect needs to be carefully considered in relation to other factors.

ground topography. Table 3 illustrates the components of the site factors knowledge base.

16 The key features of the structural factors are the size, shape, foundation type and superstructure type. The building classification method used by Yu has been employed in the structural factors knowledge base. The most likely damaging type is given the lowest rating. Table 4 shows the method.

Consultation of ESDAS

17 ESDAS consists a total of five knowledge bases, including an Introduction and Conclusion as well as the three main knowledge bases described above. When a user starts to run a Query, ESDAS asks a series of questions, which are associated with the sub - parameters of the three main factors.

18 The consultation starts in the Introduction knowledge base, and then moves to the Mining factors knowledge base by asking questions concerning mining factors. After the mining geometry have been given by the user, the system displays three screens to tell the user the position of maximum strains and also the areas of three different strain zones, which are considered to be very important since they help the user in determining the structures location in relation to the three different zones. At the end of this knowledge base, the individual certainty factor from each of the rules is eventually combined to obtain the final degree of slight, appreciable and severe damage due to mining factors. A report of this result is presented.

19 In a similar way, questions associated with site factors and structure factors are asked. After finishing all the questions, the system moves in to the Conclusion knowledge base. By combining the mining, site and structural certainty factors, the overall damage degree of slight, appreciable and severe damage can be obtained. The system finally selects the largest certainty factor as the final damage degree to the structure. Meanwhile the main contributing factors leading to the damage and recommendations for damage control are stored in two different text files, which can be presented to the user at the end of consultation. A final conclusion reached and a description of damage to the structure are also presented at the end of consultation, which are shown in Table 5.

Table 3 Components of Site factors Knowledge Base

Sub - parameters	Comments	Sources

Fault Effect	1. Structure on outcropping point:
	   The structure will probably suffer severe damage from fault effect point of view.
	2. Structure beyond outcropping point:
	   If mining is only taking place on one side of the fault, there should be no damage to the structure; however, if mining takes place on both sides of the fault, the structure will suffer normal damage.
	3. Structure within outcropping point:
	   Whether mining is only taking place on one side of the fault or both sides of the fault, the structure will suffer normal damage.
		Whittaker and Reddish (1989)

Joint Effect	It is obvious that a structure situated across a joint, which is subjected to a concentration of differential displacement, would be seriously damaged. However, a similar structure adjacent but wholly within the confines of a single block of strata would develop no damage.	
Fissure Effect	Type of bed rock / Location of surface fissures Coal Measures — Near the position of maximum tensile strain; a few occurred over the ribside Triassic Sandstone — Most occurred within 0.1 * depth of the ribside; the others were spread out further over the ribside. Permin Limestone — A wide spread; a high concentration close to the extraction edge.	Breeds et al (1976)
Ground Topography	The severity index of structure damage is lower if the site is located on a ridge, a hill slope or some other elevated area rather than an alluvial flat, on a valley floor or at the toe of a slope.	Bruhn(1982)

Table 4 Components of Structure Factors Knowledge base (After Yu et al)

Sub- parameters	Foundation		Superstructure		Length /Radius of influence		Height/length of structure	
Sub - Rating	Isolated footing	1	Brick, stone and concrete	2	< 0.1	8	< 1.0	8
	Continuous footings	4	Reinforced concrete	4	0.1 - 0.25	6	1.0 - 2.5	6
	Raft foundation	8	Timber	6	0.26 - 0.50	4	2.6 - 5.0	4
	Buoyancy foundation	16	Steel	8	> 0.5	2	> 5.0	2

Total	Rating	Class Damage
	7 -10	I
	11-20	II
	21 - 30	III
	31 - 40	IV

Table 5 Presentation at the end of a consultation of ESDAS for a case study

Final Report
Slight damage risk is   -0.774
Appreciable damage risk is   0.99
Severe damage risk is   0.890
Conclusion
The structure will suffer Appreciable damage with certainty of 0.99
Description of typical damage
Slight fracture showing on outside of the building, doors and windows sticking, service pipes may fracture.
Main factors leading to damage
Mining method; visible crack; face advance; strain effects; site location; joint existence
Measures suggested to be taken
Changing mining method to partial or full retreating extraction; Reducing face advance if possible; Keeping building from joint systems.

CONCLUSION

An expert system for assessment of structural damage due to mining subsidence is outlined. The system uses the certainty factor technique to predict the damage degree of a particular structure subjected to mining subsidence. The system also provides the user with the main factors leading to the damage, and a general description of the damage and the possible measures to be taken to control the damage.

The trial expert system under discussion is still the subject of further research. The knowledge bases within the system require further development to include all the latest developments in subsidence expertise. However, it has been demonstrated that this system has a useful role to play in the assessment of mining subsidence damage.

REFERENCES

1.   ARIOGLU. E & YUKSEL. A, Classification of house damage due to mining subsidence. House Science, 1984. Vol.8, No.4
2.   BRAUNER. G Subsidence due to underground mining. Information Circular 8572, Denver Mining Research Centre. USBM.
3.   BREEDS, C. D. A study of mining subsidence effects on surface structures with special reference to geological factors. Ph.D thesis, 1976, University of Nottingham.

4.   BRUHN. R. W, MCCANN, W. S., SPECK. R. C. & GRAY, R. E. Damage to structures above active underground coal mines in the Northern Applalachian Coalfield. First International Conference on Stability in Underground Mining, August 16 - 18, 1982, British Columbia, Canada.

5.   KAUFMANN, L. A.et al Handbook of Artificial Intelligence. 1981,Vol.1.

6.   KRATZSCH. H. Mining subsidence Engineering, Springer-Verlay, Berlin. 1983

7.   NCB, Subsidence Engineers' Handbook, 1975, National Coal Board, Mining Department, London.

8.   REN. T. DENBY. B & SINGH. R. N. Applying knowledge - based expert system to provide guidance for the safe storage of coal. 1991. Mining Science and Technology,12.

9.   SHORTLIFFE. E.. H. Computer - based medical consultation, MYCIN,Elsevier, New York,1976

10   WHITTAKER. B. N & REDDISH. D. J. Subsidence occurrence, prediction and control. Elsevier, Amsterdam, 1989.

11.   YAO, X. L. REDDISH, D. J. and WHITTAKER, B. N. Evaluation of subsidence parameters for inclined seams in UK coalfields. 10th International Conference on Ground Control in Mining, Morgantown, 1991, WV,USA

12.   YAO, X. L. Modelling of mining subsidence with reference to surface structure behaviour. Ph.D thesis, 1992, University of Nottingham.

13.   YU. Z.KARMIS. M.JAROSZ. A & HAYCOCKS. C. Development of damage criteria for building affected by mining subsidence. Proceedings, Sixth annual workshop generic mineral technology centre, mine system design and ground control, USA.

12. Probabilistic approaches for slope stability in a typical geomorphological setting of Southern Italy

C. CHERUBINI and C. I. GIASI, Politecnico di Bari, Italy, and
F. M. GUADAGNO, Universita di Napoli, Italy

SYNOPSIS. Preliminary results on the application of probabilistic methods in stability analysis are here presented.A typical geomorphological setting of Southern Italy has been considered in the analyses.

INTRODUCTION

1. In Southern Italy, landslides are very frequent, in time and in space, involving the Apennine Chain formations and those of the foredeep basin such as the "Varicoloured clays" and the "Blue clays".

2. Generally, stability analyses of natural slope are carried out during, or even better, after the instability (type A and B of the Lambe forecast, ref.1) by means of back-analyses which don't always correctly reconstruct the phenomenon.

3. It is true instead that the soils or the rocks have highly variable physical and mechanical characteristics, even within the same formation. It is therefore very difficult to apply the merely deterministic practice which gives the evaluation of safety factors for the slopes as the ratio between available resisting force and applied load. In fact, resisting force is related to the physical and strength parameters of the soil (or rock) bodies.

4. The present paper describes some preliminary results on the application of probabilistic methods in stability analysis of a slope, consisting of "Blue Clays".

GEOMORPHOLOGICAL SETTING

5. Montalbano Ionico, the studied area, is located in the Basilicata region (Fig.1) where Blue Clays widely outcrop. These belong to the Plio-Pleistocene sequence of the "Fossa bradanica" that represent the southern part of the Apennine foredeep. The post-Sicilian tectonic activity, which resulted in mostly vertical movements, and the glacio-eustatic variation of the sea level have induced the deposit of transgressive and terraced sandy-gravel sediments.

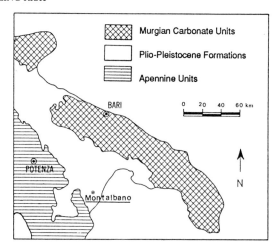

Fig. 1. Semplified structural map and location of the s⁺udied area

6. The morphological setting is, therefore, characterized by tabular reliefs where 20-40 metres thick sandy sediments overlay the blue clays. Erosional phenomena, as badlands, and rotational landslides induce the retreat of the slopes that connect the top plateau to the river plain.

7. The town of Montalbano Ionico, as the largest part of the Apennine towns, is located at the top of a tabular relief and it is subjected to slope instability.

GEOTECHNICAL CHARACTERISTICS

8. Undisturbed samples taken in boreholes and pits have allowed a geotechnical characterization of the clays. Fig.2 shows the variability of the index and physical properties of the Blue Clays. The comparison with the data of previous studies (ref.2), show that the values of the geotechnical parameters fall within the typical variation fields.

9. Fig.2 shows also the values of effective cohesion and friction angle defined in the stress range 0-0.7 MPa. Cohesion and friction angle have mean values of 49 kPa and 23° and standard deviations of 23 kPa and 2° respectively.

10. As regards the terraced sandy-gravel deposits, natural unit weight is variable between 19-22 kN/m³ as function of grain size distribution. The friction angle has been assumed as equal to 40°.

SAFETY EVALUATION

11. Safety evaluation of slope stability, as for other geotechnical problems, can be estimated by means of various calculation levels (ref.3).

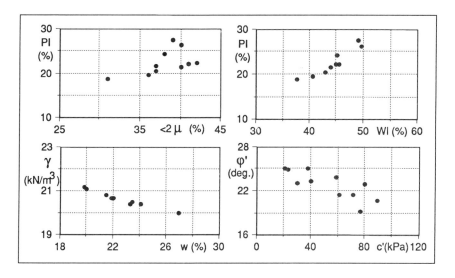

Fig. 2 Index, physical and shear strength properties of the Montalbano blue clays.

12. In the first level, such evaluation is carried out by means of the classic deterministic "Factor of Safety" resulting from the ratio between resisting (R) and overturning moments (S)

$$F = R/S. \tag{1}$$

13. In the second level, mean and standard deviations of the main geotechnical, geometrical and hydrogeological parameters are considered, in order to estimate the "performance function" G, which is usually given by the safety margin (SM)

$$G = SM = R-S. \tag{2}$$

14. Cornell (ref.4) gives as reliability index the ratio

$$\beta = \overline{SM}/\sigma_{SM} \tag{3}$$

from which collapse probabilities can be obtained. The "performance function" in the case of slope stability can be expressed as

$$G = F-1 \tag{4}$$

where F is the classic safety factor previously mentioned.

15. In the final level (ref.3) the knowledge of variables is practically complete as it is not limited to the first two moments of statistical distribution. These methods, however, are not yet totally efficient or tested.

THE STUDIED CASE

16. A second level method has been utilized for the Montalbano case. Mean and standard deviation values of effective cohesion (c') and friction angle (φ') have been utilized in the calculation.

17. In comparison with other deterministic analyses previously carried out (ref.2) the mean value of the friction angle has not changed while the cohesion one is lower (from 80 to 50 kPa).

18. The existence of a vertical fluctuation scale (δ_v) for c' and φ', equal to 2 and 5 m has been used on the basis of the literature (ref.5). This parameter, introduced in a semplified way, must necessarily be taken into consideration as it contributes to reduce variability in accordance with the Random Field Theory (ref.6).

19. A mean topographic profile, resulting from statistical analysis of Montalbano hill slopes, has been defined to perform the slope stability analyses. A pore pressure distribution has been assumed as "normal" condition (see water level in Fig.3).

20. Fig. 3 shows the Montalbano profile and the analyzed base and half slope circles, of which the test results are reported. Ten surfaces with the lowest safety coefficient have been selected. On these the probabilistic calculation has been performed. Stability analyses have been carried out with the simplified Bishop method using the Stabl-G program code of Geosoft (ref.7).

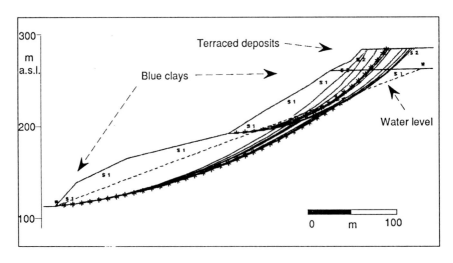

Fig.3. The analyzed mean profile of Montalbano hill.

STABILITY ANALYSIS RESULTS

21. The probabilistic calculation method utilized in the procedure is the Rosenblueth one (ref.8). The results, in terms of reliability index

$$\beta = (\overline{F}-1)/\sigma_F. \qquad (5)$$

are shown in tab. 1 for the ten different surfaces, for which, as already mentioned, the safety factors were the lowest.

22. The calculation has taken into consideration both the case in which the correlation coefficient (r) between c' and φ'is equal to 0, and the case (real) in which such coefficient is equal to -0.5.

23. As can be seen, reliability coefficients appear to be, in any case, rather high, and minimum safety factor doesn't always correspond to a minimum β value. The highest β values appear obviously when the fluctuation scale is smaller (2m) and the correlation coefficient is equal to -0.5.

24. Differences exist between the two cases of base and half-slope circles. The half-slope circles show greater reliability (β values are higher). The values of β reliability coefficients are generally acceptable compared to the "safe" values (ref.9,10).

25. This result must, however, be considered with some caution in view of the limited number of lab test at the base of statistical characterization of clayey formation, and of the deterministic use of the friction angle for the sandy top.

Table 1. Reliability index for the different studied cases.

FOOT					MIDDLE HEIGHT				
δ_v=2m r=0	δ_v=5 m r=0	δ_v=2 m r=-0.5	δ_v=5 m r=-0.5	F=R/S	δ_v=2m r=0	δ_v=5 m r=0	δ_v=2 m r=-0.5	δ_v=5 m r=-0.5	F=R/S
6.72	*3.79	9.42	* 5.31	1.099	7.13	4.67	9.83	6.47	1.174
*6.61	3.81	* 9.29	5.35	1.100	7.26	4.70	10.02	6.51	1.174
6.71	3.83	9.38	5.35	1.102	7.26	4.70	10.02	6.51	1.174
6.77	3.90	9.44	5.44	1.105	7.28	4.83	10.08	6.74	1.177
7.62	4.28	10.54	5.94	1.119	*6.99	* 4.62	* 9.49	*6.30	1.180
7.82	4.37	10.84	6.04	1.125	8.40	5.44	11.76	7.65	1.197
7.82	4.43	10.84	6.12	1.125	7.23	4.78	9.65	6.41	1.206
7.90	4.57	10.90	6.30	1.130	8.26	5.86	12.59	8.26	1.210
9.12	5.07	12.49	6.97	1.153	9.34	6.17	13.14	8.71	1.219
10.36	5.92	14.00	8.03	1.190	9.96	6.25	13.63	8.81	1.223

CONCLUSION

26. Some stability analyses have been made with traditional and probabilistic methodologies on a mean profile of Montalbano hill, consisting of blue clays and sand.

27. The results show the relevant influence of the correlation coefficient between the friction angle and cohesion and also of the values of the fluctuation step. The values of reliability coefficients are generally good or very good even with deterministic safety factor of about 1.1- 1.2.

The results so far obtained can't be considered exhaustive; in fact, further studies are under way in order to define a more complex geotechnical model, for different slope structures and heights, and, also, by adopting more evolved analysis methods.

REFERENCES

1. LAMBE T.W. Predictions in Soil Engineering. Geotechnique, 1973, 23,2, 148-222.
2. CHERUINI C. GUADAGNO F.M., VALENTINI G. Caratteristiche geotecniche e condizioni di stabilità delle Colline argillose terrazzate di Montalbano Ionico (Basilicata). Geol. Appl. ed Idrog.,1984 vol.14, 121-145.
3. GIASI C.I., CHERUBINI C. Valutazione della stabilita dei pendii in ottica probabilistica. 3° Conv. dei giovani ricercatori in Geologia Applicata. 1993, Potenza
4. CORNELL C.A. First order uncertainty analysis of soil deformation and stability. Proc. 1st ICASP, 1971, 129-144.
5. CHERUBINI C.Considerazioni sulla variabilità delle caratteristiche fisico-meccaniche dei terreni naturali. Convegno Nazionale del Gruppo AIMETA di Meccanica Stocastica, Taormina, in press.
6. VANMARCKE F.H. Probabilistic modeling of soil profiles Jour. of Geot. Eng. Div. ASCE, 1977, 103, 1227-124⁻
7. GEOS.FT Stabl/G: A Computer Analysis Program. Orange, California, 1992.
8. ROSENBLUETH E. Point estimates for probability moments. Proc. Nat. Acad. Sci. USA, 1975, Oct. 329-335.
9. FRANKE E The Eurocode-Safety approach as upright to foundations. Proc. of the 9th Danube-Eusropean Conf. on Soil Mech. and Found. Eng. Budapest. (1990) 173-182.
10. MEYERHOF G.G. Limit state design in geotechnical engineering. Struct. Safety, 1982, 1, 67-71.

13. The assessment of ground movements beneath a highway embankment under construction

R. G. V. GREEN and T. N. HARDIE, MRM Partnership, UK

SYNOPSIS

This paper describes the construction of a highway embankment in north-east Somerset in 1991/1992 where a slip surface developed in the underlying Oxford Clay. The 10m high embankment which followed the alignment of the existing trunk road was constructed on side long ground in an area where some faulting and minor folding of the Jurassic strata has occurred and where some landslipping is evident in the locality. Although the embankment design made allowance for shallow shearing in the Head/weathered Oxford Clay it was considered prudent to install some inclinometers to monitor horizontal displacement as the embankment was being constructed. These instruments enabled a relatively deep seated zone of movement to be detected which passed beneath the granular keys included near the toe of the embankment to prevent sliding in the shallow sheared zone. The paper presents some of the inclinometer data and discusses how the risk of failure was assessed leading to a decision to improve the stability of the embankment by installing piles near the embankment toe. This stabilisation was undertaken as part of the main construction contract and no significant delays were incurred to the earthworks.

INTRODUCTION

1. The recently completed A303 Mere-Wincanton trunk road improvement bypasses the villages of Bourton and Zeals, crossing both the Wiltshire/Dorset and Dorset/Somerset boundaries along its 8km length. The construction of the scheme commenced in September 1990 and the new road was opened in July 1992. The main Contractor was Wimpey Construction Ltd.

2. Much of the route crosses Upper Jurassic clays which

contained near surface slickensided shears. Consequently the design of several embankments included special measures to improve stability and the provision of a monitoring system to check the behaviour of the embankments during construction.

3.   During the construction of one of the embankments (F4) relatively deep seated lateral movements were detected by inclinometers.   This necessitated a review of the stability of the embankment and an assessment of the risk of failure was carried out based on observational methods and engineering judgement.

SITE DESCRIPTION AND GEOLOGY

4.   Embankment F4 lies between Chainage 2100 and 2350 approximately 2 km to the east of Wincanton, Somerset in an area known as Leigh Common. A public house "Hunter's Lodge Inn" lies close to the western end of the embankment.   (Grid Reference ST 743 298).   The main topographic features of the site in the vicinity of embankment F4 are shown on Fig. 1. The lower slopes of Leigh Common immediately to the south of the existing A303 are common land, this area being mainly wooded, in contrast to the surrounding agricultural land.   The elongated plateau to the south of the Common is capped with limestone from the Corralian strata, the surrounding slopes being Jurassic clays which in places are covered with a thin veneer of Head.

5.   The geology of the area is dominated by the Mere fault which passes approximately 250m to the north of the F4 embankment site. This major fault has a displacement of between 50 and 180m which to the east of Leigh Common has produced a faulted contact between Jurassic and Cretaceous strata.   In the Leigh Common area a subsidiary fault has been mapped trending NE-SW which passes close to or beneath the embankment.   In this area the Cretaceous strata are absent and either Oxford Clay or the overlying Corallian strata are found at outcrop. Although exposures are rare, dips up to 25° have been recorded in an area where the regional dips have a low angle to the east, (ref. 1).

6.   There are a number of landslips in the area some of which have been identified by the British Geological Survey and others which have been discovered during investigations for this scheme.   However none of these disturbed areas were shown to be beneath the F4 embankment. Although the ground investigation had recorded that the near surface clays contained slickensided fissures to depths of between 1 and 2m, there was little geomorphological evidence to

support this except to the south of Leigh Common where the desk study had identified an area of 'Hillwash and Surface Instability' in the steeper slopes below the limestone plateau.

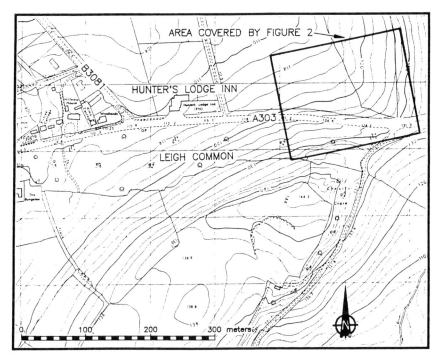

Fig. 1 Site Location Plan

7.   Embankment F4 carries both the main line dual carriageway and the B3081 side road diversion, the new alignment passing immediately to the north of the former trunk road, having crossed the old alignment near the Hunter's Lodge Inn, see Figs. 1 and 2.

8.   The higher proportion of the embankment (>4m in height) is between main line Chainage 2150 and 2350 and reaches a maximum height of 10m at Chainage 2260. The new alignment crosses side long ground with a slope mainly between 1:8 and 1:12, being generally flatter near the toe. Upslope of the embankment the slopes are steeper where Corallian strata overlie the Oxford Clay which forms the lower slopes. East of culvert 3 (Ch. 2250) which follows a former ditch beneath the embankment, the slope direction changes from NNW (approximately normal to the road centre line) to W as the road approaches the cutting near Encie

Farm (Grid Reference ST 749 300). The embankment has batters of 1:2½ and reaches its maximum height (10m) approximately where it crosses the culvert.

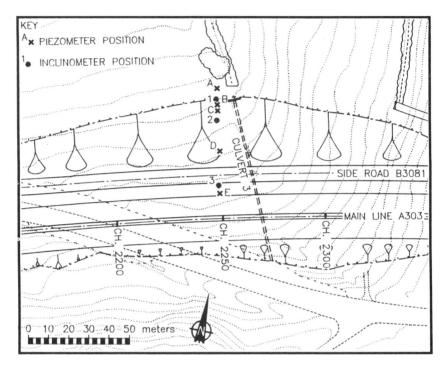

Fig. 2 Instrument Location Plan (Design)

9.   A high pressure water main which formerly crossed the site was diverted pre-contract to pass parallel to and at a distance of approximately 8m beyond the toe of the embankment.

SPECIAL CONSTRUCTION REQUIREMENTS

10.   In view of the shearing/fissuring in the upper 2m of the clay the design specified strengthening measures comprising counterfort drains and granular keys, normal to the centreline and nominally 2.5m deep. These drains and keys discharge into a 2.5m deep filter drain approximately 3m distance from the embankment toe.

11.   The side long slope was benched before the controlled placement of filling commenced. The Specification restricted the rate of placement of fill to 1.0m per week (not exceeding 0.4m per day) until the embankment reached a height of 6.0m above original ground level. Following a 'rest' period of 6 weeks filling was allowed to continue

at rate of 0.6m per week (max. 0.3m per day).

12.   No filling was permitted until a four week wait period elapsed after the installation of the pre-earthworks drainage in order to allow a period for pore pressure equilibration. The placement of fill which was mainly clay from the cutting to the west commenced in early June 1991 and reached full earthworks height at the end of October 1991.

13.   In order to assess the performance of the fill a monitoring system was specified to identify whether the fill rates specified were acceptable in terms of excess pore pressure and that shallow and deep seated movements could be detected should they occur.

14.   The initial monitoring comprised three inclinometers (1, 2, 3) and five pneumatic piezometers (A-E) approximately on a line normal to the centreline, just to the west of culvert 3 (see Fig. 2).

EMBANKMENT CONSTRUCTION

15.   During the construction of the embankment F4, lateral movement within the foundation was detected by the inclinometers installed prior to the placement of any fill. Additional instruments were installed in two stages to monitor the embankment as the construction progressed. The results of the monitoring of these instruments were used to assess the amount and extent of movement and the risk of failure and its consequences. The effect of delay/disruption to the Contract and the cost to the Client were taken into account when considering the options available for progressing the works as well as the risk of a major disruption to the trunk road and the long term performance of the new road. The key events in the construction of embankment were:

(i)   significant lateral movement detected in Inclo 1.

(ii)   decision to install Inclos 4 to 10 and piezometers F to J.

(iii) lateral movements detected in Inclos 4 to 10.

(iv)   decision to allow placement to continue to full earthworks height and install Inclos 11 to 18.

(v)   decision to carry out stabilisation measures.

The dates of these events are shown on the Key Event chart (Fig.3) and are described in more detail below.

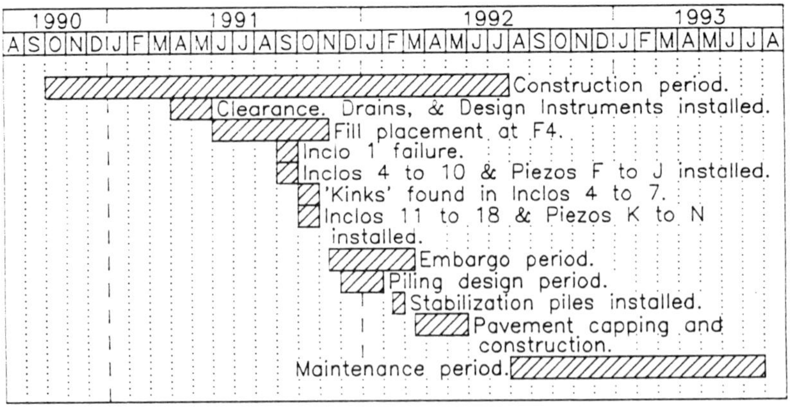

Fig. 3 Key Event Chart

16. During the early stage of construction small movements of the inclinometers were recorded but these were not thought to be of concern. However, as filling proceeded, a trend of movement was detected in Inclo 1 which caused increasing concern as the movement appeared to be accelerating during September. After 12 September it was not possible to advance the inclinometer probe below a depth of approximately 5.5m below ground level in the A-B direction (normal to road centreline). Readings continued with difficulty in the C-D direction until 20 September after which no further readings were attempted. The depth deflection profile for Inclo 1 (see Fig. 4) shows a kink developing at a depth of 5.5m. It can be seen that movement at this depth can be traced back to the start of filling, in June 1991. By September a deflection of approximately 75mm downslope over a length of 1.0-1.5m had occurred.

17. A re-appraisal was undertaken at this time and concluded that although Inclo 1 indicated that some ground movement was occurring this was not substantiated by the readings obtained from the other inclinometers, or from the piezometers where no significant excess pore pressures were recorded. This together with the fact that there had been some erroneous data from other isolated instruments along the site led to the decision to replace Inclo 1 and to increase the number of instruments thereby increasing the instrumented area. The additional instrumentation comprised seven inclinometers (Inclos 4 to 10) and four piezometers, F to J. The positions of these instruments are shown on Fig. 5. At the same time undisturbed U100 samples were taken in some of the instrumentation boreholes and were extruded and logged. The examination

156

of the U100 samples did not identify a plane of movement
although a significant amount of fissuring was evident
both above and below the zone of apparent movement.
Whilst the additional boreholes did not confirm the
existence or otherwise of a shear plane the samples taken
did reveal laminated zones within the clay on which the
indications of movement were seen.

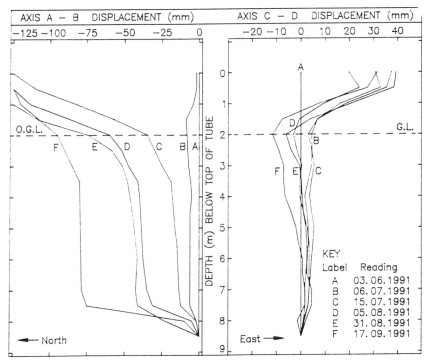

Fig. 4 Depth - displacement profile - Inclo 1

18.   The decision to allow filling to continue whilst the
      additional instruments were being installed allowed the
      construction to continue without further restrictions
      being placed on the Contractor and to allow the Engineer
      to accrue more information regarding the potential slip.

19.   Ten to fourteen days after installing these additional
      instruments depth-displacement profiles similar to that
      found in Inclo 1 were apparent in four of the
      inclinometers (Inclos 4-7 inclusive). The kinks in Inclo
      4 (adjacent to Inclo 1) and Inclo 6 at the toe of the
      embankment were at depths of about 5.5m similar to Inclo
      1. From a study of the inclinometer data it was deduced
      that lateral movement of the order of 100mm had already
      occurred near the toe of the embankment. Also there was

evidence to suggest that movement was related to filling. Selected readings of Inclo 4 are presented in Fig. 6 which show the development of a 'kink' in their profile at an approximate depth of 6m.

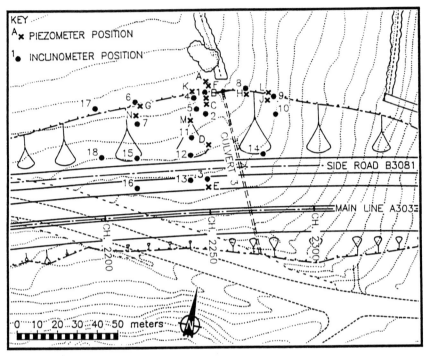

Fig. 5 Instrument Location Plan (Construction)

20.   It was now confirmed (mid October 1991) that movement within the embankment foundation was taking place and over a larger area than was being monitored at this time. The decision on how to proceed considered the following factors when assessing the risks:-

  i)   the short term (immediate) stability of the embankment which was temporarily carrying an important trunk road;

  ii)   the presence of the water main near the toe of the embankment and the risk of disruption if a 'failure' occurred.

  iii) long term stability and serviceability of the new road;

  iv)   the effect of delay or change in design on the construction costs and programme;

21.   The basis for the risk assessment was the inclinometer
       data and a knowledge of the ground conditions. At this
       time displacements in excess of 100mm had occurred and the
       rate of displacement was approximately 4mm/week. It was
       considered that if displacement continued at this rate a
       major embankment failure could eventually occur.

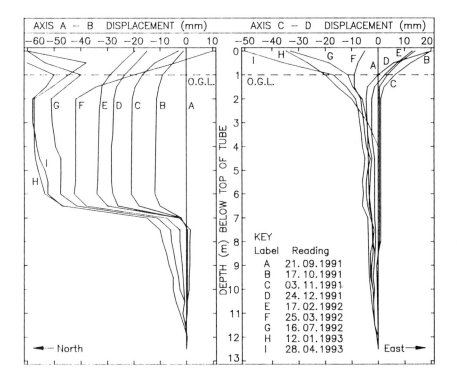

Fig. 6 Depth-displacement profile - Inclo 4

22   It was recognised that the failure mechanism would be
       complex probably involving failure along a pre-existing
       zone of movement combined with brittle failure through
       intact material. It was apparent that the average shear
       strength along the failure surface would not need to be as
       low as residual for failure to occur. When viewed in
       terms of displacement it was considered that movements of
       up to 150mm measured near the toe could be tolerated and
       that this criteria could be exceeded within the next few
       months. Thus the likelihood of stabilisation measures
       being required was indicated.

23.   At this time the embankment was approximately 1m lower
       than the design height (excluding capping and pavement

construction) and the winter earthworks embargo period was due to commence in mid November. Clearly there was advantage in bringing the embankment to full earthworks height before the embargo commenced. It was estimated that this further loading would lead to an additional movement of 10-20mm.

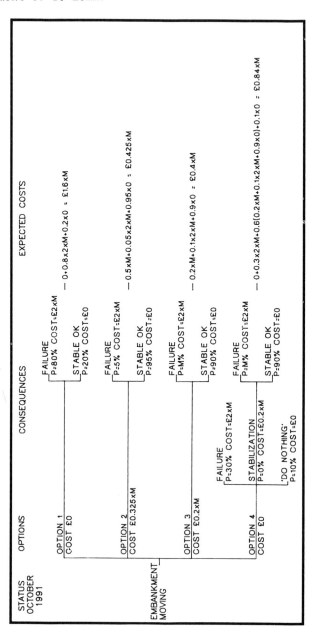

Fig. 7 Decision Chart

24. Additional instruments were installed in November to define the limits of the movement and to obtain more detailed information on the soil parameters. Small movements were recorded which were consistent with the movement already recorded and were helpful when assessing the subsequent remedial works.

25. The cost of a major failure was difficult to estimate due to several variables such as time of failure, stage of completeness, disruption of traffic, extension to the Contract and disbenefits due to late opening. It is contended that as time progresses from when significant movements were confirmed (October 1991) that the direct and indirect costs could escalate to greater than £2 million, particularly if failure occurred towards completion of the Works.

26. When assessing the stability in October 1991 it was recognised that three options were available.

    (1) Complete embankment construction ('do nothing').
    (2) Suspend embankment filling and implement stabilisation measures.
    (3) Continue filling and implement stabilisation measures during the winter embargo period.
    (4) Continue filling and monitoring. Any stabilisation measures required could be installed when and if necessary but preferably during the Maintenance Period.

27. Options 2 to 4 recognise the need for stabilisation measures, although a 'do-nothing' option is implied in Option (4). The direct costs of the stabilisation work was estimated to be similar in each case ie. approximately £0.2 million, although it was estimated that additional indirect costs of £0.125 million could be incurred if option 2 was adopted. However, each option attracts a different risk and the total costs (ie. direct and indirect costs) could vary considerably in each case.

28. The option and risks are illustrated on Fig 7 which gives the expected costs for each option. It is noted that the probability assigned to each of the consequences are judgemental. A single cost for failure (£2 million) has been used throughout. As previously discussed the total cost will vary depending on the scale and timing of a slip.

29. Option 3 presented the best combination of risk and cost, ie. a small increase in risk and the minimum delay and disruption to the Contractor. This approach also satisfied the failure criterion in that it allowed the

stabilisation measures to be installed before the displacement criteria of 150mm was exceeded. In addition confidence in the instruments was now such that it was felt that significant acceleration in the movement could be detected in sufficient time for measures to be taken to avoid a major slip.

30. It was recognised that if Option 4 was adopted the failure criteria could have been breached before the Maintenance Period commenced because of:

a) a possible reduction in the average shear strength along the shear surface if movement continued;

b) increased pore pressure/rise in ground water levels during the winter/spring periods;

c) increased loading due to capping and pavement construction when works resumed after the embargo.

31. Option 3 was therefore adopted and the design of the stabilization measures comprised a series of large diameter bored piles along the toe of the embankment. Inclinometers were installed in a number of the piles. The work was carried out in a two week period in February 1992. Post piling monitoring to date has shown that movement has virtually ceased. During this time small movements in some of the pile inclinometers has been observed as the piles have picked up load.

SUMMARY

32. Instrumentation was one of a number of special measures included in the design of embankments along this section of trunk road. Deep seated movement was detected by inclinometers installed in a 10m high embankment (F4) constructed on Oxford Clay.

33. Observations from the inclinometers showed movement within the foundation of the embankment up to 120mm being recorded by December 1991, some 8 months after filling had begun. This identified the potential for a major slip which could have led to serious disruption of the trunk road and damage to a water main. Using engineering judgement and the data from the inclinometers the risk of failure both in short term and long term was assessed.

34. Confidence in the information being produced by the monitoring system increased as the embankment construction progressed and more data became available. It was felt that the repeatability of the readings meant that any

acceleration in the movement of the embankment could be detected readily following placement of more fill allowing action to be taken if necessary. This approach allowed the Contract to proceed with no significant delay/disruption to the earthworks.

35. The continuing movement of the inclinometers led to the judgement that there was an unacceptably high risk of failure and the decision was taken to stabilise the embankment using bored piles.

ACKNOWLEDGEMENTS

The Authors wish to thank the Director General Highways of Department of Transport for permission to publish this paper. The Authors also gratefully acknowledge the assistance given by the Resident Engineer and his staff, in particular
Mr D Packer and Ms S Amys, for collecting and processing the data some of which is presented in this paper.

REFERENCES

1. British Geological Survey 1:50,000 map Solid & Drift Sheet No. 297 - Wincanton.

14. Probabilistic risk analysis applied to sudden inflows of groundwater into underground excavations

R. J. CONNELLY and J. E. DODDS, Steffen, Robertson and Kirsten (UK) Ltd, UK

SYNOPSIS. Ground water is recognised as a major planning and cost consideration in mining especially in highly fissured rock such as limestone. These considerations apply to the mine itself as well as to the environment in which it is developed. Ground water assessments for supply, dewatering or pollution issues are often viewed with scepticism by engineers due to the high degree of uncertainty attached to the basic field and analytical information. Probabilistic Risk Analysis has been applied in engineering for some years and is beginning to find application in ground water studies. A major hazard in underground mining is a sudden inflow of ground water. A probabilistic approach to assess the risk permits mine management to make rational decisions. The same technology has been applied successfully to water supply and pollution problems.

INTRODUCTION

1. Probabilistic Risk Analysis is proving to be a useful technique to assess the impact of ground water on mining or the impact of mining on the ground water environment. This paper presents the overall approach and application of Probabilistic Risk Analysis to the problem of sudden inflows to an underground mine or excavation. A particular example of a karstic environment is presented.

Impact of ground water on mining

2. Ground water affects mining in various ways in open pits, quarries and underground mines or excavations. Ground water flowing into a mine causes a number of problems depending on the quantity. These problems include; nuisance value (of the water itself and the equipment required to deal with it); uncomfortable working conditions; increased wear and tear on equipment; difficult rock

handling and transport; increased blasting costs; trafficability of roads; risk to life; risk to the mine.

3. The quantity of water in mines varies tremendously. Some are completely dry while some of the wettest mines in the world such as Konkola (formerly Bancroft) in the Zambian Copperbelt, pump several hundred Ml/day. In the UK, water quantities are not usually large but lives have been lost due to sudden inflows. Sudden inflow is a fairly common event in karstic areas due to the unpredictability of the presence of large water bearing features. West Driefontein gold mine in the South Africa and Kombat mine in Namibia suffered catastrophic inflows which resulted in loss of life and almost resulted in the loss of the mines. Many mining regions in Eastern Europe and China have histories of sudden inflow causing major problems. Alliquander (ref. 1) records that 18 serious mine flooding incidents have occurred in the Dorog coalfield in Hungary between 1950 and 1970 resulting in loss of life, loss of production and an ultimate reduction in available reserves of 40%. Loss of life is unacceptable and together with the sensitivity of mining to costs, it is most important that the risks are correctly assessed and the adequate management and monitoring systems are established to minimise the risk of catastrophe. The risk, the cost of ignoring the risk and the remedial work to reduce the risk then have to be evaluated to enable management to make rational planning decisions.

4. Additional risks to mining operations include water pressure, leading to rock mass failure; pumping cost, which is related to pumped volume and head; and water treatment. South African gold mines have been known to pump in the order of 100 Ml/day from depths of 1500 – 2000 m resulting in operating costs of £ 4 000 000/year. Water pollution legislation in most parts of the world and certainly in Western Europe, classifies the water leaving a mine site as effluent. Whatever water cannot be used on the site must be treated, usually to a very high standard. The cost of treatment can be high and is directly related to the volumes of water that require treatment.

Impact of mining on ground water

5. Any interference with soil and rock will have an impact on the natural water balance. It is important to identify the impacts

relevant to the various phases of development, production and closure of a mine.

6. Interference with existing supplies. When ground water is abstracted from an aquifer, a cone of drawdown will develop around the extraction point or area. The shape, depth and extent of the cone will depend on the aquifer characteristics and the amount of water drawn from the aquifer. Any supply borehole within this cone, will be affected. In a significant dewatering system, the area of influence can extend 10 kilometres (6 miles). A major component in the design of a mine water management system is based on predicting this cone of drawdown and designing a system to reduce the impact or provide alternative supplies.

7. Subsidence. Lowering of the ground water table increases the effective stress in a soil profile and under some circumstances can cause consolidation of the soil and settlement of structures. Special situations, such as over karstic limestone, can result in the redevelopment of dolines or the generation of sinkholes. Many areas of the world, including the UK, have numerous records of catastrophic events due to the development of sinkholes as a result of underground mining. In the gold fields of South Africa, ground water has been lowered regionally by many 10's of metres resulting in sinkholes suddenly forming and engulfing houses and mining plant. Less dramatic but equally impressive, is the settlement around the lignite mines near Cologne in Germany. The ground has subsided several metres but with little damage to structures because of the uniform settlement.

8. Steam and spring flow. Drawdown may change a stream from a situation where it is fed from the ground water to one where the stream looses water to ground water. Losses through the steam bed can be complete resulting in cessation of flow in the stream. This is an effect not only from mining but also from over exploitation.

9. Ground water pollution. Any mining activity will affect the quality of water that comes into contact with the mine. The affects range from an increase in suspended solids to high levels of metal and other chemical contamination. This problem can be managed and controlled if the chemical process and the ground water system are understood. A general objective would be to try to minimise the

amount of ground water and its contact time with the mining operations.

10. Acid rock drainage (ARD). ARD is complex reaction but is based on the oxidation of pyrite, producing a low pH environment. This in turn may result in the mobilisation of metals. The low pH water and/or mobilised metals then move away from the mine via both the ground water and surface water systems. ARD is not only related to underground metal mines, but coal mines, waste rock dumps and pyritic shale and mudstone earthworks.

11. Intrusion of poor quality water. The cone of drawdown around a mine changes the natural hydraulic gradient and can induce the flow of different water types towards the mine. This intrusion of possibly poor quality water can be lateral and/or vertical from an underlying aquifer. Dewatering wells at the Orapa Mine in Botswana, draw very good water from the main aquifer but if they are pumped at too high a rate, then poor quality water from underlying shales can be drawn upwards. The salinity of this poor water is twice that of seawater. The result of the increase in salinity of the pumped water is increased corrosion of the pumping and reticulation system; a reduction in the usability of the water; and a reduction in the disposal options available.

Mine closure

12. When a mine is closed, and the dewatering pumps are switched off, ground water levels will recover to the pre mining situation unless affected by other factors. The recovery can create a number of problems; flooding of adjacent workings; potential subsidence in backfilled areas; pollution of ground water and possibly surface water as water levels rise into shallow, weathered material; resurgence of springs that may not have flowed for several generations; change of the water balance, where people may have become used to the artificial situation created by pumping. For instance, the loss of water available for sewage dilution in rivers on cessation of pumping, as has occurred in the Nottinghamshire coalfield. ARD can also be the source of a very long term liability. The effects of mine closure on the environment are very much in the public eye at present with the visible effects of mine drainage from abandoned coal mines and working metal mines. The assessment of

the long term risk/liability of ground water recovery will therefore become increasingly important.

Summary

13. Events occurring during dewatering or after ground water recovery are varied and are associated with a variety of risks. In order to provide decision makers with information on the cost of remedial measures and the likelihood of the various remedial options being required, the risks must be assessed during the planning phases of the mining project. The assesment must therefore allow the impact of risk on project viability to be presented.

THE METHOD

14. A hazard is a condition which exists, there need not be any risk attached. Only when someone or something is exposed to a hazard is there risk.

15. The method involves the development of fault and event trees whereby various possible events associated with a failure are listed, the probability of occurrence of each event is determined and the sum of the probabilities for each fault computed. There are standard techniques in industry for the development of fault and event trees which are beyond the scope of this paper (ref. 2). The problem with ground water studies is the determination of probabilities using typically uncertain data such as hydraulic conductivities, storage, joint/cavity distribution data, etc. Figure 1, after Freeze et al (ref. 3), shows the framework for hydrogeological decision analysis on a mining project. At each stage of development of an investigation, the uncertainties in geological and hydrogeological data can be quantified using probabilistic methods.

16. There are a number of techniques for assigning probabilities to a particular event. These range from personal opinion based on experience via solicited opinion from a group of acknowledged experts, to rigid statistical evaluation of representative populations of data. Hydrogeological data is usually variable and uncertain, relative to the density of data collection. Harr (ref. 4) presents methods of assessing probabilities for uncertain data, based on the fact that an experienced person can usually estimate maximum and minimum values and an expected value for a particular variable. The argument is that a distribution function can be derived for any

variable and can be improved as additional information becomes available. These methods are discussed further in ref. 5.

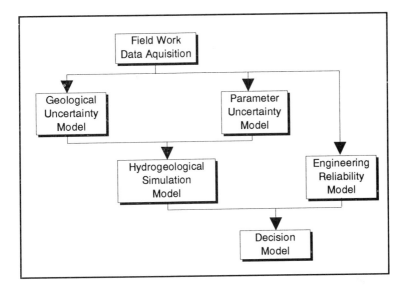

**Figure 1 :   Framework For Hydrogeological
Decision Analysis (Freeze et al 1992)**

RISK ASSESSMENT IN A KARST ENVIRONMENT

17. The major risk from ground water in an underground karst environment is of a sudden, unexpected inflow. There are two primary sources of such an event, fracture zones and cavities. In the most simple form of risk assessment, the probability of intersecting features of a certain size, which would relate to a magnitude of water problem can be reviewed. Additional aspects affecting risk can be then be added such as; locating the potential water bearing feature; and dealing with the inflow. Prior to developing the mine, the risk needs to be assessed with and without pre–dewatering. In terms of the mine development there is an intermediate consideration of partial dewatering. In this section, the various aspects of inflow are discussed with a brief description of the methodology used to assess probabilities.

Fracture zones

18. Details of the nature and distribution of jointing needs to be obtained. Any assessment of ground water in a fractured rock environment requires a good understanding of the geotechnical nature of the rock, including the nature and orientation of fractures. The methodology employed in collecting fracture data makes it amenable to statistical analysis, due to the large number of individual measurements that are made. The fracture opening is usually the most difficult criteria to measure in cored samples. Estimates of this can be made by back calculating (ref. 6) inflows/outflows during packer and other hydraulic tests. Other important observations include the nature of joint surfaces and degree of weathering (as an indication of ground water flow) and the type and nature of any joint infill, whether it be sediment or crystalline. Correct data recording will ensure that all this data can be treated statistically.

Cavities

19. The probability of intersecting a cavity is more difficult to assess than that of a fracture. The reason for this is that cavities are highly variable both in size and occurrence. Cavities though are very important, as intersecting one cavity system underground could result in loss of life and loss of income of the mine. The importance to underground inflow is the probability of intersecting a cavity within the "mining horizon". It is therefore important to understand the mode of formation and occurrence of the cavities. This can be evaluated using standard geological techniques.

20. The factors influencing magnitude and duration of sudden ground water inflow, due to cavities are; size, infilling (or lack of it), hydraulic interconnection.

21. In a recent study the likelihood of intersecting cavities was assessed using data collected during mineral exploration drilling. Data from 206 boreholes was assessed using geostatistical techniques. In order to obtain information on the spatial distribution of cavities, the data relating to the proportion of cavity in a 25 m mining zone within each borehole, was extracted from a geological data base. 2–D semi–variograms were produced from this data and the parameters used to produce a 2–D kriged block model. The model provided a reasonable guide to the relative amount of cavities

that could be expected in the different parts of the potential mining area. More importantly the modelling provided reproducible statistical data on the spatial distribution of the cavities. This study is discussed further later in the paper.

22. The size of the cavities is difficult to deduce from drilling due to the drill hole spacing usually being far larger than the size of the cavity. During mineral exploration drilling, unlike shallow site investigation drilling, it is not possible to drill many holes at a very close spacing. The possible size of the cavities is best estimated using the drill hole data available, along with data on local or regional cave systems which have been explored.

23. The nature of infilling is important in that it will control the rate of flow in the cavity. With the sudden release of pressure as a result of sudden inflow, very high velocities are created at the mouth of the opening, this in turn causes the infill material to erode, thus increasing the hydraulic conductivity of the cavity, increasing flow velocities and thus the erosion. Minor, uncontrolled inflows into underground workings can therefore increase steadily to difficult proportions.

24. Hydraulic connection must be tested by long duration test pumping, with adequate and correct instrumentation measuring pressures at various depths and distances from the test well. The importance in assessing the likely hydraulic connection between cavities or cavity zones cannot be stressed enough. The degree of connection will control the total length of time that the inflow will last and therefore the long term effects of the inflow.

Volumes of inflow
25. The likely flow volumes that would be encountered can be estimated from a review of test pumping data, calculations and if necessary modelling. In order to obtain theoretical high values, literature reviews will usually provide typical data. The duration of flow will be a function of the degree of connection and the amount of pre–dewatering. An inflow without dewatering could result in draining the full volume of storage in the overlying aquifer system. Under dewatered conditions the volume of water in storage will be small and the risk of catastrophic inflow consequently much lower.

Water quality

26. Ground water quality is assessed during the test pumping programme, both by multi level sampling and mixed samples with time, during prolonged pumping. The greatest risk in terms of sudden inflow and water quality, is whether the water removed from the mine after inflow will meet the discharge requirements of the regulators and if not, whether treatment is feasible and cost effective. Very little data is available on the quality of water entering mines suddenly. However by having knowledge of the natural variability of the water quality in the aquifer together with the nature of cavity infill material an assessment of the water quality can be made within tolerable levels of confidence. The water quality issue, is generally less important than the water quantity, as the water quantity will generally govern the cost of treatment and/or holding facilities for conditioning prior to discharge.

Human life

27. The major risk in terms of a sudden inflow is the risk to human life. Uncontrolled flooding at a high rate in certain parts of a mine could result in injury or loss of life. It is therefore important to not only understand the components of risk but also the mitigation measures. The latter would include items such as strategic sumps to provide intermediate storage where mine workings may not be suitably positioned, water doors, escape routes etc. The risk to human life is the final risk calculated from all the others.

The mine

28. The loss of production or the loss of the mine itself could arise from a major inflow. The magnitude of impact would relate to the inflow rate and duration and the contingency plans in place.

DISCUSSION

29. The key to the assessment is to develop the fault and event trees (ref. 2). These can be made as complex or as simple as required but they provide a means of logically placing all the contributory events which can result in a top event, in this case a sudden inflow. Typical examples are presented in Figures 2 and 3.

30. Figure 2 shows a simple situation. The probability of intersecting a water bearing feature is calculated, without defining how large the flow may be. The probability of intersecting the

feature is assumed to be related to the probability of intersecting either a cavity or a major fault. In a particular investigation, the probability of intersecting cavities was assessed from drilling logs using indicator kriging. Drill core data from 206 boreholes, drilled through a 25 m mining horizon was logged and any borehole intersecting a cavity greater than 0.1 m, within the mining horizon, was coded (1), while those that intersected no cavities were coded (0). Semi–variograms were calculated from this data and were used to generate an Indicator Kriged Block Model. The figures assigned to each block in the model represent the probability that if a borehole is drilled through the the 25 m zone within the block, it will intersect at least one cavity. In certain mining areas the probability was as high as 20%. In the example shown in figure 2, this value has been used.

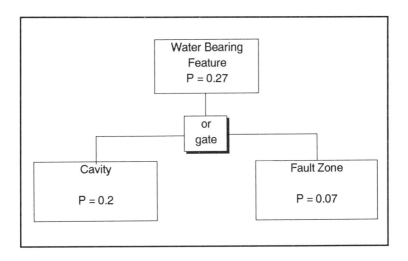

**Figure 2 :   Probability Of Intersecting A Water
Bearing Feature**

31. The probability of intersecting a fault zone was assessed from the mapped positions of major faults crossing the mining area. Hydrogeological drilling and test work had shown that certain of the major faults were conduits for ground water flow. The probability of intersection within a drive was assumed to be equal to the number

of occurances of faults per unit length of development. Because the occurance of the cavities and faults are unrelated the probability of the resulting event is equal to the sum of the probabilities of the contributing events.

32. The example given in figure 2, shows how geostatistical and spatial data can be used to obtain the probabilities of occurance of events.

33. Figure 3 shows a more complicated example of an event tree. In this case the sudden inflow is assessed in terms of the failure to identify and grout underground features. In this example a detailed statistical data set was not available in order to calculate the probability of events occurring. Probabilities were therefore assessed using "expert opinion". The fundemental reasoning and justification for this methodology is given in ref. 4. The probabilty of the top event occuring is calculated by constructing a tree of events that lead upto the top event, in this case a sudden inflow. Each contributing event is assessed by one or more experts and based on their combined experience a probability of occurance is assigned. The probabilities are then combined up the tree via and/or gates to arrive at the top event.

34. In this example only the likelihood of sudden inflow is assessed. The next stage of development would be to link this tree to a similar tree constructed to calculate the likelyhood of a certain or threshold inflow occuring.

CONCLUSION
35. Ground water data is uncertain due to geological heterogeneity. Probabilistic Risk Assessment has been developed to examine uncertainty in engineering problems and these methods are shown to have an important role to play in ground water problems, whether in works of a mining or civil engineering nature; in water supply studies; dewatering design and optimisation; or pollution problems.

36. Fault and event trees provide a means of understanding the factors which can give rise to a particular top event and then the consequences of such an event. Probabilistic methods are available to suit any type of data set, whether small or detailed. As more is

understood about a data set or the overall problem, the risk assessment can be refined.

37. The method provides a means of translating uncertainty in hydrogeological data, to numerical and therefore financial models which form a rational basis for decision making.

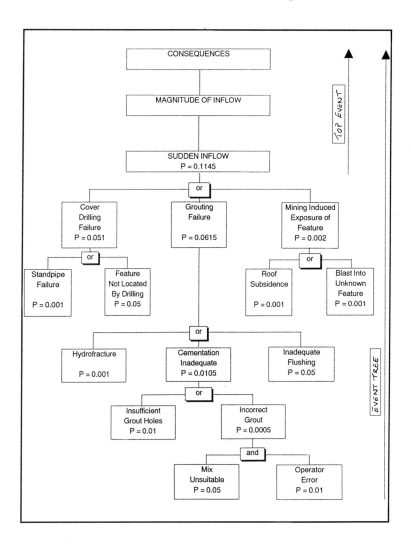

Figure 3 : Probability Of A Sudden Inflow Occuring During Underground Mining With Cover Drilling

REFERENCES

1. ALLIQUANDER A. Experience and Ideas of Development on the Control of Mining under the Karstic Water Hazard. Proceedings of the International Mine Water Association symposium, Budapest, 1982.

2. ANG A.H.S. & TANG W.H. Probability concepts in engineering planning and design. Vol II Decision risk and reliability. Wiley 562 pp.

3. FREEZE R.F. et al. Hydrogeological decision analysis. National Ground Water Association 1992.

4. HARR M.E. Reliability based design in civil engineering. McGraw–Hill 1987.

5. McCRACKEN A. Reliability based design using point estimate methods and capacity–demand models. Risk and reliability. ICE 1993. (in press)

6. HOEK E. & BRAY J. Rock slope engineering. IMM 1977.

15. Hazard and risk assessment in rockfall prone areas

A. CANCELLI and G. CROSTA, University of Milan, Italy

SYNOPSIS. Hazard and risk assessment in rockfall prone areas play an important role for urbanization and land planning purposes of mountainous areas. Although much has already been done, much has still to be done both for numerical simulation and for zoning purposes. This paper presents a comprehensive approach, based on the Rock Engineering System (ref. 1), that describes a rockfall environment by means of its controlling factors and of their mutual interactions. The rockfall magnitude, hazard and risk evaluation method allows the zonation both for regional or specific and local interest.

INTRODUCTION

1. Hazard and risk assessment are fundamental goals for zoning, planning and designing purposes. This goals cover an important role in many different problems and they are of particular interest in landslide prone areas. A variety of assessment techniques has been advanced, but only few succeeded in providing an effective prediction for areas with different morphological and geological characteristics (ref. 2, 3). Some of these techniques still remain too intricated or enigmatic to result useful even making use of computer capability for data manipulation and representation. Indeed, a simple method for zoning and planning in rockfall prone territories is still to be developed without involving any reduction or over-simplification of the complex system. In particular, many different classifications already existing describe only the broad susceptibility to landsliding without taking in account for the evolution of the phenomena and then for the hazard and risk assessment. The procedure proposed in the following is based on the Rock Engineering System (ref. 1) and leads to evaluate the intensity (magnitude) of a rockfall event and with more steps to the evaluation of the hazard, specific risk and finally the residual risk. Nevertheless, the approach allows to the user any sort of control with minor changes and restyling actions.

Previous methodology for rockfall hazard evaluation

2. Rockfalls are very difficult to be predicted and prediction itself is a complex and difficult process and goal at the same time. Prediction necessitates a certain amount of informations (geological, morphological and geotechnical site investigations, in situ monitoring, etc.), judgement and experience, imagination and sound ideas about the mechanism and the evolution of the phenomena eventually sustained by numerical analysis. Furthermore, prediction involves different degrees of knowledge, like prediction of the phenomena inception and frequency in a datum time interval, prediction of the evolution mode and of its final repercussions. Such a puzzle has been deciphered through different terms like "danger" (geometrical and mechanical severity of the phenomenon),

"hazard" (probability of occurrence of a certain event with given severity), "vulnerability" (degree of loss of a definite element, $0 \div 1$), "specific risk" (resulting by the product between hazard and vulnerability), "risk" (or probability of total losses) (ref. 4, 5, 6) and "residual risk" (or residual probability after the introduction of countermeasures). Finally, different steps are involved at different levels of prediction: temporal, geometrical and mechanical (type, kinematics, volume, velocity, travel distance).

3. Methodologies concerning rockfall hazard evaluation have been codified by the Laboratoire Central des Ponts et Chaussées (LPC, ref. 5, 7) and other researchers (ref. 8, 9). The LPC's methodology suggests a preliminary investigation, directed to define topographic, lithologic and antecedent occurrences features (volumes, frequency, consequences). The procedure continues evaluating the probability of danger onset and of the maximum allowable reach by combining some indicators (I: topography, rock discontinuity type and arrangement, vegetation and hydrology; II: topography, vegetation, passive countermeasures) starting from the simplest combination up to more complex ones when results are considered unreliable. Finally, hazard is subjectively distributed in 5 classes (none, low, medium, high and very high) and user's judgement is requested in the assignment of favourable or unfavourable role of the indicator. Pierson (ref. 8) introduces 9 parameters in its Rockfall Hazard Rating System (RHRS) for the rockfall hazard rating purposely oriented to road traffic safety. The nine discretizing parameters are: the slope height, the ditch effectiveness, the average vehicle risk (total time a vehicle will spend in a rockfall hazard area), the road eye-sight distance (also for railways), the roadway width (not available for railways), the geologic features, the block size or volume for each rockfall occurrence, the presence of water and, finally, the rockfall history. A limit of this approach for regional or local studies is to be too much specific, working only on transportation lines or sort of lineal problems.

MODELLING A ROCKFALL ENVIRONMENT

4. A system is a more or less complex object which reacts in some way to a certain input signal originating an output signal. Input signals can also be described as the causes while the output signal is the effect. From a hierarchical point of view the system is made up by a series of different elements, sometimes unified in sub-groups, interacting or not with each other but influencing the input signal. Rockfall environment can be described as such a sort of system. When examining rockfall processes, a valid approach should consider the choice of most representative elements or parameters, at which the system results more sensitive, as well as the study of their mutual interactions. In fact, some parameters, besides controlling the system (influencing the output signal), could decrease or strongly control the effect of some other characteristic parameter. In particular, this procedure has been applied in the present paper to evaluate the state of danger (geometrical and mechanical), also called the "magnitude" or intensity of the phenomenon. The entire rockfall system is described through a main matrix. Two different approaches are then proposed to evaluate, in sequence, the hazard, the specific risk and the residual risk.

5. The proposed comprehensive approach, based on the Rock Engineering System (ref. 1), allows calibration and summing-up of the main interactions between the controlling factors eventually resulting in a new rockfall hazard evaluation method. The rockfall system with its main controlling parameters and their reciprocal interactions is described through sketches in Fig. 1. This graphical representation adds more concepts to the simple revision of the parameters function, interaction and effects as reported in the literature. In particular, the sketch is able to resume all the possible interactions by visualizing them and to suggest, by means of some plots, the non-linearity of many interactions and their variability when multiple interactions are considered. A check out work is requested to the reader both on interaction representations (Fig. 1), attributed values (Fig. 2) and index tables (Table 1), to provide a complete vision of how the system

works and how much each parameter can be a controlling one. Furthermore, such a controlling work could reveal the subjectivity adopted by the authors in evaluating the interaction power and always existing in such kind of evaluation.

6. Preparatory work. The evaluation of the rockfall hazard and risk should begin with a rock mass characterization and a general slope stability assessment. Rock mass characterization by slope stability oriented classification (ref. 1, 10, 11) (see upper left hand side of Fig. 2), could be coupled with some kinematic feasibility tests (ref. 12) and geomorphological mapping. Such an introductory work could allow to evaluate the degree of instability, the probability of occurrence for rockfall events or simply the phenomena initiation and the triggering causes. This preparatory work is excluded by the main matrix because triggering causes don't play an important role in rockfall magnitude (or intensity) if we exclude perhaps the contribution of an initial velocity due to earthquake shakings or anthropic action (explosions, vibrations, etc.). On the other hand, triggering causes play an important role in recurrence time interval definition and consequently in the process of hazard evaluation.

7. The Model. Excluding slope stability oriented parameters and triggering causes, the method models the whole system by means of the main parameters and their mutual interactions connecting, physically and logically, each parameter to another (ref. 1). Three different choice levels are involved in the process. First of all is the selection of the characterizing parameters usually reported as controlling factors. This choice leads to a list of parameters, both qualitative or quantitative, constituting the leading matrix diagonal in Fig. 1. The second step involves the evaluation and coding of the interactions between each couple of parameters. The Interaction power is expressed by values ranging between 0 (no interaction) and 4 (strong interaction)(Fig. 2) according to an "Expert Semi-Quantitative method" (ESQ, ref. 1). Beyond the interaction power it might be useful to quantify the range of variation or scattering to evaluate the sensitivity of the system (as shown by plots in Fig. 1). In fact, small deviations from the mean values to the unsafe side of different parameters could induce hazardous situations even if each one of the deviations by itself would seem harmless. Again, a thorough check out work of the values reported in Fig. 1 is adviced to correct misinterpretations or misevaluations. Doing this work the user must remember that interactions must remain valid for more than a single event, taking in account also for changes induced by successive rockfalls on different parameters: surface roughness, slope material, vegetation, triggering of secondary rockfalls, etc..

8. The main parameters, around which the matrix is created, can be inferred on different bases: quotation frequency in technical literature, existing codes of practice, specific knowledge of the problem, previous experience and logical arguments. The selection of technical papers led, for this case, to a list of fifteen parameters (P_i) forming the leading diagonal of a 15x15 matrix (Fig. 1) and numbered from the top left corner to the bottom right one. The list includes parameters very similar but still maintained separated, as block motion (P3, Fig. 1) and rockfall trajectory (P4), or that are strongly interdependent as impact behavior (P7), coefficients of restitution (P8, normal and tangential) and slope material (P9). Further interdependent parameters could be the surface roughness (P11), the vegetation (P12), the soil material (P9) and the resistance coefficient (P14). Surface roughness and vegetation presence and type have been separated because of the easier definition of the former one and the multiple and complex role played by the second one (soft, flexible and breakable obstacles, deviating effects, etc.). Other elements are not introduced because easily considered within some others, for example the coupled effect of temperature and of the presence of water (change in the degree of saturation of the slope material and freezing ground) able to influence the impact, the coefficients of restitution and the resistance. Eventually, some parameters, as already in a previous paper (ref. 13), imply the idea of hazard and risk, like the maximum reach and the maximum admissible reach ratio (from field surveying,

179

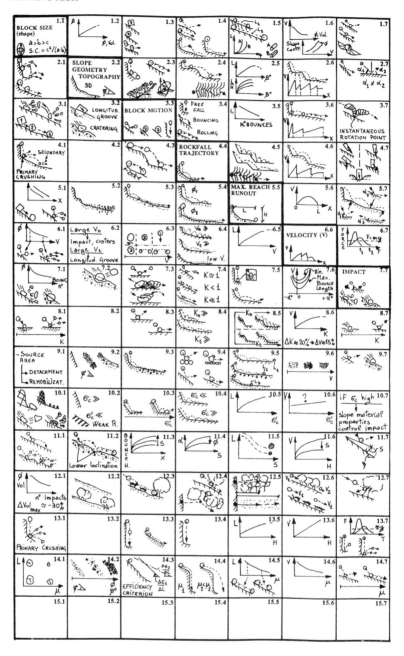

Fig. 1. Rockfall system matrix with parameter interactions represented through sketches.

180

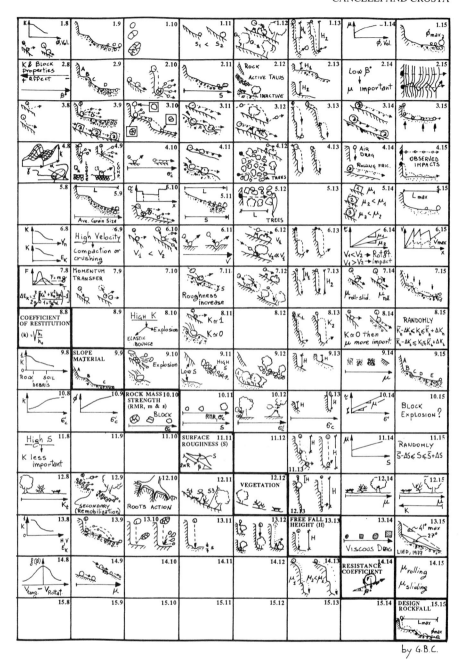

by G.B.C.

numerical, empirical methods, ref. 14, 15), or the velocity in the endangered area or the design rockfall.

ROCKFALL MAGNITUDE EVALUATION

9. Rockfall magnitude evaluation implies the attribution of numerical values to each reciprocal interaction. Then, as in the mathematics, the matrix can be described as a whole made up of rows and columns, where each element represents the influence or interaction between two parameters. As a consequence, rows and columns form the two interaction paths between each possible couple of parameters located along the leading diagonal (Fig. 1, 2). Symmetry of the two clockwise interaction paths is not a requisite at all as shown by some boxes symmetric with respect to the leading diagonal (intensity value $I_{ij} \neq I_{ji}$). Some empty boxes exist in Fig. 1 meaning that no interaction exists and consequently they result as zeros within the matrix in Fig. 2. Each row, crossing the leading diagonal in correspondence of a certain parameter, describes the influence (cause, C) played by such parameter on each of the remaining ones and consequently on the whole system. In the same way, any column describe how the other 14 parameters affect the parameter (effect, E) individuated by the same column on the leading diagonal. Any interaction will remain valid for any sort of rockfall environment being the result of the combination of mechanical, morphological and geometrical parameters. Local effect are site specific effects defined and introduced in the following. Once the matrix has been coded, summing up all the values for each row and for each column, we represent the total amounts of causes ($\Sigma_j I_{ij} = C_{pi}$, external right-hand side column in Fig. 1) and effects ($\Sigma_j I_{ij} = E_{pi}$, bottom row in Fig. 1) for each interacting parameter, respectively. Summations, as before, can be asymmetric. Such values represent the influence of the parameter on the whole system and viceversa, and plotted in a cause/effect plot point out which and how much a parameter is dominating or subordinate. A (C+E) histogram might represent the degree of interactivity for each parameter (ref. 13).

10. Parameters selection, interactions coding and some more coding work performed on each parameter allow to assess rockfall danger (magnitude or intensity) for any rockfall environment (where the value of each parameter can change) by expressing it as a Rockfall Intensity Index (RII, %). In particular, parameters weighting allows to generalize the matrix. To pursue this weighting we generated fifteen pull-down menus one for each parameter. Each pull-down menu subdivides the characteristic range for each parameter into classes to which we ascribe an index (V_i), increasing with dangerousness. Table 1 shows 15 pull-down menus where four classes, coded from 0 to 3, have been individuated for each parameter. Any other subdivision, conducted with a larger number of classes for specific site condition, could work with the only constraint of maintaining the same number of classes for each parameter. In this way we ensure that the matrix is modifiable according to user's need, requests or environmental restraint (block size, urbanization, codes of practice, presence of active or passive counter-measures, etc.). Anyway, it is suggested that no changes must be introduced after the adoption of a previous different subdivision during the zoning of a certain area.

11. Eventually, the exploitation of the matrix needs to link the general mechanical and geometrical description of the phenomenon with the site specific conditions. Weighting is such a connection (see the external left hand side column in Fig. 2) and is realized by expliciting the sum of cause and effects for each parameter as percentage of the total (see Fig. 2; $\Sigma C_{pi} + \Sigma E_{pi}$ = causes + effects = 376 + 376). Calculations must take in account for the maximum index value (3, or any other user's maximum), and so:

$$W_i - \text{Parameter weight} - \frac{(C_{pi} + E_{pi})}{(\Sigma_i C_{pi} + \Sigma_i E_{pi})} * \frac{100}{3}.$$

For any rockfall situation summing up the products between parameter indices (V_i, from

ROCK MASS RATING - SLOPE (SMR, Romana, 1992, etc.; kinematic feasibility tests)

Weight																Causes C
2,44	P1	0	3	3	4	3	2	2	3	2	2	1	1	2	4	32
1,78	2	P2	3	4	3	3	3	1	2	0	1	1	3	0	4	30
2,40	2	0	P3	3	2	3	2	2	1	1	1	1	1	3	4	26
3,02	2	0	3	P4	3	3	4	3	1	2	1	1	3	2	4	32
2,62	1	0	2	2	P5	3	1	0	2	1	2	1	0	1	4	20
2,84	1	0	2	3	4	P6	3	3	1	2	0	2	2	2	4	29
2,71	3	0	2	3	3	4	P7	4	1	1	2	1	2	1	3	30
2,22	0	0	2	4	3	4	4	P8	0	1	1	1	1	1	4	26
2,53	4	3	3	3	3	3	3	3	P9	3	3	1	0	3	4	39
1,87	3	2	1	2	2	1	2	2	2	P10	1	1	1	3	2	25
1,78	0	2	2	3	2	2	3	2	0	0	P11	0	1	3	3	23
1,33	2	0	2	2	3	2	1	1	2	1	1	P12	0	2	2	21
1,60	2	0	1	2	3	2	2	1	1	2	1	0	P13	0	3	20
2,04	1	2	2	2	4	3	2	1	0	1	0	0	1	P14	4	23
2,13	0	0	0	0	0	0	0	0	0	0	0	0	0	0	P15	0
Effects E	23	9	28	36	39	36	32	25	16	17	16	11	16	23	49	376

Fig. 2. Interaction coding matrix and parameter weights to evaluate rockfall magnitude.

Table 1. Pull-down menus with the parameters coding for magnitude evaluation.

Parameter Index	1 BLOCK SIZE	2 SLOPE GEOMETRY	3 BLOCK MOTION	4 BLOCK TRAJECTORY	5 MAX. REACH / MAX. ADMISSIBLE REACH	6 VELOCITY max. velocity in mitigated areas	7 IMPACT	8 RESTITUTION COEFFICIENT (Seismic Velocity - Vp)
0	<0.1 m3	Faible <25°	Sliding	Sliding	< 0.3	< 5 m/s	Plastic (Block/Soil)	< 0.1 (<40 m/s)
1	0.1÷0.5 m3	Steep, Channels	Rolling/Sliding	Rolling/Sliding	0.3÷0.7	5÷10 m/s	Elasto-plastic Block/Debris	0.1÷0.3 (40÷300 m/s)
2	0.5÷2.0 m3	Very steep	Rolling	Rolling & Tense parabolas	0.7÷1	10÷20 m/s	Elasto-plastic Block/Debris & Rock	0.3÷0.5 (300÷700 m/s)
3	>2.0 m3	Steep, 3D effects	Bouncing	High parabolas and 3D effects	> 1	>20 m/s	Elastic Block/Rock	0.5÷1 (700÷>2400 m/s)

Parameter Index	9 SLOPE MATERIAL prevailing along the slope profile	10 ROCK BLOCK MASS STRENGTH (RMR)	11 GROUND SURFACE ROUGHNESS Velocity Based Design	11 GROUND SURFACE ROUGHNESS Bounce Height Based Design	12 VEGETATION	13 FREE FALL HEIGHT	14 RESISTANCE COEFFICIENT (Equivalent Friction Coefficient)	15 DESIGN ROCKFALL
0	Soil (peats, soft soils, etc.)	I - II class	S > 4 block radius (R)	< 0.5 R	Dense forest - Large trees	< 5 m	> 0.8	Perfectly exact (computer assisted)
1	Fine or loose debris (morain, fluvial dep., etc.)	II - IV class	4÷2 R	0.5÷1.5 R	Trees and shrubs (rare large trees, orchards)	5÷25 m	0.58÷0.8	Uncertain (no previous events; Energy Line method)
2	Coarse or dense debris, Weak Rocks	IV - V class	2÷1 R	1.5÷3.0 R	Shrubs and small trees	25÷100 m	0.2÷0.58	Variability of 2 or more parameters
3	Sound Rock	Very Dangerous Conditions (joints, volumes, ...)	< 1 R	> 3.0 R	Absent or rare (meadows, bare land, etc.)	> 100 m	< 0.2	Extremely complex (no computational methods)

183

the pull-down menu) and their corresponding weights (W_i, $RII = \Sigma_i V_i * W_i$) allows the computation of the RII. Again, RII and the whole matrix represent the state of geometrical and mechanical danger (magnitude or intensity) of the event, with no reference to prediction or probability evaluation and risk assessment.

HAZARD AND RISK ASSESSMENT

12. The assessment of the hazard and risk level is probably the most important and more complex result at the same time. Hazard and risk definition could be done in two different ways and probably more. The first method, suggested in a previous paper to which we remand for more details (ref. 13), performs the passages by introducing, with a cascade-like system, a smaller uncoded matrix with two more parameters: the number of events and the land use. The second method evaluates the probability of occurrence of an event of any magnitude (RII) within 4 different maximum reach distances. This subdivision results in a hazard zonation along each investigated profile and not only for an entire profile as with the first method. Risk is finally obtained by the different products of the resulting hazard values with the results of another 6x6 matrix (Fig. 2).

Hazard assessment

13. The difficulties in evaluating the probability of occurrence or the recurrence interval are notorious especially for phenomena like landslides where scarceness and low quality of information are common. To assess the probability of rockfall initiation (primary or secondary falls), originating area must be individuated, slope features must be surveyed and mapped and slope profiles prepared. It must be borne in mind that the probability of occurrence will be function of the number of kinematically removable blocks, of the recurrence time of triggering events, like earthquake, rainfalls or other rockfalls, of the groundwater level together with freeze-and-thaw cycles, of the anthropic action or disturbance. Mapping blocks size and their areal distribution within the talus slope, geophysical and topographical surveyings, cliff and slope conditions surveyings (structural features) together with available historical data, both for rockfalls and for triggering causes (earthquakes, floods or rainfalls, freeze-and-thaw cycles frequency, external disturbances, etc.) give useful information to infer a rockfall scenario and to define a recurrence interval and a probability of occurrence for the events. At the same time, field surveying and numerical simulations, performed in a statistically significative number to take in account for field and mechanical data variability, will improve this scenario identifying probabilities of occurrence (summing up to 1) for fixed magnitude events within different distances from the source area. This is because not all the blocks of equal size will run the same distance along the same profile due to minor changes and disturbances (surface roughness, impacts, vegetation, etc.). In this way, broad probability values can be inferred for the occurrence of a detachment (it could be very low) and for various reach distances. Furthermore, numerical analyses with introduction of countermeasures might result in the hazard evaluation fulfilling for land-planning and mitigation purposes. Many improvements could be introduced in the methodology especially concerning probability evaluation technique.

Risk assessment

14. The proposed 6x6 risk matrix (Fig. 3) considers the L ratio (the maximum reach to the maximum admissible reach ratio), the type of impact against structures (as in ref. 9) and countermeasures, the number of impacted structures and countermeasures, the cost or the type and the estimated value of the structures. Adoption of the procedure to transportation lines should take in account for traffic parameters (ref. 8) keeping in mind that in these situations hazard and risk distribution along a lineal structure are of main interest. Weight and pull-down menus (see Table 2) are prepared for this matrix and are modifiable according to the user's needs, too. Logically, hazard generally increases uphill while risk shows an opposite trend. In fact, any rockfall running the absolute maximum

W							
7,11	MAX REACH /MAX ADM. REACH	2	2	4	4	4	16
4,90	3	TYPE OF IMPACT: STRUCTURE	0	2	2	4	11
5,39	4	3	TYPE OF IMPACT: COUNTER-MEASURE	3	3	4	17
4,17	0	1	0	N. DAMAGES-INJURIES	0	4	5
6,13	3	3	3	3	N. DAMAGED COUNTER-MEASURES	4	16
5,64	3	0	0	0	0	COST-STRUCTURE TYPE	3
	13	9	5	12	9	20	68

P	1	2	3	4	5	6
I	MAX REACH / MAX ADMIS. REACH	TYPE OF IMPACT: STRUCTURE	COUNTER-MEASURE	N. DAMAGED: STRUCTURE PERSONS	COUNTER-MEASURE	COSTS-STRUCTURE TYPE (see Table 3)
0	< 0.3	No	No	No	No	No
1	0.3+0.7	Absorbed	Absorbed	Minor	Sector	Minor
2	0.7+1	Penetrated	Penetrated	Major	Row or Multiple Sectors	Major
3	> 1	Crossed (structural failure)	Crossed (structural failure)	Injuries & Casualties	Total	Very High

Fig. 2. Interaction coding matrix and parameter weights for risk evaluation.

Table 2. Pull-down menus with parameters coding for risk evaluation.

Table 3. Classes of structures for different approaches: planning and mitigation.

	SPECIFIC RISK			RESIDUAL RISK	
INDEX	LAND USE (PLANNING)	LAND USE (MITIGATION)	INDEX	ACTIVE MITIGATION METHODS	PASSIVE MITIGATION METHODS
0	Extremely Safe (public buildings, nuclear pl., highways, etc.)	Desertic or useless areas	1	None	None
0,2	Urban Settlement, industrial plants	Low Value Crops, mule tracks, exceptional transit, etc.	0,8	Scaling & Trimming	Nets
0,4	Seasonal Settlements, industrial plants, recreational areas	High value Crops (Orchards), Automatic Industrial plants, etc.	0,6	Scaling and Reprofiling	Catch Nets, Rare Elastic Nets
0,6	High value Crops, Automatic plants, etc.	Seasonal Settlements, industrial plants, recreational areas	0,4	Anchors, Grouting	Rows of Elastic Nets or Ditches
0,8	Low Value Crops, mule tracks, exceptional transit, etc.	Urban Settlement, industrial plants	0,2	Bolting, Anchors, Grouting	Coupled Elastic Nets and Ditches
1	Desertic or useless areas	Extremely Safe (public buildings, nuclear pl., highways, etc.)	0	Reprofiling, Anchoring and Grouting	Multiple Combination of Nets, Elastic Nets, Ditches or Tunnels

distance will pass through all the individuated slope sectors, giving to these uphill areas the higher hazard values. Lower downhill risk boundary will be the absolute maximum distance, as resulted by field surveyings or numerical simulations.

15. At this point, remain to stress the different role played by the designer when a territory is already used for certain activities where the aim is to reduce the number of events through a circumspected adoption of mitigation countermeasures, or that played by the planner, when the best use and land planning must be pursued. Table 3 summarizes the different categories that can be individuated by simple logical arguments (socio-economic). These categories are differently ordered according to the type of project, planning or mitigation, respectively. In the former situation the social or strategic value of existing structures represents the design constraint. In the later circumstances the main restriction could be the need in limiting excessive countermeasures cost by assigning the safest location (with no supplementary protections and costs) to more valuable

structures. Finally, the evaluation of residual risk after the adoption and put-in-place of new active or passive countermeasures could complete a planning and designing work. This could be done by simply multiplying the computed risk values for a reducing index (in favour of safety, Table 4), function of the type and number of countermeasures, or once more for a probability of interception estimated by numerical simulations. A similar approach could be performed by addition of two more columns to the risk matrix: one with the type and another with the number of added countermeasures. Still unsolved at the end of this stage is the problem to define an acceptable risk threshold.

DISCUSSION

16. Many arguments must be focussed at this point. The adoption of the large matrix, in Fig. 1 and 2, with its relative pull-down menus (Table 1) results in the evaluation of the most probable event magnitude for each investigated site. A well performed choice of the number and value ranges for the parameter classes, adopted in the pull-down menus, could avoid further modifications of the same ranges to satisfy at some specific site conditions. In fact, the undesired consequence would be that to obtain maps not laterally juxtaponible. For example, an effective choice of block volume classes could allow to maintain them valid when investigating different areas to represent any site specific volumes. Conversely, any change could imply the attribution of the same index (i.e. $V_i = 0 \div 3$) to different volume intervals, moving from an area to another, resulting in magnitudes of different meaning even for a single parameter change. This procedure is unacceptable for regional mapping purposes where interest is toward a widespread magnitude comparison. For example, censoring the block volumes used in the analyses at a lower and upper limit to eliminate blocks too small to be dangerous or too large to behave or evolve like a simple rockfall, could be an approach. The volume range, being still too wide, could be subdivided in more classes (more than 4) by remembering that the number of classes must be constant for all the pull-down menus to permit weighting. Regarding the hazard and risk evaluation some distinctions have been done. Adoption of the first approach (Cancelli & Crosta, 1993) leads to a lateral zonation of the slope, based on a single event of maximum magnitude for each profile. Conversely, the evaluation of the probability of occurrence for various distances or L ratios and the 6x6 matrix allow for longitudinal slope subdivisions, beyond the lateral one.

17. A consequence of the methodology is that through the passages (from magnitude to hazard up to the specific and residual risk) the values will decrease, for generally favourable conditions, remaining constant for the most unfavourable ones. Then the comparison of different maps is of major importance to point out the reasons that induce variation. A problem of great interest remains the determination of threshold values to distinct between dangerous or safe areas, or the so-called acceptable risk. On the basis of logic arguments, the degree of acceptable risk is connected with sustainable costs, socio-economic criteria, acceptable risk increase after subsequent events and recurrence interval. The idea is that a correct and widespread use of the method in areas subjected to different rockfall environments could help in finding out most valuable hazard and risk limits, expecially if followed by precise socio-economic considerations. Anyway, still remain the problem that urbanization is a continually developing process, even if planned, and this means a continuous increase in the number of structures potentially at risk. Time is in fact the most problematic side of all these approaches.

18. One more need in the methodology is to improve the interaction power values attribution. In fact, the interval from a value to the following one (from 0 to 1, from 1 to 2, etc.) is not always constant or expressed by a linear relationship and adoption of more intervals (for example: $0 \div 10$) can't solve the problem eliminitating this inexactness. The most evident example, but this consideration is true for any interaction and any index in the pull-down menus, is the evaluation of costs from structural damages up to loss of human lives. Another aspect of the same problem is that of the subjectivity of the value

attribution, expressing also this idea of non linearity of the interaction trends. A partial solution that has been proposed above and already tried by the authors is to compare matrices from different compilers. Other solutions could involve the definition of a mean value and a standard deviation for each value or the adoption of a fuzzy mathematics approach or, again, the evaluation of analytical relationships for each couple of interacting parameters (plots in Fig. 1).

EXAMPLES OF ACTUAL ROCKFALLS

19. A variety of maps (magnitude, hazard, specific and residual risk maps) can be produced through adoption of the methodology, valid for phenomena of different size and behavior. To verify the methodology we have looked for some actual rockfall situations. Two sites located on the eastern side of the Como Lake: Varenna, at half-length of the lake, and Piona, at the very northern extreme in a secondary sound, have been selected.

On May 1987, a rockfall at Varenna caused two casualties along the shoreline road. The slope topography is resumed in Fig. 4a, with some profile traces and the 1987 rockfall path. Rockfalls are common in the area and block volumes, from talus surveying and rock mass characterization (limestones pertaining to RMR classes III and IV, ref. 10), range between 0.5 m^3 and 15 m^3. The steep slope surface is represented, for its entire width, by scarcely to densely vegetated talus material with rock exposures. Few old passive

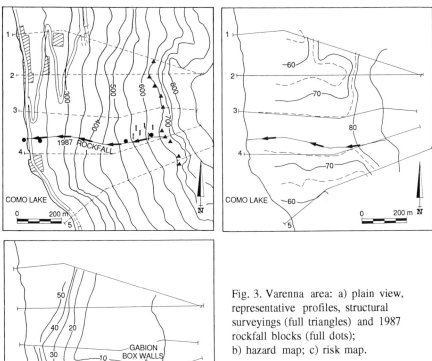

Fig. 3. Varenna area: a) plain view, representative profiles, structural surveyings (full triangles) and 1987 rockfall blocks (full dots); b) hazard map; c) risk map.

187

countermeasures (box gabion catch walls) had been already placed at the foot of the more rockfalls prone cliff. Figures 4b and 4c show the results of analyses for hazard and risk evaluation conducted with the presented methodology in combination with some rockfall numerical simulations and subdividing the results on the base of four L ratio classes (<0.3; 0.3÷0.7; 0.7÷1.0; >1.0). An evident high hazard corridor (75%) surrounds the actual 1987 rockfall path even if all the slope is characterized by a high up to very high rockfall hazard. The risk map (fig. 4c) shows the trend of risk contours and two main zones are evident: the large area to the NW with risk larger than 50% related to the evident urbanization and that bounded by the sharp bend in the contour lines associated with the presence of the gabion boxes and their damaging. Contours bending is a good representation for the presence and uncomplete success obtained with the old defensive countermeasures. In fact, well dimensioned passive structures (like catching walls and nets, ditches, etc.) might ensure that no block will pass through them and that minimum damages, possibly with no need of maintenance works, will be induced. Clearly, this is not the case of non continuous box gabion catch walls. Consistently with the roads and residencial areas location, the lower slope sector is highly exposed to rockfall hazard excepted for the southern side where a rock shed ensures a good protection. A final consideration regards the increased capability in slope discretization as a consequence of numerical simulations. In fact, adoption of a simplicistic empirical approach (ref. 14, 15) would result in a total lack of longitudinal zoning of the slope.

Farther northward, the Piona sound area (see fig. 5a) is subject to small rockfalls along the shoreline road but it is endangered by larger rock volumes. Furthermore, the old shoreline road constituted, up to a few years ago, the only transit to Valtellina and Switzerland along the eastern side of the lake. Slopes are steep to very steep, covered by gneissic blocky debris generally vegetated with trees and with subordinated channels (profile trace 6). Rock mass ratings (RMR) for gneissic rock masses range from II to III class with only few IV class sectors, while block volumes from debris slope surveying and rock mass classification resulted between 0.05 m^3 and 15 m^3. No active or passive countermeasures are placed in the area. Field surveying revealed low probability of block detachments from kinematic feasibility tests in the area of profile 2 and for such a reason we gave a 0.2 probability of occurrence (decreasing the hazard) at the phenomena of more probable magnitude. Same as before, two maps (Fig. 5b, c) have been derived on the base of the same L ratio subdivision of the profiles. The hazard map (Fig. 5b) displays one absolute maximum along profile 5 and three sub-maxima in correspondence of profiles 3, 6 and 1 in decreasing order. Derived risk results homogeneously distributed (Fig. 5c), higher for profile 3 where hazard was constant and high for all the profiles. Three diminishing relative risk maxima occur at profile 6, 4 and 1, respectively, while profile 2 denotes a low risk sector. The Piona sound area, differently by that of Varenna, is a good example of a rockfall hazard zoning performed in absence of precise information about antecedent events.

CONCLUSIONS

20. Rockfall hazard assessment and mitigation is one of the most important problems to be faced and solved in Engineering Geology and Rock Engineering for alpine areas. Theoretical, experimental and numerical researches have been done allowing for a good comprehension and modelling of all the mechanical (kinematic, static and dynamic) aspects of this complex phenomenon. Besides qualitative judgement criteria, semi-quantitative (ref. 7, 8, 9) and quantitative (ref. 2, 3) estimates of the hazard level have been recently proposed. According to the semi-quantitative approach (ESQ, expert semi-quantitative method), a new comprehensive matrix method, based on the Rock Engineering System (ref. 1), is proposed. This method allows to compute a rockfall intensity index (RII) and to evaluate, by successive steps, the hazard, the specific risk and

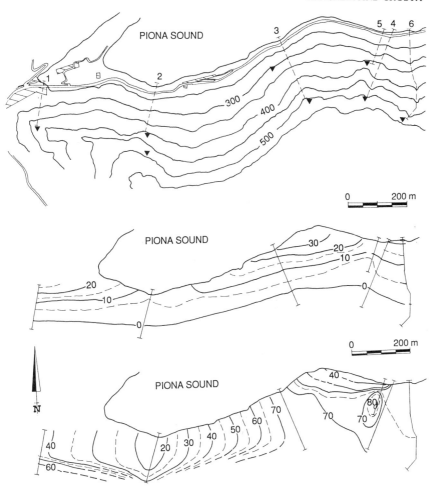

Fig. 4. Piona Sound area: a) plain view, representative profiles and structural surveyings (full triangles); b) hazard map; c) risk map.

the residual risk after the adoption of mitigation countermeasures. The suggested procedure can be modified by the user according to distinctive site conditions (e.g. geology, extension of the investigated area, block size, economic criteria and importance of different elements at risk, existing countermeasures, etc.). Two examples seem to show the capability of the method to discretize slopes in sector of different hazard. For planning purposes calculations could be easily implemented for small areas on simple software packages (Microsoft Excel), or for regional zoning on Geographical Information System (GIS) packages (ARC-INFO, etc.). Furthermore, GIS could allow for the introduction of more complicated and valid analyses with a widespread and precise evaluation of topographic changes, controlling statistical functions and with a natural

189

propension to maps superposition or juxtaposition. Finally, the definition of the degree of acceptable risk still remains the main problem and the only suggestion is in the definition of socio-economic criteria involving analyses of costs, damages, subsequent acceptable increase of risk and recurrence time intervals.

ACKNOWLEDGEMENTS

The authors are grateful for his suggestions to dr. A. Carrara. The research has been supported by MURST 40% funds.

REFERENCES

1. HUDSON J.A. Rock Engineering Systems: Theory and Practice, p. 185. Ellis Horwood, 1992
2. CARRARA A. Multivariate models for landslide hazard evaluation. Mathem. Geol., 1988, v. 15, 403-426.
3. CARRARA A. et al. Geographical information systems and multivariate models in landslide hazard evaluation. Proceedings 6th ICFL, Aug. 31st -Sept. 12th, 1990, Milano, Italy. Ricerca Scientifica ed Educ. Permanente, 1990, suppl. 79b, 17-28.
4. VARNES D.J. Landslide hazard zonation: A review of principles and practice. Natural Hazards, 1984, 3. UNESCO, 63.
5. EINSTEIN H.H. Special lecture. Landslide risk assessment procedure. Proceedings 5th Int. Symp. on Landslides, Lausanne, 1988, II: 1075-1090.
6. HARTLEN J. and VIBERG L. General report: Evaluation of landslide hazard. Proceedings 5th Int. Symp. on Landslides, Lausanne, 1988, II: 1037-1057.
7. L.P.C. Eboulements et chutes de pierres sur les routes. Methode de cartographie. Groupe d'Etudes des Falaises (GEF), Lab. Central Ponts-Chausse'es. Rapport de Recherche, 1978, n° 80: 63 pp.
8. PIERSON L.A. The Rockfall Hazard Rating System. Proceedings Nat. Symp. on Highway and Railroad Slope Maintenance, Assoc. Engng. Geologist, Chicago, 2-3 October, 1991, 1-22.
9. OBONI F. and ANGELILLO V.T.G. Risk maps for rockfall prone areas: Environmental/human aspects and remediation projects. Proceedings Environ. Management, Geo-Water & Engineering Aspects, Chowdhury & Sivakumar (eds.), Balkema, 1993, I, 715-720.
10. BIENIAWSKI Z.T. The Geomechanics Classification in Rock Engineering Applications. Proceedings 4th Int. Cong. Rock Mech., ISRM, Montreux, 1979, vol 2, 41-48.
11. ROMANA M. SMR classification. Proceedings 7th Int. Symp. Rock Mechanics, Aachen, 1991, 955-960.
12. MATHESON G.C. Rock stability assessment in preliminary site investigations. Graphical methods. Transport and Road Research Laboratory, Report 1039, 1983, Crowthorne, Berkshire.
13. CANCELLI A. and CROSTA G. Rockfall hazard in Italy: assessment, mitigation and control. Key Lecture. Proceedings Environ. Management, Geo-Water & Engineering Aspects, Chowdhury & Sivakumar (eds.), 1993, Balkema, vol. II (pre-print).
14. LIED K. Rockfall problems in Norway. In: Rockfall dynamics and protective work effectiveness, Pubbl. ISMES Bergamo, 1977, 90, 51-53.
15. ONOFRI R. and CANDIAN C. Indagine sui limiti di massima invasione di blocchi rocciosi franati durante il sisma del Friuli del 1976. Reg. Aut. Friuli-Venezia Giulia, 1979, CLUET, 42 pp.

16. Probabilistic evaluation of allowable bearing capacity considering the influence of fluctuation scale

C. CHERUBINI, Politecnico di Bari, Italy

SYNOPSIS. The allowable bearing capacity is an important element in the design of shallow foundation and can be evaluated using several available deterministic methods.
Some mrthods have been developed, in recent years, to determine allowable bearing capacity on the basis of probabilistic procedures. The probabilistic approach accounts for the randomness of various geotechnical parameters and is normally based on a probability of failure or a reliability index criterion.
Probabilistic methods can be classified into various categories. To apply them is necessary to know mean, variance and fluctuation scale of each geotechnical parameter involved.

FOREWORD

1. The allowable bearing capacity of shallow foundations resting on loose soils is usually evaluated on the basis of the already known ultimate bearing capacity: the value of the selected safety factor F is mostly between 2.5 and 3.0.

2. Although this computation procedure has been tested many times, it nevertheless shows its limitations if one takes into account the variability of geotechnical parameters which must be included in the computation model. Based on these considerations, a number of probabilistic or semi-probabilistic methodologies have been developed in which the variability of the geotechnical parameters is dealt with by introducing the corresponding mean values and standard deviations into the computation model.

3. However, when these methodologies were applied without having regard to the influence of the fluctuation scale on the reduction of variance (Li, 1992), the results obtained were often highly impracticable, and thus unacceptable. As a

consequence, the use of probabilistic methods in geotechnics was viewed with suspicion and lack of confidence.

4.   By critically reviewing the results obtained to date and by proposing a computation example, this paper attempts to clarify the problem.

PREVIOUS SOLUTIONS

5.   Many solutions are available for evaluating the bearing capacity by probabilistic methods: having analysed the parameters c, $\emptyset$ and γ statistically, one can find the pdf of the ultimate bearing capacity (qult). These solutions are listed in the following paragraphs, with a brief comment where necessary, in relation to the strength parameters of the soil, namely:

- Cohesionless soil.
6.   The solutions proposed to solve this problem are by Cherubini et al. (1988), Cherubini (1990), Easa (1992). With the first two solutions, only the variability of the friction angle is considered. With Easa's solution, one can also consider the variability of the unit weight: if this variability is high - a rather rare finding indeed - it may have an influence on the qult (bearing capacity) frequency curve and thus on the levels of probability related to qall as evaluated deterministically.

- Cohesive soil.
7.   The solution proposed by Easa (1991) appears to be quite easy to manipulate: by using it, one can examine both the variability of cohesion and that of the unit weight. According to this Author, if the soil unit weight is really high, it can affect the probability of failure when this has been defined by evaluating deterministically the allowable bearing capacity.

- Soil with both cohesion and friction angle.
8.   Countless solution have been proposed, based on different techniques such as The Point Estimated Method (P.E.M.), the Monte Carlo simulation method, the First Order Second Moment (F.O.S.M.) method, etc etc. A great many studies have been published in this connection, among them: Biarez and Favre (1983), Bennet et al. (1989).
9.   This same problem is also discussed by Harr (1987), Rethati (1988), Smith (1986). Of special interest are those cases where the possible, and generally negative $(-0.24 \leq r(c,\emptyset) \leq -0.70)$ correlation between cohesion and friction angle is

taken into account (see harr, 1987).

10. A work by Favre and Genevois (1987) deserves special attention. These two workers utilize the finite element method in a probabilistic evaluation. Specifically, they analyse the spatial variability of the deformability and stress parameters in a strip foundation resting on field level. Besides the variability of c, ∅, E and γ, they also consider the effects of two fluctuation scales δ (vertical and horizontal) upon the four parameters, and conclude that the variability of the soil parameters has remarkable effects on the bearing capacity, especially in extreme cases: a strong scatter of the parameters, a strong positive correlation among them, a high fluctuation scale with respect to the foundation's characteristic dimensions. The scatter of data relative to the bearing capacity found by those Authors in connection with the effect of the fluctuation scale is between 10 and 100 times as low as when δ = ∞. The conclusions reached by Favre and Genevois should be given careful consideration even though the fluctuation scales selected by them do not seem to be realistic in all cases. In particular, the horizontal fluctuation scale data appear to be lower than those actually reported in literature. Compare, for example, the works by Keaveny et al. (1989) and Vickremesinghe and Campanella (1993).

11. In another noteworthy study (Kayalar, 1988), the bearing capacity is computed starting from the data obtained from a large number of dynamic penetrometric tests. This Author bases his computations on a Capacity - Demand Model wich evaluates the reliability index β. The model variabilities are the same as those observed in the measurements taken at 20 cm intervals.

12. Instead, the effect, of the fluctuation scale is not considered.

13. Having available a sufficiently large number of data on 12 variously spaced verticals, however, enables the vertical fluctuation scale to be evaluated - at least as a first approximation - and the results obtaied by the Author to be modified. More details, in this connection, are given in the following paragraph.

THE INVESTIGATED CASE

14. The data used here are derived from the abovementioned work by Kayalar (1988). Table I summarizes the readings from 12 penetrometric tests performed at the depths -2.00 to -10.00 m by 20 cm steps.

15. The evaluations of the bearing capacity are

obtained through the worker's knowledge of Rd, i.e.
the Dynamic Strength of a heavy German penetrometer
(DIN 4094, see Sanglerat, 1972): the Rd values are
taken into account down to a depth equal to the
width B of the investigated foundation (varying
from 1 to 8 m). According to Sanglerat (1972), the
allowable bearing capacity can be expressed by
means of

$$qall = \frac{Rd}{20}.$$

while the ultimate bearing capacity is taken equal
to

$$qall = \frac{Rd}{8}$$

with a safety factor obviously equal to 4.

16. Kalayar develops his probabilistic
computation by considering:

a) square foundations 1, 2, 3, 4, 5, 6, 7, 8 m
wide;
b) variability of the capacity C (i.e. qult in the
study case) derived from the Rd values measured
by soil strips equal in width to the
foundations;
c) a 50% variability of Demand D (i.e. qall);
d) correlation between Capacity and Demand with a
correlation coefficient r = 0.75;
e) evaluation of failure probability according to
the expression (Harr, 1977) based on the
computation of the reliability coefficient β
(and on the subsequent, pf computation on the
basis of a normal and beta pdf), namely

$$B = \frac{\bar{C} - \bar{D}}{\sqrt{(\sigma c^2 + \sigma d^2 + 2\ r_{CD}\ \sigma c\ \sigma d)}}$$

17. The failure probabilities obtained by
Kalayar range from 11% for the smaller foundations
(1.00 - 2.00 m) to about 3% for foundations up to 8
m wide.

18. Conversely, the following proposed changes
to the computation imply:

a. that the case where C and D are not correlated
should also be considered;
b. that the value of the Demand coefficient of

variation should be reduced from 50% (highest value) to 0% (lowest value);

c. that the influence of the vertical fluctuation scale upon actual variance should be considered, according to the expression developed by Vanmarcke (1977), as a function of the investigated section length.

$$\Gamma^2(L) = 1 \qquad\qquad \text{for } L < \delta$$

$$\Gamma^2(L) = \delta/L \qquad\qquad \text{for } L \geq \delta$$

19. The fluctuation scale δv is estimated according to the simplified approach proposed by Vanmarcke (1977), later used also by Salembier (1978), after eliminating any Rp trends that might develop with depth.

20. In the case in point, the Rd data relative to the penetrometric measurements reveal a trend that increases with depth (approximately from -2.00 to - 8.00 m), while for the remaining 5.00 m the trend is practically constant, with minor fluctuations about the mean value. This fact has been verified by applying the "Runs Test" (Wonnacott and Wonnacott, 1977). Next, the least square straight line was determined for the first section (between -2.00 and -5.00 m), while between -5.00 and -10.00 m the fluctuation was estimated to be around the mean value. The fluctuation scale value was computed by using the simplified relation

$$\delta = \frac{\overline{d}}{\sqrt{\pi/2}} \qquad \text{with } \overline{d} = \frac{\Sigma d i}{n}$$

21. Other more precise methods of evaluating δi are now available. See, e.g., Vickremesinghe and Campanella (1993), Keaveny et al. (1989).

22. The reason why a simplified approach has been used here is justified by the fact that this work is mainly intended to point out the orders of magnitude of the probability values one can obtain by involving the fluctuation scale or else without it.

23. Table II shows the fluctuation scales evaluated by 1.00 m wide soil strips and by taking into account separate or aggregated verticals.

24. Note that the fluctuation scale varies in average as one proceeds from a 1 m strip (-2.00, - 3.00) to a wider strip up to 8 m (-2.00, -10.00 m). These are precisely the δv values utilized to reduce variance according to the above mentioned relations developed by Vanmarcke (1977).

25. The effect of the horizontal fluctuation scale was not considered.

26. The final results are shown in fig. 1 in terms of foundation width and percent failure and probability, as estimated with the normal law with respect to a deterministically computed qall. The upper part of the diagram shows results that can be obtained without reducing the variance, including the results with CV(D) = 50% and r_{CD} = 0.75 which, however, are not very different from the results relative to lower CV(D) values and with no correlation between Capacity and Demand.

27. Instead, the results obtained by taking into account the reduction of variance with r = 0.75 and 0 and with different values of the Demand D coefficients of variation are presented in the lower part of the diagram.

28. Fig. 1 also shows the probability levels for the Ultimate Limit States 1 and 2 established in the Eurocodes and the value proposed by Meyerhof (1982) for "onshore foundations". It is in any case evident that the influence of the fluctuation scale is quite remarkable and increases in importance with the increasing width of foundation, hence with the thickness of the mass being considered while the pf value is several times lower then it would be if δ = ∞. The results are also affected by the variability of Demand and by the different values of the correlation coefficient between C and D.

29. Thus, should the fluctuation scale parameter not be taken into account, this might lead to an overestimation of the failure probability while adding to the foundation safety, this would nevertheless be unacceptable for correct geotechnical design.

CONCLUSION

30. Having analysed the above described computation example with two different methods - the classical probabilistic approach and the modified version which takes into account the vertical fluctuation scale δv - we were able to evaluate that the corresponding computed failure probabilities differ widely, often by as much as several orders of magnitude. This is also confirmed by the relatively few works already published in this connection.

31. Thus, by introducing the vertical fluctuation scale, even though by a simplified evaluation method, the failure probabilities were reduced to acceptable values which compare fairly well with the frequencies observed in actual reality.

32. We feel we can rightly state, in the words

of Mostyn and Li (1993), that "it is now time to abandon models that do not take account of the spatial correlations of data and to move forward to models based on random fields".

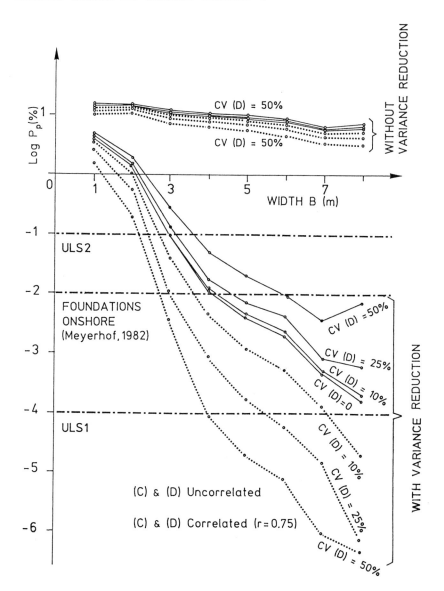

Fig. 1 - A comparison between failure probabilities at qall with and without considering the effect of the fluctuation scale and the correlation between Capacity and Demand with respect to foundation width.

	PENETRATION LOCATION											
Depth (m)	P1	P2	P3	P4	P5	P6	P7	P8	P9	P10	P11	P12
2.0-2.2	13	13	19	13	25	32	13	19	13	13	25	19
2.2-2.4	32	13	19	19	25	25	19	45	19	19	25	25
2.4-2.6	57	32	19	19	19	6	32	45	19	19	19	57
2.6-2.8	83	38	19	19	13	6	32	19	19	19	38	32
2.8-3.0	102	45	19	38	6	19	25	70	19	77	45	64
3.0-3.2	95	53	30	83	6	18	41	71	24	83	18	77
3.2-3.4	124	47	47	119	12	18	41	65	30	77	53	59
3.4.3.6	142	77	41	119	30	24	41	65	30	65	47	47
3.6-3.8	124	89	36	119	59	36	36	89	36	30	59	47
3.8-4.0	89	71	36	89	24	71	36	83	24	18	59	36
4.0-4.2	50	55	44	67	39	72	55	83	33	72	67	55
4.2-4.4	72	83	50	50	39	94	67	55	22	89	33	72
4.4-4.6	83	83	72	100	50	105	78	28	28	89	55	78
4.6-4.8	94	100	83	128	55	67	83	94	39	100	50	78
4.8-5.0	100	83	105	139	44	33	78	28	67	89	61	67
5.0-5.2	115	89	99	125	31	26	78	31	63	104	83	89
5.2-5.4	109	83	104	125	26	21	57	31	52	57	83	63
5.4-5.6	99	94	94	125	26	31	78	57	47	68	63	63
5.6-5.8	125	99	115	120	16	42	94	57	52	78	73	68
5.8-6.0	125	89	115	125	36	26	78	31	52	16	63	68
6.0-6.2	133	93	123	108	69	118	54	29	84	25	69	64
6.2-6.4	123	113	113	108	54	128	88	29	59	39	84	79
6.4-6.6	128	108	84	113	59	64	108	34	49	34	88	88
6.6-6.8	88	128	79	133	54	34	39	34	59	29	98	93
6.8-7.0	20	103	69	147	49	34	79	54	49	29	108	93
7.0-7.2	56	74	74	144	65	42	70	33	60	37	112	112
7.2-7.4	93	84	107	116	56	51	112	33	70	51	98	79
7.4-7.6	60	79	70	112	56	88	102	70	93	70	107	42
7.6-7.8	33	65	56	102	60	84	88	107	79	74	107	33
7.8-8.0	70	88	60	93	56	88	74	107	74	70	107	23
8.0-8.2	110	106	106	93	57	75	71	115	71	75	106	35
8.2-8.4	102	115	128	115	75	79	75	146	66	79	115	44
8.4-8.6	79	110	110	115	66	79	79	160	53	110	93	53
8.6-8.8	57	115	106	110	62	57	71	160	53	106	57	79
8.8-9.0	53	115	71	110	75	57	62	160	79	128	71	88
9.0-9.2	59	105	55	115	71	63	42	160	67	97	59	67
9.2-9.4	67	109	63	101	67	63	42	160	55	76	55	59
9.4-9.6	71	84	71	80	67	59	34	130	63	63	35	42
9.6-9.8	84	84	71	67	71	63	42	84	71	76	59	46
9.8-10	101	80	88	55	71	59	42	84	88	63	68	29

Tab. I - Rd values obtained at each measurement point. $(\times 10^2 \ KN/m^2)$

DEPTH (m)	δ_v FOR DIFFERENT LOCATIONS												$\bar{\delta}$
	P1	P2	P3	P4	P5	P6	P7	P8	P9	P10	P11	P12	
2 - 10	0.64	0.40	0.64	0.58	0.50	0.54	0.46	1.06	0.46	0.50	0.71	0.54	0.5858
2 - 9	0.70	0.40	0.46	0.62	0.52	0.70	0.35	0.94	0.46	0.56	0.80	0.46	0.5808
2 - 8	0.66	0.37	0.60	0.69	0.54	0.69	0.40	0.48	0.48	0.60	0.80	0.43	0.5617
2 - 7	0.57	0.40	0.40	0.50	0.43	0.66	0.35	0.52	0.35	0.57	0.50	0.43	0.4733
2 - 6	0.54	0.29	0.46	0.54	0.29	0.54	0.46	0.46	0.46	0.35	0.35	0.35	0.4242
2 - 5	0.80	0.26	0.48	0.60	0.30	0.60	0.48	0.48	0.40	0.48	0.48	0.34	0.475
2 - 4	0.73	0.40	0.40	0.54	0.40	0.54	0.40	0.80	0.32	0.54	0.40	0.32	0.4825
2 - 3	0.40	0.40	0.40	0.80	0.40	0.40	0.40	0.40	0.26	0.40	0.40	0.20	0.405

Tab. II - Computed vertical fluctuation scales based on measurement readings.

REFERENCES
1. BENNET R.M., HOSKINS J.D. and KANE W.F. Reliability based analysis of shallow foundations. 5th Int. Conf. on Structural Safety and Reliability ICOSSAR, 1989, pp. 321 - 329.
2. CHERUBINI C., CUCCHIARARO L. and GRECO V.R. A comparative probabilistic analysis of shallow foundation bearing capacity. Symposium on reliability based design in Civil Engineering. Lausanne, 1988, vol. 2, pp. 135-143.
3. CHERUBINI C. A closed form probabilistic solution for evaluating the bearing capacity of shallow foundations. Canadian Geotechnical Journal, 1990, Vol. 27, pp. 526-529.
4. CHERUBINI C., CUCCHIARARO L. and GIASI C.I. Probabilistic analysis of shallow foundations bearing capacity. Int. Conf. on Soil Mech. and Found. Eng. Chile, 1991, pp. 971-980.
5. CHERUBINI C., CUCCHIARARO L. and GERMINARIO S. Computerized probabilistic methods for the computation of bearing capacity of shallow foundations. Proc. Intern. Conf. "Geotechnics and Computers". Paris, 1992, pp. 198-195.
6. EASA S.M. Discussion on the article : A closed

form probabilistic solution for evaluating the bearing capacity of shallow foundations (by Cherubini C., 1990). Canadian Geotechnical Journal, 1991, Vol. 29, p. 918.
7. EASA S.M. Exact probabilistic solution of two parameter bearing capacity for shallow foundations. Canadian Geotechnical Journal, 1992, Vol.29 n. 5, pp. 867-870.
8. FAVRE J.L. and GENEVOIS B. Effect de la variabilitè spatiale des parameters du sol sur la variance de la capacitè portante des foundations superficelles. Proc. V ICASP. Vancouver, 1987.
9. HARR M.E. Reliability based design in civil engineering. Mc Graw Hill Book Company, N.Y., 1987.
10. LI K.S. Some common mistakes in probabilistic analysis of slopes. Proc. 6th Int. Symp. on Landslides. Christchurch, New Zeland, 1992, pp. 475-480. Balkema.
11. KAYALAR A.S. Statistical evaluation of dynamic cone penetrometer test data for design of shallow foundations in cohesionless soils. Penetration testing ISOPT I. Orlando, U.S.A., 1988, pp. 429-434.
12. KEAVENY J.M., NADIM F. and LACASSE G. Autocorrelation functions for offshore geotechnical data. 5th Int. Conf. on Structural Safety and Reliability. ICOSSAR, 1989, pp. 263-270.
13. MAC ANALLY P.A. Reliability of the bearing capacity design of shallow footings in sands. 4th ICASP. Firenze, 1983, pp. 1545-1550.
14. MEYERHOF G.G. Limit state design in geotechnical engineering. Structural Safety n. 1, 1982, pp. 67-71.
15. MOSTYN G.R. and LI K.S. Probabilistic slope analysis. State of play. Proc. of the Conference on probabilistic methods in geotechnical engineering. Canberra, 1993, pp. 89-109.
16. RETHATI L. Probabilistic solution in geotechnics. Elsevier, Amsterdam, 1989.
17. SALEMBIER M. Tentative d'evaluation probabiliste du niveau de securitè des ouvrages. Proc. of the 7th ECSMFE Vol. 1, Brighton, G.B., 1979, pp. 149 - 156.
18. SANGLERAT G. The penetrometer and soil exploration. Elsevier Publishing Company. Amsterdam, 1972.
19. SINGH A. How relable is the factor of safety in foundation engineering?. Proc. of the 1st ICASP, Hong Kong, 1971, pp. 126 - 132.
20. SMITH G.N. Probability and statistics in civil engineering. Nichols Publishing Company. New York, 1986.
21. TUKEY, J. Exploratory data analysis. Addison

Wesley Publishing Company, 1977.

22. VANMARCKE E.H. Probabilistic modelling of soil profiles. Journ. of Geot. Eng. Div. ASCE 103 (H), 1977, pp. 1227-1246.

23. VICKREMESINGHE D. and CAMPANELLA R.G. Scale of fluctuation as a description of soil variability. Proc. of the Conference on probabilistic methods in geotechnical engineering. Canberra, 1993, pp. 233-239.

24. WONNACOTT T.H. and WONNACOTT R.J. Introductory Statistics. Wiley, N.Y., 1977.

17. Geostatistical interpolation techniques for geotechnical data modelling and ground condition risk and reliability assessment

D. GILES, University of Portsmouth, UK

SYNOPSIS. The concepts of risk, risk management and reliability of decision are becoming increasingly important in ground engineering. The engineer now requires that the risk associated with a particular project, analysis, or test result be quantified in such a way as to support a particular design or interpretation. Geostatistical modelling techniques can be used in many aspects of ground engineering for ground condition assessment. These techniques provide a formal quantitative estimate of the reliability of the interpolation of the data and provide the engineer with an important risk delineation tool.

INTRODUCTION

1. Recent initiatives (ref. 1) have meant that an increasing volume of geotechnical data is becoming available to the engineer in a digital format. The vast majority of this data will in some way be spatially referenced. This development, coupled with the ease with which the data can be input into a computer system, will provide the engineer with new opportunities for the comprehensive spatial modelling of geotechnical data that were previously too time consuming or not easily achievable. This paper sets out to review the spatial data modelling options available and in particular the geostatistical algorithms that can be used for the data interpolation. Only geostatistical techniques provide a formal quantitative estimate of the reliability of the interpolation of the data. This error of estimation resulting from the interpolation process has great potential for quantifying the reliability of a particular interpretation or analyses and as an engineering risk delineation tool.

2. This paper will consider the available geostatistical techniques and will provide examples of the use of the error of estimation resulting from the interpolation process. In particular Universal Kriging techniques will be detailed as a means of quantifying the risk associated with certain ground conditions and for delineating areas of potentially unsuitable ground and areas of potential risk and hazard to engineering works.

Risk and reliability in ground engineering. Thomas Telford, London, 1993

SPATIAL DATA INTERPOLATION

3. Very often in ground investigation data is collected from a series of sample points, usually boreholes or trial pits, which will be located in a manner that is possibly not ideal for the potential project in question. The most optimal sites for investigation may be occupied by existing structures or affected by utilities. Very often too, the ground engineer is more concerned with the 'unknown' ground conditions between the investigation sites and sample points. One method available to the ground engineer for quantifying this unknown is to undertake some form of data interpolation between the sampled points. This process will involve taking data from the discrete, known observational localities and utilising this data to mathematically model data at a series of unknown localities. This data modelling usually takes the form of interpolating the data, onto a regularly spaced grid, which can subsequently be contoured. Numerous interpolation algorithms are available to 'grid' the data in this manner but as far as their use in risk and reliability assessment is concerned, they have serious drawbacks. The engineer must know the error or factor of safety associated with any calculation or engineering design. This requirement must be maintained in any sub-surface modelling or data interpolation as it is in, for example, any slope stability calculation. The risk and reliability associated with any geotechnical data modelling must be known and quantified before any engineering decisions can be made utilising that model.

4. Standard data interpolation techniques such as weighted interpolators or least-squares polynomial methods give no quantitative indication of the error or reliability associated with the data interpolation. Furthermore these traditional techniques fail to take account of the spatial continuity of the observed data, they assume independence of the sample points (ref. 2), a situation which is obviously not true when dealing with the vast majority of sub-surface data. To minimize the risk in the data modelling and to increase the reliability of the model the ground engineer requires an interpolation method that includes the spatial component of the observation point and includes a measure of the spatial continuity of the data. An additional requirement is for a quantitative 'feel' of the reliability and error associated with that data interpolation. Geostatistical methods provide all of these requirements.

GEOSTATISTICAL INTERPOLATION TECHNIQUES

5. The term geostatistics is now widely applied to a special branch of applied statistics originally developed by the French geomathematician Georges Matheron and by the South African mining engineer D.G. Krige (refs. 3-4). They devised numerical methods to treat problems that arose when conventional statistical theory was used in estimating changes in ore grade within a mine. However, because geostatistics is an abstract theory of statistical behaviour (ref. 4) it is applicable to many circumstances in different areas of geology and of ground engineering. Geostatistics can be considered as the modelling of spatially referenced data.

6. Geostatistical techniques have three major advantages over the more classical data interpolation methods. Firstly, they consider the spatial dependency between the sample or observational points. The spatial coordinate, ie the grid reference of the data point, and the spatial relationship to the other sample data points are utilised in the data interpolation process. Secondly, these techniques preserve the observed field data values, ie they honour the data points in the interpolation, that is to say that they are an exact interpolator. This is obviously of paramount importance when dealing with ground investigation data as the only known 'facts' are the data emanating from the boreholes, although the cross-validation procedures described later offer a very useful check on the actual sampled data and can be a very helpful mechanism in highlighting sample or test error or data misinterpretation. Thirdly, perhaps the most important advantage of the geostatistical methods, is that together with the estimated value a measure of the uncertainty associated with that estimate is given.

GEOSTATISTICAL MODELLING PROCESS
7. Geostatistical data modelling and interpolation can be considered as basically comprising of four component stages
(a)   the determination of the spatial correlation between sample points
(b)   the modelling of that spatial variation
(c)   the cross-validation of that model
(d)   the interpolation of the observed data points onto a regular grid utilising the modelled spatial variation within the data, and the spatial dependency between the observation points.

Determination of spatial correlation
8. The determination of the spatial correlation between sample points requires the undertaking of an analysis of the spatial continuity within the data set. The basic tool that is used to determine and model any spatial correlation within the data is the semi-variogram. The semi-variogram is a plot of the spatial dependency between samples, the semi-variance, along a specific 'support' (ref. 4). The support can be considered as the size, shape, orientation and spatial arrangement of those samples under consideration. The semi-variogram describes the variation within a spatial data set as a function of distance and direction. Mathematically, the semi-variance is defined, for a specified distance interval, as follows

$$\gamma_h = \frac{1}{2n} \sum_{i=1}^{n-h} \left(x_i - x_{(i+h)} \right)^2$$

Where γ_h = experimental semi-variance
            x_i = sample measurement at location i
            $x_{(i+h)}$ = sample measurement at h intervals away
            n   = number of sample points

The semi-variogram itself (Fig. 1) consists of several component parameters which all have an influence on the data interpolation process (ref. 5). These paramters are

9. Range. As the separation between data sample points increases the corresponding semi-variance will also generally increase. At some distance the separation between the sample data points will no longer cause an increase in the semi-variance between the pair of sample points. The semi-variogram will therefore reach a plateau. This distance at which the semi-variogram reaches a plateau is called the range.

10. Sill. The sill is the value of semi-variance that is reached at the range, it is therefore the semi-variance of the 'plateau' of the graph.

11. Nugget Effect. If two sample points or data observations are spatially very close together then it could be expected that the semi-variance value should be approaching zero as theoretically their data values should be virtually the same. There are however geological and indeed geotechnical circumstances where this may not be the case. Factors other than just simple sampling error may affect the data values. For example, two sub-surface level values separated by a fault could have markedly different values, despite being spatially close together. Two undrained shear strength test values from samples at the same levels in two closely adjacent boreholes also could have differing values, possibly indicating a sudden change of soil lithology and soil properties. These factors could give rise to a 'nugget effect' on the semi-variogram, so called from the origins of geostatistics in the mining industry. This short scale variability may cause a discontinuity at the origin of the semi-variogram.

12. To calculate an experimental semi-variogram to describe the spatial relationships within a data set, two properties of the variable of interest are required, the spatial coordinates of the variable in one, two or even three dimensions, and secondly the measured parameter value itself. As previously stated the semi-variogram describes the variation within a spatial data set as a function of distance and direction. This directional component is important and can be used to ascertain whether the spatial continuity of the data set is the same in all directions. It is possible that geological and geotechnical variables show a different variability in different directions. Semi-variograms can be calculated for data pairs along a specific orientation with a given tolerance or for all data pairs regardless of the orientation The semi-variogram which best describes the spatial continuity within the data set is usually used for the spatial continuity modelling.

13. After the calculation of the experimental semi-variogram from the observational data a model must be fitted which will describe and provide the semi-variances at any given data separation, not just from the separations of the known data points (Fig. 2). A variety of mathematical models are available for the semi-variogram fitting but for most geological

data, such as stratigraphic levels or isopach thicknesses, a spherical model suffices. A spherical model rises from the origin (or slightly above if a nugget effect is detected) and continues smoothly to an upper limit, at the range, and then continues at a constant level, the sill value. Other models that are available include a linear model (a model with only one parameter, the slope) or an exponential model. Refs 4-6 provide further examples of semi-variogram models. The semi-variogram model will provide the interpolation equations with the necessary parameters and information about the spatial continuity within the data set.

14. One very important factor to consider when generating experimental semi-variograms and their subsequent modelling is that these representations and models of spatial continuity are only valid on data that do not exhibit any trend or 'drift' (ref. 6). Obviously with many geological or geotechnical data sets some element of trend will be present within the data. To correctly generate and model the semi-variogram any trend must be analysed and if present removed and the semi-variogram generated and modelled on the remaining residual variation within the data set. Any trend within a data set is usually determined by a polynomial trend surface analysis with the goodness of fit of the potential trend surface being tested by analysis of variance (ANOVA) techniques (ref. 4).

Semi-Variogram Cross Validation

15. Once a semi-variogram model has been fitted to the experimental, ie field data, it is possible to validate the model to ascertain whether or not it correctly reflects the true variation within the spatial data set. This cross-validation process involves each sample being removed in turn from the data set and its value estimated via the geostatistical model. This estimated value is then compared to the true value and an error statistic is calculated. The range of these errors determines the goodness of fit of the semi-variogram model to the field data. This cross-validation procedure can also be a very useful process in highlighting anomalies within the data set and can be used to pinpoint sample points that do not 'conform' to the model. These may be sampling errors or more significantly true anomalies representing some potential 'risk' or inconsistency within the data. For example, a borehole penetrating a scour feature would not conform with the regional model or a weak shear strength test result would also be detected by its non conformity with its neighbours. After the semi-variogram model has been validated the data is ready for the actual geostatistical interpolation process, colloquially referred to as the kriging of the data, so called after its originator D Krige.

Kriging

16. As has already been discussed, the semi-variogram is the basic data analysis tool that is used to measure the spatial correlation within a data set. The kriging equations are used to make the interpolations from the observed data values, using the parameters supplied by the semi-variogram model, onto a regular grid (ref. 7). The general form of the kriging

estimator is identical to that of other interpolation methods used to calculate grid node values (ref. 8). The difference between kriging and the other weighting interpolators is in the calculation of those weights. In the inverse distance method the contribution of each observation depends on its geographical distance to the node being calculated. Each weight in this method is computed separately. The calculations in kriging estimators are much more complex. More parameters are utilized in the estimation process. The appropriate weights are calculated from the solution of a series of simultaneous equations, importantly with kriging the calculated weights depend not only on the distances between a node being estimated and a data observation, but on the distances between data observations as well, ie the spatial relationships of the data points to each other is a crucial element of kriging. The basic assumption in the kriging process is that each sampled location (borehole, trial pit etc) will be taken and will be weighted according to its spatial relationship with the location being estimated. Another major advantage of the kriging process is that every point that is estimated will have an error value, known as the standard error, associated with the estimation of that point. The reliability of the estimate depends not only on how far the observational data points are from the unsampled location but again on how far the samples are from one another. The reliability of the estimated value will also be dependent on the actual continuity of the sampled values within the study area, as characterized by the semi-variogram model. These standard error values generated by the kriging estimation process are useful in delineating areas of geological uncertainty arising out of the basic interpolation procedure. The standard error values can be contoured just as the main interpolated parameter can. Areas of these resultant contour maps can be highlighted according to their statistical reliability. This can give an added aid to the analysis of the geological or geotechnical risk. Areas of sparse data are given a quantified visual aid as to their reliability. The kriging process itself mathematically minimizes the formula for the standard errors to find a set of weighting factors which will produce the greatest reliability, ie the lowest standard error.

17. A number of different kriging systems are available depending on the original data set and the type of interpolation and modelling that is required. Table 1 (after ref. 9) summarises the basic kriging systems available.

UNIVERSAL KRIGING FOR TUNNELLING RISK ASSESSMENT

18. In any tunnelling project the engineer must assess the extent, both lateral and vertical, of the preferred tunnelling medium and be fully aware of the precise location of any unfavourable ground conditions. The delineation of hazards such as granular strata, water bearing horizons or any alluvial, glacial or periglacial features, such as buried channels, pingo remnants or scour features, will be of a major concern. The traditional practice for a geological assessment along a tunnel alignment is to present the available ground investigation data as a long section. Boreholes will

Table 1. Available Kriging Systems

Kriging System	Comment
Simple or Ordinary Kriging	Simplest form of kriging. Used in data with no trend or drift present. Used where the variance is constant throughout the data, and where the mean value is the same, on average, over the various sub-areas of the data
Universal Kriging	Kriging of data where there is a trend or 'drift' present. Trend is analysed and removed, and the semi-variogram modelled on the residual variation within the data set. Trend is reinput into the modelling at the interpolation stage. Utilizes an enlarged set of kriging equations which include the trend element in addition to the normal kriging weights
Disjunctive Kriging	All of the previous systems are linear methods. Disjunctive kriging considers non-linear estimations. A mathematically complex method
Co-Kriging	Where two highly correlated variables have been measured both variables are used together to estimate each variable in turn thus providing a richer set of data. Cokriging is best used where one variable, which can be measured only with great expense or difficulty, is correlated with another variable that is easily measured at low cost
Lognormal Kriging	Used with highly skewed data. Essential that the data have a log-normal distribution. Used where high outlying data values appear in a small data set where they exert a totally disproportionate effect
Indicator Kriging	Instead of using raw data values, 'indicator' values are used. The indicator values are then modelled
Probability Kriging	Utilizes the uniform distribution of the data. Reduces order relationship problems to a degree which makes them negligible
Soft Kriging	All of the previous systems use 'hard' data, ie samples which have been actually measured. However, at some locations the behaviour, if not the value, of the variable may be known, for example data maxima and minima. Soft kriging allows this 'extra' data to be utilized

have been sunk at set intervals along or as close to the tunnel alignment as possible, and the intermediate geology and ground conditions interpreted as best possible. This approach is obviously very limited with regard to any overall geological risk associated with that tunnel. No account is taken of the surrounding regional picture or as to the accuracy of the intermediate interpretation. In no way has the risk and reliability of the interpretive model been quantified.

19. One approach to overcome these inadequacies is to utilise a wider information base of existing geological and geotechnical data from the

project region and to undertake a geostatistical assessment of that data to produce an interpolated model. By using geostatistical modelling this regional overview of the project area can be developed with the added advantage of having the risk and reliability of that model quantified in such a way as to positively aid any engineering decisions taken from it.

20. As previously stated, any geological risk analysis project should concern itself with the highlighting and delineation of that geological risk. The main geological risks to any tunnelling project could be considered as

(a)   granular or water bearing horizons
(b)   faulting or other structural features
(c)   buried channels, scour features, other glacial, periglacial or alluvial hazards.

What can also be considered as a form of 'risk' are insufficient data to make a sound judgement on the ground conditions. Some form of quantification of data inadequacy would be an aid to the risk and reliability of any overall study.

21. To create a geological risk model for a tunnelling project, data would be required for a significant envelope around the tunnel alignment. This data will usually be in the form of existing borehole information acquired as part of the project desk study, which is used to compliment new data from the project ground investigation. These data will have been interpreted geologically or geotechnically depending on the detail of the risk analysis study required, and incorporated into some form of data management system (ref. 10). The data would then be available for the geostatistical modelling and analysis.

22. Consider a project where the requirement was for a tunnel to be constructed and remain within the preferred tunnelling medium of a stiff clay and to avoid underlying strata of variable soft clays and loose water bearing sands and other granular soils. As an aid to the overall risk analysis the levels to the various stratigraphic horizons of interest could be modelled to delineate the best tunnelling window where the unfavourable ground conditions could be avoided and to highlight the potential chainages where these ground conditions could affect the alignment. As with any geostatistical analysis and interpolation, an appropriate kriging system should be used for the data set in question. In this particular case the stratigraphic levels of the key horizons affecting the tunnel are being considered. With a geological surface a trend could be expected to be present within the data set. The data would probably be normally distributed with no undue proportion of outlying data values. From Table 1, Universal Kriging provides the correct kriging system of equations for this type of data. If Universal Kriging techniques are to be used correctly, any trend within the data set must be analyzed, removed and the spatial continuity within the data calculated and modelled on the residual variation remaining. The trend component of the model is reinput into the calculations at the interpolation stage. The geostatistical modelling procedure, as previously stated, would comprise of the following stages

(a)   trend surface analysis
(b)   semi-variogram calculation and modelling
(c)   semi-variogram model cross-validation
(d)   interpolation, utilising Universal Kriging equations, of the data to produce a resultant grid together with an associated grid of the standard error resulting from that interpolation.

The semi-variogram model cross-validation procedure allows the opportunity to highlight potential anomalies or inconsistencies within the data. The cross-validation process involves removing each data point in turn from the data set and estimating the value of that point using the remaining data. Once this estimate is calculated, it can be compared with the true sample value and a statistical magnitude of error calculated. This can then be plotted, either as a graph with a plot of true value against estimated value, or shown spatially, Fig. 3, using proportional symbols to highlight the magnitude of the error. The larger the symbol, the greater the error of the estimation and the greater the potential for a data point that is not conformable with its neighbours, possibly highlighting some form of geological risk, uncertainty or hazard. This type of plot can also be of great use for detecting erroneous data values, particularly those with an incorrect geological interpretation.

23. After cross-validation the data can be interpolated or kriged onto a regular grid. The estimation process produces an interpolated grid together with a grid of the associated standard error. Both of these grids can be contoured. The geostatistical methods provide this formal quantitative estimate of the reliability of the interpolated data allowing areas of statistical uncertainty to be highlighted. Any standard error which is larger than the sample standard deviation denotes an unreliable prediction. These areas can be considered as of being statistically unreliable and of potential uncertainty with regard to the estimated surface levels in those areas. Fig. 4 shows a typical contoured geological surface together with the contoured grid of the standard error. As kriging is an exact interpolator, a standard error of zero is calculated at the individual data points. Fig. 5 shows areas of the contoured standard error grid where the standard error is greater than the sample standard deviation. This is highlighting the unreliable predictions and improving the reliability of any decisions made using this model. The engineer can see which areas of the geological surface are statistically reliable and which areas can be considered statistically unreliable. These areas of unreliable predictions have 'quantified' the risk for the engineer on any use that is made on the interpolated data for those particular regions.

24. The grid of the standard error values can also be used in other ways. It is possible to take a profile of the standard error along the tunnel alignment. Fig. 6 shows this profile and the tunnel chainages for which the estimates of those particular horizon levels may not be reliable. Further use of the standard error can be made for delineating risk and reliability by utilising standard statistical theory. Statistical theory states that there is a 95% probability that the true value lies within an interval defined by

plus or minus twice the indicated error value from the estimated value. For example

Estimated level $= 14.80$ m

Standard error (from that estimation) $= 0.6$

95% probability that the true elevation lies between 14.68 m and 14.92 m

This theory can be utilised for risk prediction. Fig. 7 shows the 95% confidence interval for the top of a potentially hazardous horizon which could affect the proposed tunnel alignment. The figure shows tunnel chainages where there is a possibility of encountering a potential granular or water bearing horizon at tunnel level. The profile has enabled areas of risk to be delineated as well as highlighting areas of high standard error where more data is required to improve the reliability of the model.

25. The use of Universal Kriging and the construction of standard error profiles and the 95% confidence limits have provided the ground engineer with a quantified tool for the risk and reliability assessment of the proposed engineering works.

SUMMARY

26. Geological risk analysis studies are becoming an essential component of any ground engineering projects. The advent of electronic data interchange standards for ground investigation data has greatly improved the ease with which this information can be incorporated into computer systems and made available for analysis and modelling. All of this data will in some ways be spatially referenced and will provide the ground engineer with the opportunity to undertake the comprehensive spatial modelling of the data at their disposal.

27. It is proposed that only geostatistical techniques offer a reliable and robust set of modelling and interpolation algorithms for these data sets as they offer the engineer a formal quantitative measure of the errors associated with the estimation and modelling process. These techniques allow for the spatial dependency and continuity of the data to be assessed and modelled, as well as providing useful tools for risk quantification and delineation.

REFERENCES

1. ASSOCIATION OF GEOTECHNICAL SPECIALISTS The electronic transfer of geotechnical data from ground investigations, A.G.S. London, 1992.
2. NOBRE M.M. and SYKES J.F. Application of Bayesian Kriging to subsurface characterization. Can. Geotech. J., 29, 1992, 589-598.
3. BURROUGH P.A. Principles of Geographical Information Systems for land resources assessment, p.194, Clarendon Press, Oxford, 1986.
4. DAVIS J.C. Statistics and data analysis in geology, p.646, John Wiley & Sons, New York, 1986.
5. ISSAKS E.H. and SRIVASTAVA R.M. An introduction to applied geostatistics, p.561, Oxford University Press, New York, 1989.

6. CLARK I. Practical geostatistics, p.129, Applied Science Publishers, London, 1979.

7. NATHANAIL C.P. and ROSENBAUM M.S. The use of low cost geostatistical software in reserve estimation. From Annels A.E. (ed.) 1992, Case histories and methods in mineral resource evaluation. Geological Society Special Publication No 63, 169-177.

8. OLEA R.A. Kriging, understanding alloys intimidation. Geobyte, October 1992, 12-17.

9. ROYLE A.G. A personal overview of geostatistics. From Annels A.E. (ed.) 1992. Case histories and methods in mineral resource evaluation. Geological Society Special Publication No 63, 233-241.

10. GILES D.P. The geotechnical computer workstation: The link between the geotechnical database and the geographical information system. Géotechnique et Informatique, Paris 1992, 685-690.

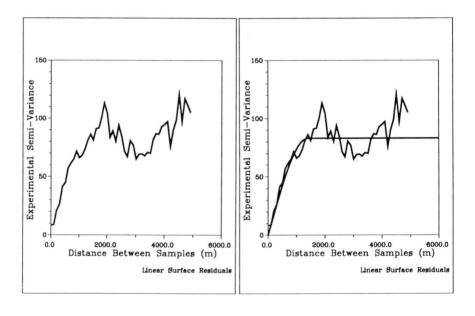

Fig. 1. Experimental Semi-variogram   Fig. 2. Experimental Semi-variogram
with spherical model

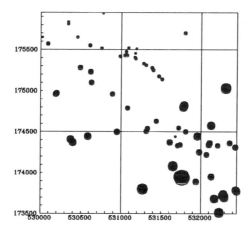

Fig. 3. Proportional symbols highlighting the magnitude of the Standard Error

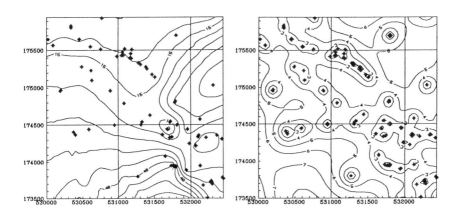

Fig. 4. Contoured surface with associated Standard Error

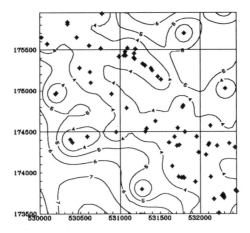

Fig. 5. Contoured Standard Error highlighting areas of statistical unreliability

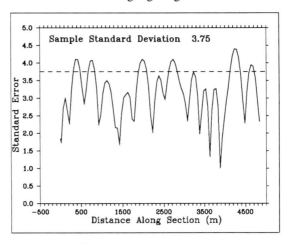

Fig. 6. Standard Error profile

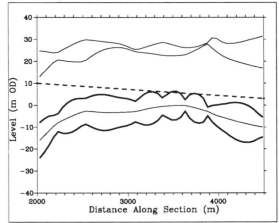

Fig. 7. 95% confidence interval highlighting tunnel chainages at potential risk

214

18. Hazard associated with old stone mineworkings: a case history from Combe Down, Bath

A. B. HAWKINS and B. J. McCONNELL, Engineering Geology Research Group, University of Bristol, UK

SYNOPSIS

The paper describes the geotechnical hazard assessment of the shallow mineworkings under Combe Down, Bath, undertaken to identify areas of potential risk to life, property, public open spaces and highways. It discusses the philosophy behind the hazard assessment and considers the results in relation to calculated and perceived risk. It is concluded that for Combe Down mines, engineering judgement is more applicable than a purely frequentist probability approach.

INTRODUCTION

1. In the Combe Down area of Bath development has taken place with little consideration of the oolitic freestone workings of up to 8.5 m in height which exist at a depth of between 4 to 8 m below the surface. Considerable areas of the old workings are accessible and surveying during the past three years has revealed progressive deterioration of the mine roof and pillars. A geotechnical assessment of the conditions within the workings has allowed identification of the most hazardous areas. However, the familiarity of the local residents with the existence of the mines has significantly reduced the perceived risk and the local population are often less concerned with the hazard presented by the mines than with the short term inconvenience for the local community during any stabilisation works.

THE COMBE DOWN MINES

2. Quarrying for oolitic freestones on and surrounding the Combe Down plateau, south of Bath, has taken place since Roman times but it was not until the early eighteenth century that major subsurface mining began, to win building stone from the Great Oolite. As their closure in 1860 predated the Coal Mines

Regulation Act of 1872, there are no mine plans or records and little historical documentation of these workings.

3. The mines are extremely shallow, being only 4 to 8 m below ground. Up to 8.5 m of rock was extracted by room and pillar techniques. As the stone was removed along pre-existing discontinuities in the Combe Down Oolite, there is little regularity in pillar size, shape or layout and room widths vary from 2 to 12 m. As the freestone was much in demand for facing and architectural finishes, only the largest and best quality blocks were required; the inferior material (discards) was simply backstowed within the workings. This has resulted in an extremely uneven mine floor with the subsurface void varying from 0.2 to 8.5 m in height.

4. The extent of the potential hazard presented by the mines was appreciated in the 1970s when the workings were exposed during the excavation of service trenches. Subsequently several shaft caps failed and a significant crownhole subsidence occurred. As a result, a preliminary survey and assessment of the Firs/Byfield Mines was initiated in the late 1980s. This has been followed by a more extensive assessment which is continuing.

5. To date the survey has identified approximately 16 hectares (40 acres) of workings compared with previous estimates (ref. 1) of in the region of 10 hectares (25 acres). In some areas, large pillars were left where the roof is highly fractured. In other areas, there is clear evidence of more recent sawing of the stone indicating extensive pillar robbing early this century which has resulted in some pillars being severely tapered at the base (Fig. 1). Extraction percentages were extremely high throughout the workings. A mean value of 86% has been calculated but in areas where pillar robbing took place or very slender pillars were left by the miners, extraction exceeds 95%.

6. The stability of the workings is generally very poor. A high percentage of the roof beds have suffered collapse, reducing the remaining roof cover to as little as 2 m in places. With such a shallow overburden thickness, the vertical stresses are generally too low to cause pillar failure on a large scale but 20 to 30% of the pillars are showing varying degrees of distress.

DEVELOPMENT AT COMBE DOWN

7. Until 1769, the area of Combe Down consisted of only eleven mine management houses, most of the miners living in the Avon valley, north of the plateau. The growth of the community began around the turn of the nineteenth century, the chapel being built in 1815 and the village church in 1830. Mining ceased in about 1860 (ref. 2) and with time, the existence of the old workings attracted less attention.

8. As there appear to have been few incidents of ground subsidence, it is understandable that the developing community of Combe Down eventually expanded over the old mine workings.

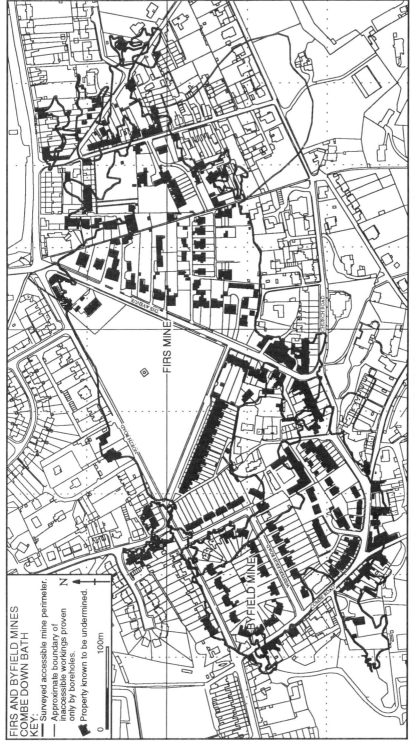

Fig.2: Map showing accessible boundary of the Firs/Byfield Mines and overlying properties

Although builders were probably aware of the existence of the mines, normal strip footings were typical and it was not until the 1950s that raft foundations were first used for some developments over the western part of the old mine workings. Some of the more recent housing development has taken account of the significance of the mines with the construction of piled foundations or underground stone built foundations, in some cases filled with concrete. For any new development, the City Council now requires a site investigation and an appropriate foundation design.

COMPARISON WITH OTHER MINES

9. The workings in Combe Down are unusual in that they are extremely shallow and accessible, yet have a significant overlying development (Fig. 2). Whilst a cover in the order of 6 m is normal, in many parts of the mines collapses have extended for up to 4 m above the mine roof bed. Consequently little competent rock remains beneath the topsoil/weathered rock horizon which has been shown in trial pits to extend to a depth of 2 m. Indeed, in some areas the thickness of rock capable of forming a "bridging" mine roof has been proved by survey to be no more than one metre

10. An advantage of this small thickness of roof cover however is that overburden stresses are relatively low, reducing the load taken by the pillars. This is in contrast to the mines at Valkenburg described by Price and Verhoef (ref. 3) and visited by the authors where the overburden is up to 50 m thick. The major collapse which occurred in 1988 in the mines at Heidegroeve, in which the Germans had a war-time underground factory, resulted from a failure of the pillars (ref. 4). Pillar failure is also believed to have been the cause of the 200 x 300 m surface depression at Cow Pasture Mine in 1978 where the limestone was extracted at a depth of 150 m (ref. 5).

11. Although for coal mines it was previously considered that 6 to 10 times the extracted thickness was sufficient to ensure that bulking would prevent migrating voids reaching the surface, events at Bathgate and in the Pittsburgh area have indicated this is not a realistic criterion (see ref.6 for summary).In the case of the Bathgate mines, although the collapsed workings were at a depth of 30 m up to 150 mm of subsidence occurred within a period of two weeks, following an almost instantaneous drop in the order of 75 mm.

12. At Combe Down the thickness and nature of the overlying rock would not permit sufficient bulking to arrest migrating voids, except where the mines are almost totally backfilled with discards. Although the discontinuities originally developed as tectonic fractures, many of these were subsequently opened by the Quaternary process of cambering along the edges of the elongate but narrow plateau. Throughout the mines, the roof beds are comprised of discrete, discontinuity-bounded blocks. The removal

or failure of one of these "keystone" blocks generally results in a roof bed collapse.

RECORDED SUBSIDENCES

13. A number of subsidences have occurred periodically since the closure of the Combe Down mines. Relatively few collapses have been well documented however and verbal accounts from the local population have provided valuable additional sources of information (Table 1).

Date	Failure type	Location	Details
1917	Crownhole	The Avenue	Beneath a house
1920	Crownhole	North Rd	Collapse of part of the tram route
1970	Crownhole	Junction Church Rd /Summer Lane	Related to installation of sewerage system
1972	Crownhole	North Rd	Large hole in back garden
1984	Crownhole	Shaft Rd	Surface collapse at a time when heavy lorries were delivering fill for the levelling of an adjacent playing field
1986	Shaft cap	Westerleigh Rd	A hole appeared in private garden fracturing sewer pipe.
1990	Shaft cap	Westerleigh Rd	3.7m diameter air shaft collapsed, 3 m from house, fracturing sewer pipe laid across shaft.
1990	Shaft cap	Firs Field	Tree blown down revealing 4.6 m diameter open shaft
1992	Cap over old crownhole	Combe Rd Close	An old crownhole had been partly backfilled and partly capped. A 2 m diameter hole formed when the cap failed.
1992	Shaft cap	North Rd	2 m diameter shaft cap failed due to settlement of underlying fill.

Table 1: Recorded subsidences in the Combe Down area

HAZARD ASSESSMENT

14. Evidence within the workings indicates that a number of crownhole collapses occurred during the period of mining or shortly thereafter but there are no historical records of these events. On present information, no subsidence events since closure of the mines have resulted in death or injury to persons although they involved inconvenience or impairment as defined by Cole (ref. 7).

15. Although various workers have put forward criteria on which the hazards posed by old workings can be established (ref. 8), these have generally been broad brush assessments based on data obtained indirectly as the mines were not accessible. At Combe Down, however, it has been possible to study the state of the pillars and overlying roof beds throughout much of the

workings, except in areas where the discards reach within 0.5 m of the roof.

16. Detailed surveys have been made throughout the accessible mined area to assess the potential hazard in terms of the implications for life, property, highways, services and public open spaces. The following factors were considered significant: remaining roof cover, room width, pillar deformation, presence of gulls, floor to roof height, nature of discontinuities, sagging of roof beds and concentration of collapses.

a)   REMAINING ROOF COVER

17. In order to establish the exact thickness of the roof cover, levelling surveys were carried out on both the ground surface and the mine roof; the density of points being related to the irregularity of the mine roof. This irregularity is particularly pronounced as a consequence of the bedded nature of the overlying Great Oolite. Where discontinuity-bounded blocks from the Combe Down Oolite have fallen, significant steps occur and the mine roof may vary in height by over 2 m within a smaller horizontal distance. The varying strength of the overlying Twinhoe Beds produces a different discontinuity pattern however, which in a number of areas has inhibited the upward migration of the voids.

18. All the roof falls which have migrated upwards for more than 0.5 m have been surveyed and the overlying roof thickness determined. Most of these collapses have occurred since the placement of the discards and in some areas have fallen across the tramways.

b)   ROOM WIDTH

19. Rooms within the Combe Down mines have spans up to 12 m wide. From a study of collapsed old workings exposed in the high walls of eighteen opencast coal sites, Garrard and Taylor (ref. 9) suggest collapse height = 2.68 x span width. Such a relationship is not applicable to the different geology of the Combe Down area and, because of the thin roof cover in these mines, would imply that rooms over 2 m in width would all be problematical.   Unlike many of the deeper mine workings such as Hoorsenburg mine at Limburg, little stress-induced tensile fracturing of the roof beds is visible in the Firs/Byfield mines. Nevertheless, the jointed nature of the roof beds and the condition of the supporting pillars give cause for concern in many of the larger rooms.

c)   PILLAR DEFORMATION

20. As the mine workers extracted blocks along pre-existing discontinuities, the pillars are irregular in both spacing and shape. Pillar size varies considerably, from several metres to less than one, either due to the original discontinuity arrangements and/or as a result of pillar robbing. All the pillars within the workings contain

tectonic fractures and in some cases these discontinuities divide the pillars vertically into two or more discrete sections.

21. Due to the thin roof cover (4 to 8 m), the loadings on the pillars within the workings are relatively low but clearly some of the pillars have suffered significant creep deformation. This deformation generally manifests itself as stress-induced fractures, spalling (Fig. 3) or by the visible displacement of sawn faces.

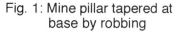

Fig. 1: Mine pillar tapered at
base by robbing

Fig. 3: Example of severely
distressed mine pillar

22. Using normal tributary area analysis it is estimated that 20 to 30% of the pillars are overstressed, particularly in the areas of greatest extraction. However in view of the discontinuity pattern within the rock mass, the true loading on the pillars will vary from that calculated by mathematical tributary calculations.

23. For the purposes of the hazard assessment, the pillars have been classified in terms of post-mining deformation:

Class 1   No visible signs of mining-induced fracturing
Class 2   Slight stress-induced fracturing visible on the pillar surface
Class 3   Some spalling concentrated in localised areas
Class 4   Significant stress-induced fracturing and spalling of the pillar sides
Class 5   Pillar has failed but remains upstanding, supporting only a residual load.

24. Depending on the stiffness of the general roof cover, violent collapse related to a single pillar could occur. In addition, the failure of one pillar will increase the stress on adjacent supports,

giving rise to a domino effect such as occurred in the Heidegroeve mines (ref. 4) and greatly extending the influence of any initial single pillar failure.

d)   PRESENCE OF GULLS

25. The valleyward lowering of the surface strata in the Combe Down plateau area during the Quaternary has resulted in the extension of natural discontinuities, frequently referred to as gulls. Within the mines, gulls of up to 0.5 m in width can be seen, the longest being proved over a distance of more than 150 m. In many cases the gulls are infilled with a clay-rich material. In some areas the infill has been removed, presumably by percolating water, revealing the vertical extension of the features to within a shallow depth of the ground surface.

26. The alignment of the extension gulls is related to the topography of the area and as a consequence of their formation during cambering processes, they are more frequently found towards the edges of the plateau. Gulls can be seen both in the roof beds and in some cases passing through pillars. Where the room alignment is coincident with the trend of the gulls, significant roof failures have occurred as these dilated fractures have reduced the frictional resistance between the blocks.

e)   FLOOR TO ROOF HEIGHT

27. The floor to roof height is a key controlling factor in whether a rock fall will migrate upwards or become choked by bulking. The bulking factor will depend on whether a number of blocks fall together as a unit onto an almost flat surface, retaining their relative positions, or whether the blocks fall independently and tilt such that significant voids are created. In the former case the bulking may be less than 10%, while in the latter, estimates of 40 to 60% have been made.

28. Where the discards are within 0.5 m of the mine roof, only a limited depth of subsidence could occur; hence it is unlikely that a catastrophic failure would be manifest at the surface. However, over more than three-quarters of the workings, bulking would have an insignificant effect and crownhole collapse could occur. In view of the height of the present mine voids and the thinness of the roof cover, the possibility of a sudden, relatively deep collapse cannot be discounted, with the associated risk to life and property.

f)   DISCONTINUITIES

29. An unusual feature of the Combe Down mines is the highly fractured nature of the roof beds which at some horizons consist of stronger, more thinly bedded limestones than at the mined level of the Combe Down Oolite. The main fracture orientations are N070° and N140°. Where these are coincident with the long axis of rooms, this trend has had a significant effect on roof stability.

g)   SAGGING OF ROOF BEDS

30. Dilation is clearly occurring within the roof beds, most notice-ably at the edge of collapses where beds have separated, in some cases by up to 100 mm. In some areas, the sagging of the roof beds is apparent but careful inspection has indicated that other, less pronounced deflections have occurred. The extent of the sagging is related to the size of the room, the thickness of the roof bed strata, the discontinuity geometry and the frictional resistance between the blocks which affects the ability of the roof beds to cantilever out from the supporting pillars.

h)   CONCENTRATION OF COLLAPSES

31. Where the density of roof collapses in any particular area is pronounced, care has been taken to assess whether any specific geological conditions prevail in that area. Where collapses are in close proximity, the competence of the roof cover will have decreased, which may contribute to further instability.

HAZARD RATING SYSTEM

32. The hazard assessment was an iterative process, the criteria being continually revised in the light of new findings or calculations. A weighting system was devised to take account of the relative importance of each of the eight hazard assessment factors in the specific areas being studied (ref. 2).

33. The classification system used by Ove Arup and Partners for the mines in the West Midlands was not considered appropriate as the lowest risk of subsidence over the Combe Down mines is greater than their "very low" rating. Indeed, a "very low" rating would be applicable to the surrounding areas as, unless they are known to have been quarried, they may also be undermined.

34. There is insufficient data to support the reliability of a frequentist probability analysis, hence the most significant influence on the hazard rating assigned to a specific area was an engineering judgement based on the conditions within the mines.

MINIMISING THE RISK

35. The potential risk posed by the Combe Down mines is currently being assessed. It is clear that the existence of the underground workings creates a hazard as defined by Blockley (ref. 10): "a set of conditions ..... with potential for initiating an accident sequence..". As discussed above, the assessment of the hazard is currently being considered in terms of a numerical system, to be described in a subsequent paper.

36. "Risk" is a combination of the likelihood of this "accident sequence" actually occurring and the severity of the consequences. This can be discussed in a variety of fields; Cole (ref. 7) uses life, property and money. The degree of risk related to

each field will depend on a number of different factors, such as accessibility to personnel, existence of superstructures or the interruption of services. In addition the perception of "risk" will depend on such considerations as the background knowledge of the individual and the degree of his or her involvement.

37. As the work is ongoing, in this paper the discussion on the assessment of risk is restricted to the action taken in respect of property and highways.

   a)   Where a high hazard rating has been assigned, underground inspections are carried out on a monthly basis.

   b)   In the case of the highways, the consequences of a subsidence are graphically illustrated by Figure 3 in Edmonds, Green and Higginbottom (ref. 11) which shows a double decker bus up-ended into a hole in a road overlying chalk mines. In view of this, within the village of Combe Down the highway authority have attempted to minimise the risk by imposing a 7.5 tonnes weight limit over the mined area and in one case, only limited access is permitted.

PERCEIVED RISK

38. One of the major difficulties in initiating action to minimise risk is the extent to which it is perceived as such. Some of the older residents of Combe Down, who may even have found the mines an interesting "playground" as children, do not consider the mines to be a significant hazard. The paucity of crownhole collapses and lack of distress to structures overlying the mines is frequently cited, to support this view, although it is realised that recent shaft cap failures have occurred. This familiarity with the existence of the workings has instilled an attitude in older residents which varies from "of little concern" to "circumspect" and in most cases the risk is "voluntary" (Cole, 1993).

39. Although the existence of mines covering at least 10 ha is referred to in a book on the village of Combe Down published locally in 1963 (ref. 1), new property owners may not necessarily have been aware of this when they moved into the area. Further, until the present study, no detailed survey of the mines had been undertaken and no assessment of their condition made. For these newer residents, the risk is "involuntary" and hence both their perception and level of tolerance to it may be lower than that of the longer-term residents.

40. As a result of the current assessment, it is considered necessary to undertake stabilisation works. This will undoubtedly have a direct impact on the people of Combe Down and to many of them, the threat to their peaceful, village lifestyle appears to present a greater hazard than that of the unseen, underground workings. Apart from the implications for property transactions, the factors of greatest concern include the possibility of pollution associated with the nature of the material proposed for the infilling,

the increased traffic flow associated with the stabilisation works, the extent to which restrictions will be placed on roads and open spaces and the possible destruction of a breeding ground for the rare Horseshoe Bat within the mines.

41. In an attempt to allay such fears and minimise the disturbance to the residents, Bath City have commissioned an Environmental Impact Assessment which is currently being undertaken. In addition, newsletters are distributed by the City Council and public meetings held to both inform the residents and allow them the opportunity to raise their concerns and ask questions.

42. The relative importance of the issues involved varies considerably for both individuals and groups. Cole (ref. 7) discusses the difference in attitude according to the amount of information available, the degree of reliability ascribed to it and whether or not the risk is imposed or voluntarily accepted. In turn, the attitude of the individuals/groups will affect the action they consider appropriate. In a situation such as is presented by the disused stone workings beneath Combe Down, "attitudes" may well have a significant influence on the remedial measures which are undertaken. It is to be hoped that these attitudes will be characterised by the maximum objectivity and that no catastrophic event will occur before appropriate precautions are taken to reduce the hazard and minimise the risk currently posed by these mines.

CONCLUSIONS

43. The shallow depth of the overlying roof cover existing above voids of up to 8.5 m high in the Combe Down area of Bath creates a potential hazard and hence risk to life and overlying properties, highways and areas of public space.

44. Although no catastrophic collapse has occurred in the last 50 years, crownhole collapses and shaft cap failures have been recorded. Mapping within the mines has detailed the major roof failures and a hazard assessment has been carried out based on eight major factors which significantly affect the stability of the disused workings. Weighted hazard ratings have been used to designate the most likely areas of future collapse.

45. Observations have shown that the mines are progressively deteriorating and the risk to life and property is likely to increase with time, particularly in view of the limited roof bed thickness and the fact that it is not possible to assess the extent to which roof bed dilation is progressing upwards, with the potential for a sudden collapse in areas of past failures and/or elsewhere.

46. In view of the paucity of catastrophic failures in Combe Down during the past 100 years, it is not considered that a frequentist probability approach will give a realistic prediction of future subsidence activity in the area and engineering judgement based on observations within the accessible mines must be the most important factor in the risk assessment.

ACKNOWLEDGEMENTS

Some of the work reported was carried out for the City of Bath. The authors are grateful for permission to publish this but point out that any views expressed are those of the authors.

REFERENCES

1. ANON. Combe Down History. pp 68. Members of the Combe Down Women's Guild. 1963.
2. FROGGATT, M.T., HAWKINS, A.B. & McCONNELL, B.J. The Disused Stone Mines at Combe Down, Bath. Quarterly Journal of Engineering Geology, 1994, Vol 27.
3. PRICE, D.G. & VERHOEF, P.N.W. The stability of abandoned mine workings in the Maastrichtian Limestones of Limburg, The Netherlands, 193-204. Engineering Geology of Underground Movements, Geological Society, 1988 .
4. PRICE, D.G. The collapse of the Heidegroeve: a case history of subsidence over abandoned mine workings in Cretaceous calcarenites. Chalk, 503-509. Thomas Telford, London, 1990.
5. COLE, K.W., BRAITHWAITE, P.A., DAUNCEY, P.C. & SEAGO, K.L. Removal of actual and apprehended dereliction caused by abandoned limestone mines in the West Midlands of England. Building on marginal and derelict land. 171-196. Thomas Telford, London, 1986.
6. EVANS, R.T & HAWKINS, A.B. Significance and treatment of old coal workings at Llanelli Hospital, South Wales. 188-206. Ground Movements and Structures (ed Geddes, J.D), Pentech Press,1985.
7. COLE, K.W. Considerations of risk and reliability. 35-37. Ground Engineering, January 1993.
8. COLE, K.W. Building over abandoned shallow mines. A strategy for the engineering decisions on treatment. 14-30, Ground Engineering, May 1987.
9. GARRARD, G.F.G. & TAYLOR, R.K. Collapse mechanisms of shallow coal-mine workings from field measurements. 181-192. Engineering Geology of Underground Movements, Geological Society, 1988.
10. BLOCKLEY, D.I. Engineering safety.p475. McGraw Hill, 1992.
11. EDMONDS, C.N, GREEN, C.P. & HIGGINBOTTOM, I.E. Review of underground mines in the English chalk: form, origin, distribution and engineering significance. Chalk, 511-519. Thomas Telford, London, 1990.

19. Application of risk assessment in tunnel feasibility studies

J. J. CONWAY, SubTerra Engineering Ltd, UK

SYNOPSIS.   This paper describes an application of risk-assessment techniques to tunnel feasibility studies, illustrated by the investigation of three potential alignments for a tunnelled river crossing in the western USA.   The objective of the study was to assess the probable costs of tunnelling as an alternative to bridge construction.   The first phase of the study involved estimation of excavation and primary support costs.   To facilitate this, probabilistic models for the geology, rockmass conditions, rock support requirements, and tunnelling costs were developed for each alignment, and this process forms the subject of this paper.

INTRODUCTION

1. As a feasibility level study, data collection activities were limited to a desk-review of topographic and geological maps, regional geological reports, mining and construction records, and anecdotal information, with no opportunities to visit the site or carry out detailed investigations. As is usually the case with this type of study, most of the information available was descriptive or qualitative, requiring considerable application of engineering judgement and experience before useful conclusions could be drawn, and it was clear that the results would be subject to appreciable uncertainty.   A risk-based approach was adopted as a means of coping with this uncertainty, and providing a consistent framework for the application of judgement.   By presenting results in the form of a broad range of possible outcomes it was intended to highlight the uncertainties in the estimates, and avoid the danger of a single value being given undue weight by the Client.

2.   The geological model was based on longitudinal sections of the alignments, with probabilities assigned to occurrence of specific geological units, depth of weathering, location or orientation of controlling structures, frequency of minor structures, and thickness of superficial

deposits. The rockmass classification and support prediction model was based on a probabilistic implementation of the NGI Q-system, while the cost model took the form of a Bill of Quantities with variable unit costs.

GENERAL APPROACH

3. The probabilistic models were developed using the risk analysis program, @RISK, linked to a LOTUS 1-2-3 spreadsheet. @RISK provides a wide variety of Probability Density Functions (PDFs) which can be entered into spreadsheet cells or formulae with user defined parameters. These PDFs are used as model variables in place of the usual deterministic values, using Latin hypercube sampling techniques to randomly assign values to the variables. By iteratively evaluating each spreadsheet model many hundreds of times, and storing the results, a PDF or CDF (Cumulative Distribution Function) of possible outcomes is obtained.

4. Of the wide variety of PDFs available in @RISK, only a limited number were used in the analysis described here. In particular, extensive use was made of the Triangular Distribution, which often proves useful when little or no hard data is available, and a 'best-guess' approach must be adopted. This PDF is defined by minimum, most likely and maximum values for the variable in question, these values forming the vertices of a triangle of unit area. The skew of the distribution can be controlled by varying the most likely value relative to the minimum and maximum values. Use was also made of the histogram, poisson, discrete, and normal distribution @ RISK functions.

5. For each alignment four options were investigated, including (i) twin tunnels each carrying three highway lanes; (ii) twin tunnels each carrying three highway lanes and a light railway; (iii) a single tunnel carrying six highway lanes; and (iv) a single tunnel carrying two light railway lines for possible use in conjunction with the first and third options. Although variations in tunnel span or geometry influenced the excavation volume, supported perimeter, and costs, the modelling approach and geotechnical assessment were essentially the same for each option, only the third option, a single 16m span tunnel, will be discussed in detail here.

6. The Client indicated the general areas in which the tunnel portals should be located, based on existing infrastructure development, and anticipated traffic flows. In order to more closely define the portal locations within these general areas, and thus provide a starting point for the study, three alignment criteria were established. Firstly, and fairly arbitrarily, a minimum rock cover of one tunnel diameter would be

required where the tunnels passed below the river, secondly, track or road gradients could not exceed specified maxima, and thirdly, portal sites would be selected which maximised the rate of increase in rock cover. In addition, to minimise the length of tunnel passing below the river and immediate flood-plain area, the tunnels in this area would be aligned as nearly at right-angles to the river as possible.

7. For modelling, the tunnel alignments were each divided into 100m long segments which were assumed to be practically homogeneous in terms of their geological or geotechnical characteristics. When using this modelling approach in later phases of investigation and design, for example after an initial phase of site investigation, the segment lengths can be progressively reduced to provide better resolution, in line with the improved data availability and, during construction, models with segments as short as five metres may be needed to make full use of the continuously growing data base.

8. PDFs were assigned to each variable affecting the tunnelling conditions and costs within each segment. Each iteration of the model produced excavation and support costs for each segment, which were summed to give the overall cost for the tunnel. Each simulation involved 1000 iterations, the results of which were stored to produce the output PDFs and CDFs.

GEOLOGICAL MODEL

9. The purpose of the geological model was to assign each segment to a geological formation, subdividing these into engineering and hydrologic units as appropriate. Input parameters included ground elevation above the alignment, tunnel elevation, solid geology, or inferred solid geology, at surface, structural controls on solid geology at the tunnel horizon, thickness of superficial materials, and hydrological regime.

10. Geological mapping indicated the area to be underlain by bedrock comprising;

o   an Upper Clastic Unit (UCU), consisting of consolidated alluvial gravels, sandstone and siltstone,

o   a Lower Clastic Unit (LCU), consisting of tuffaceous sandstone, andesitic tuffs and agglomerates, with local volcanic mud-flow breccias, and

o   a Volcaniclastic Unit (VC) consisting of late mesozoic agglomeratic tuffs and lapilli tuffs.

11. To the NW of the river, which runs through the area from NE to SW, these rocks form low rolling hills, and occur at or close to the surface, while to the SE of the river they are extensively mantled by pleistocene and holocene alluvium.

12. Information from a nearby dam site indicated that weathering of the volcaniclastics resulted in an appreciable loss of strength and development of weakened joint coatings in the upper 15m to 30m of the rockmass. The formation was thus divided into two engineering units on the basis of whether it was weathered (VCw) or fresh (VCf), using a simple depth-of-cover criterion to distinguish between these units. This criterion took the form of a triangular distribution indicating the minimum, most-likely and maximum values of depth of weathering in metres.   There was no detailed information on vertical or lateral variations within the UCU and LCU to justify subdivision of these rocks into additional engineering units.

13.   Two further engineering units were established which were independent of lithology or weathering grade, but rather were dependent on depth of cover. For rock cover of less than 1 tunnel diameter (Unit 5), it was assumed that rib support would be required regardless of rock quality, and for no rock cover (Unit 6), the alignment would be in cut-and-cover or open cut, thus defining the extent of portal earthworks. Table 1 summarises the relationships between geological units, weathering grade, depth of cover, and engineering unit.

Table 1. Engineering Units

Geological Unit	Depth of Rock Cover	Engineering Unit
Upper Clastic Unit	n/a	1 - Upper Clastic Unit
Lower Clastic Unit	n/a	2 - Lower Clastic Unit
Volcaniclastics	< 15 / 20 / 30	3 - Weathered Volcaniclastics
Volcaniclastics	>15 / 20 / 30	4 - Fresh Volcaniclastics
n/a	< 1 diameter	5 - Portal rib zone
Alluvium	nil	6 - Portal earthworks zone

14. Structural controls on the distribution of the engineering units at tunnel horizon were believed to be limited to a regional fault on Alignment A, and the dip of bedding along the NW section of Alignment B. The effects and modelling of these structural controls are described

in more detail in the appropriate sections below. Away from the influence of these structures, surface geology could be directly projected the tunnel horizon.

15. The alluvium, which had been extensively reworked by placer mining operations, occupied the river channel and flood plain, and formed a series of low terraces to the SE of the river. The thickness was believed to vary from about 6m to 15m, although mining records suggested that it could be up to 27m deep locally. The thickness of this deposit was important since it would control both the vertical alignment of the tunnel where it passed below the river channel, and the length of the southern portal approaches, to be constructed in open cut, or as cut-and-cover tunnels. In the north, close to the channel, the deposit was known to be particularly thin, while to the south it became progressively thicker, particularly below the alluvial terraces. A series of triangular distributions was developed to model the uncertainty in the thickness of this unit, and also to reflect the broad trend of variation [Table 2].

Table 2. Alluvium Thickness PDFs

Alignment	River Channel	Floodplain	Terraces
A	0	2 / 5 / 10	5 / 9 / 15
B	2 / 5 / 10	2 / 5 / 15	5 / 10 / 20
C	2 / 5 / 10	2 / 5 / 15	5 / 15 / 20

16. Four hydrological units were identified from consideration of the geology, topography, drainage patterns, and discussions with local well drillers. These units included the river channel and its immediate area, the flood plain area, the alluvial terraces, and the hills to the NW of the river. The likely range of depth to the water table was estimated for each unit, and input to the model as a set of triangular distributions [Table 3].

Alignment A:

17. Mapping suggested that Tunnel Alignment A would pass predominantly through the volcaniclastics. Towards the SE end of the tunnel, the regional fault referred to in Para. 14 was shown continuing beneath alluvial cover "within 300ft" of the position indicated, bringing either the UCU or LCU into contact with the volcaniclastics, and a triangular distribution (-100m / 0m / +100m) was used to model the location at tunnel horizon. Thus, to the NW of the predicted position of the fault the tunnel would be driven in volcaniclastics, while to the SE

Table 3. Groundwater Depth PDFs

Hydrologic Unit	Description	Depth PDF
1	Channel	0
2	Floodplain	0 / 5 / 8
3	Terraces	5 / 8 / 12
4	Hills	8 / 12 / 15

it would have an equal probability, modelled using a simple discrete distribution, of being driven in either the Upper or Lower Clastic Unit. The geological model for Alignment A is summarised in Table 4.

18. In addition to the regional fault, minor faults or shears were fairly common within the volcaniclastics, and believed to have a mean spacing of about 45m, with an assumed poisson distribution. They were expected to vary in width from about 1m to 15m, with a typical value of about 5m.

19. Based on prior experience in this size of tunnel, it was believed that the narrower faults (less than about 3m) would have a minimal effect on tunnelling, while wider faults would require cautious excavation and heavier support measures. To model the effect of these faults on tunnel costs, they were treated as discrete features which would effect tunnelling conditions locally, without impacting rock quality in the segment as a whole.

20. The poisson distribution was used to predict the occurrence of faults in each segment, and a test was conducted to estimate which would exceed the assumed critical 3m width, based on the triangular distribution of widths. The total length of features above this threshold was calculated for each segment, and used to calculate the additional costs of tunnellimg assuming rib support would be required.

21. In addition to their effect on support requirements, these faults presented a risk of inundation by water if intersected below the river channel or flood plain. This risk can be defined in terms of the rate of inflow and the pumping capacity, pc;

$$P \text{ [inundation]} = P \text{ [inflow]} > pc, \text{ where} \qquad (1)$$

$$P \text{ [inflow]} = P \text{ [f]} . P \text{ [qf]} . P \text{ [lf]} . wp \qquad (2)$$

where P[f] is the probability of intersecting a fault, P[qf] is the probable specific discharge of the fault, P[lf] if the probable length of the intersected fault, and wp is the wetted perimeter.

Table 4. Geological Model For Alignment A.

Segment	Crown Elev.	Surface Elev.	Total Cover	Alluvium Thickness	Rockhead Elev.	Rock Cover	Lithology	Weathered Depth	Eng. Unit	Hydrologic Unit
1	55.8	64	8.2	0.0	64.0	8.2	3	16.7	3	4
2	47.4	68	20.6	0.0	68.0	20.6	3	16.7	4	4
3	39.0	68	29.0	0.0	68.0	29.0	3	16.7	4	4
4	30.6	68	37.4	0.0	68.0	37.4	3	16.7	4	4
5	22.2	62	39.8	0.0	62.0	39.8	3	16.7	4	4
6	13.8	54	40.2	0.0	54.0	40.2	3	16.7	4	4
7	5.4	40	34.6	0.0	40.0	34.6	3	16.7	4	4
8	-3.0	28	31.0	0.0	28.0	31.0	3	16.7	4	4
9	-3.0	22	25.0	5.7	16.3	19.3	3	16.7	4	2
10	-3.0	22	25.0	5.7	16.3	19.3	3	16.7	4	2
11	-3.0	22	25.0	5.7	16.3	19.3	3	16.7	4	1
12	-3.0	22	25.0	5.7	16.3	19.3	3	16.7	4	1
13	-3.0	23	26.0	5.7	17.3	20.3	3	16.7	4	2
14	-0.3	26	26.3	9.7	16.3	16.6	3	16.7	3	3
15	5.3	28	22.8	9.7	18.3	13.1	3	16.7	3	3
16	10.8	30	19.3	9.7	20.3	9.6	2	16.7	?	3
17	16.3	30	13.8	9.7	20.3	4.1	2	16.7	2	3
18	21.8	30	8.3	9.7	20.3	-1.4	1		1	3
19	27.3	30	2.8	9.7	20.3	-7.0	1		1	3

Shading denotes cell values which change during simulation.

22. Specific discharge is a function of the permeability of the fault infill, and an estimate of the likely range of this parameter was required. The data suggested three types of fault infilling; (1) fault gouge consisting of rock blocks and crushed rock in a cohesive matrix, (2) fault breccia consisting rock blocks in a non-cohesive matrix, and (3) zones of open-jointing and matrix-free breccia. PDFs of the relative frequency of each infill type, and estimated ranges of permeability, are presented in Table 5. In general, the permeability of the fault zones with Type 1 infill type is of a similar order to that estimated for the host rockmass, so these zones would have little impact on overall inflows. However, even a narrow zone of Type 3 could result in very high rates of inflow.

23. Because the consequences of inundation would be serious, the risk would be mitigated by specifying a program of probe drilling during construction. Depending on the results of drilling, appropriate ground treatment measures could then be adopted. Thus, estimated costs for pre-treatment of the ground, rather than remediation costs, were included in the cost model, based on equation (2).

Table 5.   Fault Zone Permeability PDFs

Infill	Frequency	Permeability*
1	85%	1E-05 / 1E-04 / 1E-03
2	10%	1E-01 / 1E-02 / 1E-03
3	5%	1 / 1E-01 / 1E-02

* cm/sec

Alignment B:

24. Geological mapping indicated that Tunnel Alignment B would be portalled at its north-west end in the UCU, passing down into the LCU, with an uncertain length of alluvium at the south-east portal.   The location of the transition between the UCU and LCU at tunnel horizon was dependent on, and sensitive to, the dip of the contact, which was both gentle and quite variable.

25. By digitising a large number of points mapped on the contact, and calculating apparent dips from randomly selected sets of three-points, a histogram of transition locations was developed and input to the model using the @RISK histrogram function.

26. The length of the alignment to be constructed in the alluvium was modelled using the PDFs in Table 2.

Alignment C:

25.   The mapping suggested that Tunnel Alignment C would pass entirely through the LCU except at its south-eastern end where an unknown length would be driven through alluvium. Again, the length to be driven in alluvium would be controlled by the thickness of this deposit, and would be excavated as cut-and-cover or open cut.

ROCKMASS CLASSIFICATION AND TUNNEL SUPPORT MODEL

26. A probabilistic implementation of the NGI rockmass classification system (Ref. 1) was used as the basis for modelling tunnel support requirements. This rockmass classification system is a widely accepted empirical means of assessing tunnel support requirements, and is of particular use in the pre-construction stages of tunnelling projects.

27. The system uses six parameters to calculate rockmass quality, or Q-value, from the following relationship;

$$Q = RQD/Jn \ x \ Jr/Ja \ x \ Jw/SRF. \quad\quad (3)$$

28. In this expression, RQD is the rock quality designation, Jn is a value related to the number of joint sets present, Jr is a value related to the joint roughness, and Ja is a value related to the condition of the joints. The first two quotients broadly reflect the block size and shear-strength of the rockmass. Of the remaining two parameters, Jw reflects the adverse effects of water pressure on stability, while the SRF, or Stress Reduction Factor, reflects the effects of the local stress regime on stability. By substituting PDFs for each of these parameters, a PDF of Q-values is obtained.

29. Within a particular engineering unit, RQD, Jn, Jr and Ja are often somewhat independent of location within the rockmass, whereas Jw and SRF are clearly location dependent. The Q-value was therefore developed in two steps; firstly an 'unreduced' Q-value, based on only the first two quotients, was calculated, and subsequently 'reduced' by inclusion of the third quotient. PDFs for the unreduced Q-value parameters are summarised in Table 6.

Table 6. Rockmass Classification PDFs for Unreduced Q-value

Engineering Unit	RQD	Jn	Jr	Ja
Upper Clastic Unit	36 / 60 / 100	1 / 3 / 9	1.5 / 1 / 4	1 / 2 / 3
Lower Clastic Unit	45 / 80 / 100	3 / 6 / 9	1 / 2 / 3	1 / 2 / 3
Volcaniclastic Unit	45 / 80 / 100	1 / 6 / 12	1 / 1.5 / 3	2 / 3 / 6
Volcaniclastic Unit	35 / 70 / 90	1 / 6 / 12	1 / 1.5 / 3	1 / 2 / 3

30. The Joint Water Reduction factor, Jw, was somewhat easier to derive in that the unreduced Q-value provided a partial description of the rockmass. From previous experience in the broad types of hydrologic regime and rockmass conditions assumed, values of Jw were assigned, and are summarised in Table 7.

31. The Stress Reduction Factor, SRF, was assigned on the basis of overburden depth and rock-strength, in accordance with normal Q-system practice. It was considered unlikely that UCU or LCU would exhibit significant loosening or other stress related problems, and they were deterministically assigned an SRF of 1.0. In the case of the stronger, higher modulus volcaniclastics it appeared possible that loosening of the rockmass could result in reduced block stability. Strength PDFs were derived for the VCw and VCf, and used to determine a critical depth

Table 7. PDFs for Joint Water Reduction Factor

Engineering Unit (PDF type)	Hydrological Unit			
	1	2	3	4
Upper Clastic Unit (Discrete)	---	---	---	1, 80% 0.66, 20%
Lower Clastic Unit (Triangular)	0.66 / 0.5 / 0.1	0.66 / 0.5 / 0.2	1 / 0.66 / 0.2	1/ 0.66 / 0.5
Volcaniclastic (F) (Triangular)	0.66 / 0.5 / 0.1	0.66 / 0.5 / 0.2	1 / 0.66 / 0.2	1/ 0.66 / 0.5
Volcaniclastic (W) (Triangular)	0.66 / 0.33 / 0.1	0.66 / 0.33 / 0.2	1 / 0.66 / 0.33	1/ 0.66 / 0.5

below which these problems might be encountered. Thus, depending on the depth of rock cover, determined probabilistically from the alluvium thickness, an SRF of 1.0 or 2.5 might be assigned [Table 8].

Table 8. PDFs for Unconfined Compressive Strength (UCS), and SRF

Engineering Unit	UCS	UCScrit	SRF
Upper Clastic Unit	---		1.0
Lower Clastic Unit	---		1.0
Weathered Volcaniclastics	25 / 40 / 70	70	If UCS < UCScrit, 1.0 else 2.5
Fresh Volcaniclastics	40 / 70 / 100	160	If UCS < UCScrit, 1.0 else 2.5

32. Linking the geological model and the rockmass classification model, PDFs of Q-value were obtained for each segment, and tunnel profiles showing the resulting Q-values are presented in Figure 1. This figure indicates the expected Q-value, Q-value at +/- 1 standard deviation, and also the 5% and 95% confidence limits.

33. Deriving the Q-value is an intermediate step in calculating the cost per segment. The next step involves assigning an empirically derived support category to each segment on the basis of rock quality, excavation span, and the purpose of the excavation.

34. The categories are defined in some detail by the NGI system and might indicate, for instance, the spacing of rockbolts and shotcrete thickness required for stability. There is often an overlap between the support requirements indicated for adjacent categories, this lack of clear-cut boundaries reflecting the derivation of these categories from actual

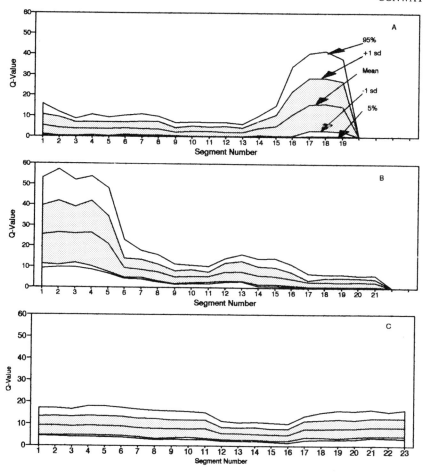

Figure 1. Q-value Profiles Along Tunnel Alignments

field experience. For practical implementation, it is usual to simplify the number of categories to a manageable number of support classes, and in the present case a set of four support classes were developed from the eight or so original support categories.

COST AND QUANTITIES MODEL
35. The cost and quantities model took the form of a simple Bill of Quantities. Quantities for excavation and overall support requirements were based on the support classes predicted for each segment, while PDFs for unit costs were derived from discussions with contractors and prices from recently completed projects (a detailed breakdown of these costs cannot be included here).

36. Additional input included probabilistic data on the occurence and effects of the fault zones on Alignment A. The effect of these zones on support requirements was described in Para. 20.

37. Costs associated with the risk of inundation of the tunnel included probe drilling, and pre-treatment of the ground. It was not anticipated that probe drilling would represent a significant proportion of overall costs, and an allowance for this activity included as a simple lump sum item. Inflow rates (from Equation 2), infill type (from Table 5), and the estimated extent of the fault zones, were used to develop cost PDFs for pre-treatment of the ground (ie. grouting) on the basis of prior experience. These cost PDFs, in the form of triangular distributions, considered grout volume, grouting pressures (and hence equipment type), drilling requirements, and overall impact on tunnel progress, again, however, a detailed breakdown of these costs cannot be included here.

38. Figure 2 presents CDFs of excavation and primary support costs for each alignment. One of the surprising results indicated by this figure is the relatively limited range of costs predicted for each alignment, and hints at an insensitivity of costs to the range of ground conditions anticipated. This may be partly explained by the generally high overall rock quality; since the relationship between Q-value and support category is logarithmic, the reduction in Q-value may have to be considerable before a lower support category is indicated.

39. Taking mean costs, Alignment B is clearly the most favourable, reflecting mean Q-values which are above, or close to, 10 for much of the alignment, only falling off in the area of shallow alluvial cover at the SE end. At the NW end, the deeper rock cover results in improved Q-values and lower support costs for some 500m to 600m. Alignment A costs are somewhat higher, reflecting the mean Q-value of around 5 for the volcaniclastic rocks, although a marked improvement occurs in the UCU/LCU to the SE of the regional fault. The effects of minor faulting on this alignment are also reflected in the costs. Alignment C is the least favourable tunnel option. This is in part a reflection of the greater length of this tunnel alignment, and in part a reflection of the lower overall Q-values, which remain consistently below 10.

40. The Clients estimate of bridge construction costs was purely deterministic. Since the main source of uncertainty as regards the bridge option was likely to be foundation costs, and these represented a relatively small proportion of the overall costs, this approach was reasonable, although it made direct comparison between the two options difficult.

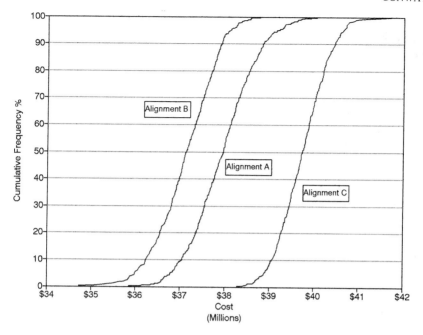

Figure 2.   Excavation and Support Costs

41. Further data and analysis would have been required to achieve the level of confidence in the tunnel costs that already existed for the bridge costs, including an analysis of the sensitivity of the tunnel costs to specific factors, providing a focus for site investigation work.   In the event, the bridge option appeared significantly less costly than any of the tunnel options, and no further analysis of the attendant risks was instructed.

CONCLUSIONS

42. The constraints of data availability can be severe in the early phases of a project, and considerable experience and engineering judgement must be applied before useful conclusions can be drawn.

43. When a small number of variables are involved, it may be satisfactory to simply consider the upper and lower bounds of the problem, and make a subjective assessment of the expected outcome. However, once the number of variables becomes large, and capable of interacting in complex and non-obvious ways, a more systematic approach is required. Risk assessment techniques provide a framework for such an approach.   Developing the simple rules governing the interaction between individual variables, and assigning PDFs to these

variables, focuses the attention of the engineer in a way which otherwise be lacking, and provides a consistent basis for the application of judgement.

44. The cost of applying risk-based techniques in the early phases of a project are likely to be negligible compared to the potential benefits. The models described here were set-up and run in the space of three days, including the time to review what limited data was available, and develop the PDFs. Risk analysis software is readily available, and the analyses require only modest run-time on modern PCs. Once the models have been established they can be continuously refined as more data becomes available during various phases of investigation, through into construction. Such models have proved to be valuable decision making aids during construction, and form an excellent basis for the evaluation of contractual claims related to unforeseen ground conditions.

REFERENCES

1. BARTON, N., LIEN, R., and LUNDE, J. Engineering Classification of Rock Masses for the Design of Tunnel Support Systems. Rock Mechanics, 1974, vol. 6, 189-236.

20. Decision analysis for liquefaction ground improvement

S. G. VICK, Consultant, USA, and B. D. WATTS, Klohn-Crippen
Consultants Ltd, Canada

SYNOPSIS. Decision analyses have been used on three major projects in Vancouver, Canada to evaluate the need for ground improvement to prevent seismic liquefaction. The potentially liquefiable foundation soils are the loose to compact sands of the Fraser River Delta. The decision analysis procedure employed for these projects included review of past performance of similar structures on liquefied soils, Failure Mode and Effects Analysis to identify important seismic failure modes for structures and groups of structures, and Bayesian decision analysis. In all three cases, the decision analysis yielded a defensible and well-documented decision not to improve the foundation soils.

INTRODUCTION
1. Seismic liquefaction produces effects on structures that are perhaps best known from the classic bearing capacity failures and tilted apartment buildings in Niigata, Japan. Less recognized but more widely damaging is the effect of liquefaction-induced lateral spreading, a phenomenon only beginning to be quantitatively understood. While it is possible to prevent both of these phenomena by densifying the liquefiable ground using such means as vibroflotation, blasting, or dynamic compaction, the uncertainties related to the degree of seismic hazard, the magnitude of lateral spreading, and the extent of resulting damage to structures, can make it difficult to decide whether ground improvement, along with the considerable cost it entails, is warranted in any particular case.

2. Decisions under uncertainty, similar in nature to the seismic ground improvement decision, are routinely addressed in other fields of engineering, business, and even law by the application of Bayesian decision theory. These techniques are not new, having been developed and first applied more than 20 years ago. That they have failed to win widespread acceptance in ground engineering can be attributed to the geotechnical community's familiarization with relative frequency,

"statistical" probability interpretations, at the expense of subjective degree-of-belief (or "judgmental") probability concepts. Bayesian decision analysis and the application of judgmental probability to geotechnical uncertainties have been recently applied to seismic ground improvement decision making for several major projects in Vancouver, British columbia, Canada. The purpose of this paper is to present three such case histories to illustrate the utility of the procedures in ordinary geotechnical practice.

LIQUEFACTION HAZARD IN THE FRASER RIVER DELTA

3. Much of the recent population growth in the Vancouver area and the infrastructure required to serve it has occurred in the Fraser River Delta, which contains liquefaction-susceptible sands and silts (ref.1). Although Vancouver has not experienced a damaging earthquake within historic time, seven earthquakes within the magnitude range 6.0 to 7.5 have occurred within 250 km within the past 100 years (ref. 2). An essential tool in characterizing the likelihood of liquefaction due to these soil and earthquake conditions is the computer program PROLIQ, which combines the Cornell-McGuire procedure for seismic hazard assessment with the Seed method for level-ground liquefaction assessment (ref. 3). For a specified silt content and corrected blowcount $(N_1)_{60}$, PROLIQ yields the probability of seismic conditions producing liquefaction by summing the contributions of acceleration and magnitude from all seismic source zones that affect the site.

4. Liquefaction can produce both vertical and horizontal displacement of the ground surface. Of these, lateral movements may be more severe, producing a continuum of effects ranging from flowslide displacements of tens of metres on slopes exceeding several degrees, to "lateral spread" displacements of several centimetres to several metres on virtually level ground. The mechanics of lateral spreading are not yet well understood. Quite different soil behaviour models have been developed by some researchers (ref. 4 and ref. 5) while empirically-based prediction procedures have been proposed by others (ref. 6 and ref. 7). These methods can yield widely varying estimates of lateral spread displacements. At present, only engineering judgement guided by applicable case histories can be used to evaluate the results.

5. Similarly, the structural effects of various magnitudes of lateral displacement are subject to great uncertainty. Within broad ranges, some types of structures can be judged more vulnerable to lateral movement than others based on the type of foundation system, the fragility of lateral connections, and the nature of equipment they may contain. Again, however, the assessment of structure performance or the

degree of damage produced by a particular magnitude of lateral displacement is largely a matter of informed judgement.

6. A number of methods are available to preclude such damage to structures by preventing liquefaction in the first place, but the thickness, stratigraphy, and silt content of soils in the Fraser River Delta have the practical effect of limiting these to vibro-replacement, dynamic compaction and explosive compaction. In local practice, vibro-replacement is performed using a vibrating probe to form stone columns on typical spacings of about 2.5 m. Stone columns have been installed to 25 m depth with substantial increases in density of the host soils provided the silt content was less than 20%. Dynamic compaction also gives acceptable results to about 10 to 12 m depth provided the upper soft floodplain silts are excavated and replaced before compaction. The effectiveness of blast densification is more uncertain, but substantial cost savings can be achieved under suitable conditions with two passes of blast holes on about 3 m spacing. In either case, the depth of treatment has an important influence on cost and the degree of reduction in liquefaction hazard, with deeper but more costly treatment producing greater reduction in the potential for both liquefaction and lateral movement of soils that underlie the treated zone.

DECISION ANALYSIS METHODOLOGY
7. Decision analyses performed to evaluate liquefaction ground improvement for projects in the Fraser River Delta share several components. Applied in stepwise fashion, these elements provide a common framework for the analysis methodology.

Compilation of seismic performance data
8. The first step is to review the performance of similar types of structures in previous earthquakes. A thorough understanding of the nature and degree of structural damage produced by actual shaking is essential to identifying the failure modes of concern and validating the ultimate outcome of the analysis by field experience.

Failure Modes and Affects Analysis
9. Most complex systems contain multiple components that may have different responses to, or different tolerances for, failure initiator events. Developed originally for use in the nuclear power industry, Failure Modes and Effects Analysis (FMEA) qualitatively assesses the factors for each system component individually (ref. 8). In this way the FMEA provides the basis for generalizing the behaviour of certain similar types of structures, and identifying other structures with special behaviour or attributes which require special consideration external to the decision analysis.

243

10. For example, Fig. 1 shows the FMEA for the Annacis Wastewater Treatment Plant case history subsequently discussed. Prepared with the assistance of structural design engineers for the plant, it indicates that one structure, the Cl/SO_2 reagent building, could pose an offsite safety hazard due to seismic failure and another, the dewatered sludge building, contains movement-sensitive equipment. Otherwise, most other structures have generally similar exposed responses, damage thresholds, and repair characteristics for liquefaction-induced lateral movements. Hence, the FMEA showed that the ground improvement decision could be evaluated for all structures collectively in the plant, with a few exceptions requiring individual evaluation based on their special characteristics. Additional, the FMEA often serves to identify simple measures that can be taken to reduce movement sensitivity of individual structures, such as structural stiffening and fusible links.

Decision Trees
11. Once individual structures have been evaluated, a decision tree is constructed for the most significant structure or group of similar structures using techniques well established in the literature (ref. 9 and ref. 10). For the liquefaction ground improvement decision, the tree begins with a set of branches representing the individual treatment methods or depths identified. Propagating branch sets typically include a liquefaction parameter, a horizontal movement parameter given liquefaction and a damage parameter given movement. Ranges of lateral spread displacement are assigned to each movement state and damage states are defined in terms of repair or replacement cost together with facility downtime.

12. A probability of occurrence is then assessed for each such parameter state, using PROLIQ to derive liquefaction probability as previously described. Judgemental probabilities are assigned for remaining parameters using a structured approach to interrogation of experienced geotechnical and structural engineers familiar with the project (ref. 11).

Decision Evaluation
13. The decision tree is supplemented by a cost matrix that gives, for each end branch, the direct costs for repair of liquefaction damage, indirect costs due to revenues lost during the repair period, and quantifiable costs of environmental damages. Multiplying by the corresponding end branch probabilities and damage costs yields the "risk cost" for each ground treatment option. This is added to annualized ground treatment cost to give total cost of the option.

STRUCTURE/COMPONENT	PROBABLE FAILURE MODE DUE TO GROUND MOVEMENT	FAILURE EFFECTS ON EFFLUENT QUALITY	FAILURE EFFECTS ON SAFETY	SENSITIVITY TO MOVEMENT	MOVEMENT DAMAGE THRESHOLD	MOVEMENT DESTRUCTIVE THRESHOLD	MOVEMENT CONFIDENCE FACTOR	RELATIVE EASE OF REPAIR	RELATIVE COST OF REPAIR*	RELATIVE TIME FOR REPAIR	CONFIDENCE FACTOR ON REPAIR	MITIGATING MEASURES/COMMENTS
1	2	3	4	5	6	7	8	9	10	11	12	13
LIQUID STREAM												
Influent pump station	rotation	critical	low	low	>1 m vert.	>10 m vert.	high	simple	low (7%)	short	high	Connection integrity critical. Bypass provisions necessary to route flow to solids contact basin.
Trickling filters	structural collapse	moderate	low	moderate	>10 cm vert. >10 cm. horiz.	>1 m	moderate	moderate	moderate (8%)	long	moderate	Rigid slabs could be provided.
Solid contact basins	cracking or horizontal separation	low	low	low	0.3 m vert. >10 cm. horiz.	several m vert. 1 m horiz.	high	simple	low (8%)	short	high	Fusible links could be considered to isolate cracking for easier repair. Base could be reinforced to prevent horizontal separation.
Secondary clarifiers	cracking or horizontal separation	moderate	low	moderate	0.3 m vert. >10 cm horiz.	several m vert. 1 m horiz.	moderate	moderate	moderate (21%)	moderate	low	Damage severity and repair depends on number of units affected.
Secondary effluent conduits	shearing, buckling or tensile rupture	low	low	low	>1 m	several m	high	difficult	moderate (2%)	long	low	Assumes steel pipe, fusible links. Assumes uncontrolled secondary effluent release with remaining processes functioning.
Disinfection	cracking	low	low	low	0.3 m vert. 10 cm. horiz.	several m	high	simple	low (7%)	short	high	Assumes design of structure as secondary rigid containment facility. Assumes fail-safe suction feed lines.
Chlorine/SO₂ reagent storage	cracking	low	high (onsite and offsite toxic gas hazard)	low	several cm	>1 m	high	simple	low	short	moderate	Assumes design of structure as secondary rigid containment facility. Assumes fail-safe suction feed lines.
Dewatered sludge bldg	collapse	low	moderate (collapse hazard to workers)	high	10 cm vert. 10 cm horiz.	1 m vert. 1 m horiz.	low	moderate	high (14%)	long	low	Movement sensitivity and repair factors reflect elevated centrifuges.

Fig. 1 – FMEA for Annacis Wastewater Treatment Plant

245

14. Ground treatment alternatives are typically compared using an expected monetary value (EMV) decision rule whereby the preferred option is that with lowest total cost. Sensitivity studies are performed to confirm that the outcome does not change for reasonable variations in key probabilities or estimated costs. The EMV criterion defines only the minimum level of protection warranted because it does not address monetary risk aversion, unquantified environmental or institutional factors, public safety, or post-earthquake lifeline considerations. As such, it provides only the minimum level of protection warranted, and evaluation of those factors external to the analysis may justify supplemental ground improvement. Even so, these decision evaluation procedures and criteria have provided useful guidance, as illustrated by the following three examples.

CASE HISTORIES
Annacis Treatment Plant
15. This secondary sewage treatment plant expansion is being constructed on liquefaction-susceptible Fraser River Delta soils at a cost of $400 million. Not only is the plant itself at risk from liquefaction, but its loss or damage could affect an important and commercially valuable salmon fishery. However, vibro-replacement could cost up to $40 million, and informal evaluation of the need for ground improvement failed to provide sufficient rationale and adequate documentation of the basis for the decision.

16. Performance of similar concrete treatment plant structures in previous earthquakes shows that their rigid monolithic nature generally provides a high degree of resistance to damage by liquefaction-induced lateral movements. This experience provided important background for the FMEA, which has been previously discussed and presented on Fig. 1. With a few exceptions, the FMEA showed that the structures were sufficiently similar in behaviour to allow the ground improvement decision to be generalized over the plantsite as a whole.

17. The resulting decision tree is shown on Fig. 2 and portrays three ground improvement options: no ground treatment, partial treatment to 10 m, or treatment to the full 22 m depth of liquefiable soils. The cost matrix includes both plant repair costs and the computed value of losses to the fishery during the period required for repairs.

18. Fig. 2 indicates that the no treatment option has the lowest total cost, and this decision has been adopted for the plant as a whole. Essentially, the decision analysis shows that for the particular soil conditions and structures

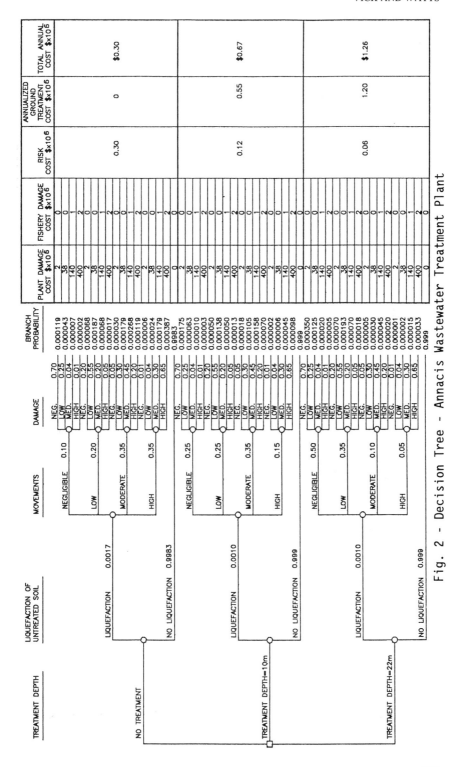

Fig. 2 - Decision Tree - Annacis Wastewater Treatment Plant

247

involved, the risk of liquefaction damage does not warrant the high cost of ground improvement over the entire plant site. Ground improvement has, however, been adopted for certain individual structures on the basis of life safety considerations, offsite hazards, and sensitive or costly equipment. Another outcome of the analysis derived from FMEA is to indicate the importance of structural rigidity in lateral movement resistance, which has led to changes in structural design and detailing.

Lulu Treatment Plant

19. Fig. 3 shows the decision tree for a similar but smaller secondary expansion for the Lulu treatment plant that will cost about $50 million. Also located on liquefaction-susceptible Fraser River Delta soils, the layout of plant structures leads to a somewhat different suite of ground improvement alternatives.

20. Plant process considerations require placement of site grading fill to heights up to 5 m above existing grade. Should liquefaction in the underlying Fraser River Delta soils occur, driving stresses imposed by the fill slopes could result in flowslides with movements far exceeding those produced by lateral spreading. One option is therefore to perform no ground treatment, but to flatten the site grading fill slopes to reduce the potential for these large movements. Another option, again directed toward flowslide potential, is to improve the ground only around the perimeter of the site to confine and restrain liquefied soils. A third general option is to improve the ground beneath each individual structure, and this can be done using vibro-replacement with stone columns or blast densification.

21. The cost matrix on Fig. 3 shows that for the Lulu plant, ground improvement only around the site perimeter is the option having lowest total cost. Compared to the no-treatment outcome for the Annacis case, this example illustrates that ground improvement precedents cannot necessarily be transferred from one site to another, even for similar types of structures. Details of site conditions - in this case the site grading fill - and the new uncertainties they impose can, however, be readily incorporated and accounted for in the decision analysis.

Vancouver International Airport Runway

22. Vancouver International Airport is currently undergoing a major expansion to enable it to better serve future air traffic from the Pacific Rim. Of the structures involved, an FMEA has led to specification of ground improvement for the terminal building on the basis of public safety, and also for

TREATMENT OPTION	LIQUEFACTION	MOVEMENTS	DAMAGE	BRANCH PROBABILITY	PLANT DAMAGE COST $x10^6	FISHERY DAMAGE COST $x10^6	RISK COST $x10^6	ANNUALIZED GROUND TREATMENT COST $x10^6	TOTAL ANNUAL COST $x10^6

NO TREATMENT (SLOPE FLATTENING) — LIQUEFACTION 0.0016, NO LIQUEFACTION 0.9984

MOVEMENTS	DAMAGE	BRANCH PROB	PLANT DAMAGE	FISHERY DAMAGE	RISK
NEG 0.05	NEG 0.95	7.60×10^{-6}	0.30	0.00	0.0000228
	LOW 0.03	2.40×10^{-6}	6.30	0.00	0.0000151
	MOD 0.01	8.00×10^{-7}	21.00	0.14	0.0000159
	HIGH 0.01	8.00×10^{-7}	60.00	0.29	0.0000482
LOW 0.10	NEG 0.90	1.44×10^{-4}	0.30	0.00	0.0000432
	LOW 0.08	1.28×10^{-6}	6.30	0.00	0.0000806
	MOD 0.01	1.60×10^{-8}	21.00	0.14	0.0000338
	HIGH 0.01	1.60×10^{-8}	60.00	0.29	0.0000965
MODERATE 0.175	NEG 0.30	8.40×10^{-5}	0.30	0.00	0.0000252
	LOW 0.60	1.68×10^{-4}	6.30	0.00	0.00106
	MOD 0.08	2.24×10^{-5}	21.00	0.14	0.000474
	HIGH 0.02	5.60×10^{-6}	60.00	0.29	0.000338
HIGH 0.175	NEG 0.10	2.80×10^{-6}	0.30	0.00	0.00000840
	LOW 0.40	1.12×10^{-4}	6.30	0.00	0.000706
	MOD 0.40	1.12×10^{-4}	21.00	0.14	0.00237
	HIGH 0.10	2.80×10^{-5}	60.00	0.29	0.00169
FLOWSLIDE 0.50	NEG 0.05	4.00×10^{-5}	0.30	0.00	0.0000120
	LOW 0.10	8.00×10^{-5}	6.30	0.00	0.000504
	MED 0.50	4.00×10^{-4}	21.00	0.14	0.00846
	HIGH 0.35	2.80×10^{-4}	60.00	0.29	0.0159

TOTAL 0.0329 — ANNUALIZED GROUND TREATMENT COST 0 — TOTAL ANNUAL COST 0.0329

PERIMETER TREATMENT (STONE COLUMNS) (OPTION 1) — LIQUEFACTION 0.0016, NO LIQUEFACTION 0.9984

MOVEMENTS	DAMAGE	BRANCH PROB	PLANT DAMAGE	FISHERY DAMAGE	RISK
NEG 0.20	NEG 0.95	3.04×10^{-4}	0.30	0.00	0.0000912
	LOW 0.03	9.60×10^{-6}	6.30	0.00	0.0000505
	MOD 0.01	3.20×10^{-6}	21.00	0.14	0.0000676
	HIGH 0.01	3.20×10^{-6}	60.00	0.29	0.000193
LOW 0.20	NEG 0.90	2.88×10^{-5}	0.30	0.00	0.0000864
	LOW 0.08	2.56×10^{-6}	6.30	0.00	0.000161
	MOD 0.01	3.20×10^{-6}	21.00	0.14	0.0000676
	HIGH 0.01	3.20×10^{-6}	60.00	0.29	0.000193
MODERATE 0.49	NEG 0.30	2.35×10^{-5}	0.30	0.00	0.0000706
	LOW 0.60	4.70×10^{-5}	6.30	0.00	0.000296
	MOD 0.08	6.27×10^{-6}	21.00	0.14	0.00133
	HIGH 0.02	1.57×10^{-6}	60.00	0.29	0.000945
HIGH 0.10	NEG 0.10	1.60×10^{-5}	0.30	0.00	0.00000480
	LOW 0.40	6.40×10^{-5}	6.30	0.00	0.000403
	MOD 0.40	6.40×10^{-5}	21.00	0.14	0.00135
	HIGH 0.10	1.60×10^{-5}	60.00	0.29	0.000965
FLOWSLIDE 0.01	NEG 0.01	1.60×10^{-7}	0.30	0.00	0.0000000480
	LOW 0.04	6.40×10^{-7}	6.30	0.00	0.00000403
	MOD 0.25	4.00×10^{-6}	21.00	0.14	0.0000846
	HIGH 0.70	1.12×10^{-5}	60.00	0.29	0.000675

TOTAL 0.00971 — ANNUALIZED GROUND TREATMENT COST 0.01 — TOTAL ANNUAL COST 0.0197

STRUCTURE TREATMENT (STONE COLUMNS) (OPTION 2) — LIQUEFACTION 0.0, NO LIQUEFACTION 1.0

MOVEMENTS	DAMAGE
NEG 0.84	NEG / LOW / MOD / HIGH
LOW 0.11	NEG / LOW / MOD / HIGH
MODERATE 0.03	NEG / LOW / MOD / HIGH
HIGH 0.01	NEG / LOW / MOD / HIGH
FLOWSLIDE 0.01	NEG / LOW / MOD / HIGH

RISK COST 0 — ANNUALIZED GROUND TREATMENT COST 0.185 — TOTAL ANNUAL COST 0.185

STRUCTURE TREATMENT (BLASTING) (OPTION 3) — LIQUEFACTION 0.0005, NO LIQUEFACTION 0.9995

MOVEMENTS	DAMAGE	BRANCH PROB	PLANT DAMAGE	FISHERY DAMAGE	RISK
NEG 0.74	NEG 0.95	3.52×10^{-4}	0.30	0.00	0.000105
	LOW 0.03	1.11×10^{-5}	6.30	0.00	0.0000699
	MOD 0.01	3.70×10^{-6}	21.00	0.14	0.0000782
	HIGH 0.01	3.70×10^{-6}	60.00	0.29	0.000223
LOW 0.15	NEG 0.90	6.75×10^{-5}	0.30	0.00	0.0000203
	LOW 0.08	6.00×10^{-6}	6.30	0.00	0.0000378
	MOD 0.01	7.50×10^{-7}	21.00	0.14	0.0000159
	HIGH 0.01	7.50×10^{-7}	60.00	0.29	0.0000452
MODERATE 0.07	NEG 0.30	1.05×10^{-5}	0.30	0.00	0.00000315
	LOW 0.60	2.10×10^{-5}	6.30	0.00	0.0000132
	MOD 0.08	2.80×10^{-6}	21.00	0.14	0.0000592
	HIGH 0.02	7.00×10^{-7}	60.00	0.29	0.0000422
HIGH 0.03	NEG 0.10	1.50×10^{-6}	0.30	0.00	0.000000450
	LOW 0.40	6.00×10^{-6}	6.30	0.00	0.0000378
	MOD 0.40	6.00×10^{-6}	21.00	0.14	0.000127
	HIGH 0.10	1.50×10^{-6}	60.00	0.29	0.0000904
FLOWSLIDE 0.01	NEG 0.01	5.00×10^{-8}	0.30	0.00	0.0000000150
	LOW 0.04	2.00×10^{-7}	6.30	0.00	0.00000126
	MOD 0.25	1.25×10^{-6}	21.00	0.14	0.0000264
	HIGH 0.70	3.50×10^{-6}	60.00	0.29	0.000211

TOTAL 0.00133 — ANNUALIZED GROUND TREATMENT COST 0.082 — TOTAL ANNUAL COST 0.0833

Fig. 3 - Decision Tree - Lulu Wastewater Treatment Plant

249

certain other small structures due to the cost of sensitive electronic and radar components they contain. The remaining feature of the expansion is a third parallel runway. Its construction cost is expected to be $64 million, while ground improvement could cost up to $27 million, or almost half again as much. Although airports serve important post-earthquake disaster relief functions, outlying facilities could serve Vancouver in this capacity. Therefore, the runway improvement decision is based strictly on economic factors.

23. As currently designed, the runway pavement consists of unreinforced 6 m by 6 m concrete slab construction. Earthquake experience shows that these slabs tend to crack or tilt, and separate at joints under the influence of liquefaction-induced lateral spreading. Combined with aircraft landing tolerances limiting allowable pavement deformations to less than about 2 cm, the runway is clearly subject to substantial damage under even small liquefaction effects. Moreover, this damage is not easy to repair and could require complete replacement of affected portions of the runway. In this case, a significant effect of damage would be lost airport revenues during the reconstruction period which could rival damage costs for the runway itself.

24. These factors are reflected in the decision tree for runway ground improvement on Fig. 4. The ground improvement options include both vibro-replacement with stone columns and blasting to either 8 m (partial) or 12 m (full) depth of the liquefiable soils. The no-treatment option also incorporates a length parameter which represents the proportion of the runway over which liquefaction - and therefore movement damage - could occur, and which reflects spatial variability in soil properties over its 3 km length.

25. The total costs on Fig. 4 indicate that ground improvement for the runway cannot be justified by economic factors alone. In this case a primary reason is the difficulty of precluding even small movements that could seriously damage the runway.

CONCLUSIONS
26. The decision approach described consists of three fundamental elements: review of the performance of related types of structures in previous earthquakes; qualitative assessment of individual structure characteristics by Failure Modes and Effects Analysis, and Bayesian decision analysis using subjective, degree-of-belief probability to quantify those key uncertainties that can only be assessed on a judgemental basis.

COST MATRIX

TREATMENT OPTION	RUNWAY LIQUEFIED LENGTH	P[L]	DAMAGE	P[D|L]	ANNUAL BRANCH PROBABILITY	RUNWAY DAMAGE COST $x10^6$	RUNWAY CLOSURE COST $x10^6$	RISK COST $x10^6$	ANNUALIZED GROUND TREATMENT COST $x10^6$	TOTAL ANNUAL COST $x10^6$
NO TREATMENT (OPTION 0)	<15%	0.0030	LOW	0.05	0.00015	0.06	2.80	0.120	0	0.120
			MED	0.15	0.00045	0.42	3.87			
			HIGH	0.80	0.00240	2.24	6.02			
	15% – 58%	0.0021	LOW	0.05	0.000105	0.30	3.66			
			MED	0.15	0.000315	2.04	5.38			
			HIGH	0.80	0.00168	10.91	11.19			
	58% – 100%	0.00161	LOW	0.05	0.000081	0.66	5.16			
			MED	0.15	0.000242	4.42	7.53			
			HIGH	0.80	0.001288	23.62	18.93			
	NO LIQUEFACTION	0.99329			0.99329	0.00	0.00			
TREATMENT TO 12m DEPTH WITH VIBRO STONE COLUMNS (OPTION 1)	100%	0.00026	LOW	0.10	0.000026	0.83	6.02	0.00993	0.807	0.817
			MED	0.25	0.000065	5.59	8.60			
			HIGH	0.65	0.000169	29.90	22.37			
	NO LIQUEFACTION	0.99974			0.99974	0.00	0.00			
TREATMENT TO 8m DEPTH WITH VIBRO STONE COLUMNS (OPTION 2)	100%	0.00092	LOW	0.10	0.000092	0.83	6.02	0.03515	0.537	0.572
			MED	0.25	0.00023	5.59	8.60			
			HIGH	0.65	0.000598	29.90	22.37			
	NO LIQUEFACTION	0.99908			0.99908	0.00	0.00			
TREATMENT TO 12m DEPTH WITH EXPLOSIVE COMPACTION (OPTION 3)	100%	0.00026	LOW	0.10	0.000026	0.83	6.02	0.00993	0.168	0.178
			MED	0.25	0.000065	5.59	8.60			
			HIGH	0.65	0.000169	29.90	22.37			
	NO LIQUEFACTION	0.99974			0.99974	0.00	0.00			
TREATMENT TO 8m DEPTH WITH EXPLOSIVE COMPACTION (OPTION 4)	100%	0.00092	LOW	0.10	0.000092	0.83	6.02	0.03515	0.129	0.164
			MED	0.25	0.00023	5.59	8.60			
			HIGH	0.65	0.000598	29.90	22.37			
	NO LIQUEFACTION	0.99908			0.99908	0.00	0.00			

Fig. 4 - Decision Tree for Parallel Runway

251

27. The general structure of this approach applies to a wide variety of geotechnical structures and ground behaviour decisions. In the case of soils in the Fraser River Delta subject to seismic liquefaction and related lateral movement phenomena, the immediate effect of this approach has been to produce savings in potential ground improvement costs of up to $70 million (or almost 15% of the related project costs) compared to full ground treatment, and to provide a systematic and documented basis for the ground improvement decisions. Clearly these outcomes have been related to the types of structures evaluated, site-specific soil conditions, and seismic hazard specific to the Fraser River Delta, and these results cannot be generalized to other structures, projects or settings. In every case, however, the approach has led to insights into the nature of the problem and engineering solutions that could not have been derived from more conventional informal decision making assessments.

28. In a larger sense, the case histories illustrate how formal decision analysis techniques are currently being applied to everyday ground engineering problems. Analytical methods for accurately predicting all aspects of ground behaviour, especially under seismic loading, are unlikely to ever be perfected, and new uncertainties will arise as analysis techniques continue to evolve. Even if these uncertainties can never be surmounted, understanding their nature and their effects on engineering decisions is at least as valuable. Systematic approaches and probabilistic methods that quantify engineering judgement are a powerful tool for doing so.

ACKNOWLEDGEMENTS
The authors wish to thank the Greater Vancouver Regional District and the Vancouver International Airport Authority for permission to publish this paper.

REFERENCES
1. WATTS B.D., SEYERS W.C. and STEWART R.A. Liquefaction susceptibility of Vancouver area soils. Geotechnique and Natural Hazards, BiTech Publishers Ltd., 1992, 145-158.

2. ROGERS G.C. The earthquake threat in southwest British Columbia. Geotechnique and Natural Hazards, BiTech Publishers Ltd., 1992, 63-70.

3. ATKINSON G.M., FINN W.D.L. and CHARLWOOD R.G. Simple computation of liquefaction probability for seismic hazard applications. Earthquake Spectra, 1984, vol. 1, no. 1, 107-124.

4. BYRNE P.M. A model for predicting liquefaction-induced displacements. Proc. Second International Conference on Recent Advances in Geotechnical Earthquake Engineering and Soil Dynamics, 1991, vol. 2, 1027-1035.

5. BAZIAR M.H., DOBRY R. and ELGAMAL A-W.M. Engineering evaluation of permanent ground deformations due to seismically induced liquefaction. National Center for Earthquake Engineering Research, 1992, Technical Report NCEER-92-0007.

6. BARTLETT S.F. and YOUD T.L. Empirical prediction of lateral spread displacement. Proceedings from the Fourth Japan-U.S. Workshop on Earthquake Resistant Design of Lifeline Facilities and Countermeasures for Soil Liquefaction, 1992, Technical Report NCEER-92-0019, vol. I.

7. HAMADA M.I., TOWHATA I., YASUDA S. and ISOYAMA R. Study on permanent ground displacement induced by seismic liquefaction. Computers and Geotechnics, 1987, vol. 4, 197-220.

8. McCORMICK N.J. Reliability and risk analysis; methods and nuclear power applications, Academic Press, Inc., 1981.

9. BENJAMIN J.R. and CORNELL C.A. Probability, statistics and decisions for civil engineers, McGraw-Hill Book Company, 1970.

10. ANG A.H-S. and TANG W.H. Probability concepts in engineering planning and design, Volume II - decision, risk and reliability, John Wiley & Sons, Inc., 1984.

11. VICK S.G. Risk in geotechnical practice. Geotechnique and Natural Hazards, BiTech Publishers Ltd., 1992, 41-62.

21. Cost overrun in construction dewatering

T. O. L. ROBERTS and M. E. R. DEED, W. J. Engineering Resources Limited, UK

SYNOPSIS. Construction dewatering is a well established method for providing dry stable conditions for excavations below standing groundwater level. Construction dewatering is a specialist technique and is normally carried out under sub-contract. A database has been prepared giving the tender programme and tender value compared to the actual construction programme and final contract value for over 130 dewatering projects completed over the last 11 years. This database has been used to identify the prime causes of cost overrun for dewatering projects.

INTRODUCTION

1. Major excavation works in granular soils which extend below the standing groundwater level will often require measures to control groundwater to maintain the excavation stability and to provide dry working conditions. Control of groundwater can be accomplished by physical exclusion using such techniques as interlocking steel sheetpiles, diaphragm walls, grouting and ground freezing. However, control of groundwater can also be achieved by dewatering using wellpoint, deepwell and ejector systems and it is only these methods which are the subject of this paper. These techniques involve the installation of an array of wells normally located around the perimeter of a proposed excavation. The well system is pumped continuously to lower the groundwater to below the excavation formation level during the construction period. On completion of the works the dewatering system is switched off and the groundwater level is allowed to recover.

2. Dewatering techniques have been used for construction purposes for at least the last 150 years. The first fully documented project being by Robert Stevenson for the Kilsby tunnel on the London to Birmingham railway in 1836 (ref. 1). This project is interesting since it is also the first well documented case of cost overrun caused primarily by failure to adequately control groundwater. The contract to construct the tunnel was valued at £98,988.00 and the final cost of the works proved to be £291,030.00. Since Stevenson's time the techniques have been greatly refined

Risk and reliability in ground engineering. Thomas Telford, London, 1993

and the modern methods are described in detail by Powers
(ref. 2) and by Sommerville (ref. 3).

3. Dewatering systems are characterised by the method of
pumping employed,

      wellpoint systems, vacuum lift using suction pumps

      deepwell systems, electric submersible pumps

      ejector wells, jet pumps installed in each well driven
           by a central surface multi-stage high pressure
           supply pump

4. These three methods are used for over 90 percent of
the construction dewatering projects in the UK. Each of the
three methods has advantages and limitations of use. These
have been examined by Roberts and Preene (ref. 4) who
prepared a diagram showing the range of application of each
of the techniques relative to the two most important design
parameters, the soil permeability and the drawdown
requirements. The other factors which influence cost are
the excavation plan size and the required duration of
pumping.

5. It should of course be perfectly possible to establish
the proposed excavation geometry and the required duration
of pumping at the early planning stage of a project and
certainly prior to the appointment of a dewatering sub-
contractor. On this basis the primary cause of cost overrun
in construction dewatering would be expected to be
inadequate assessment of the hydraulic characteristics of
the sub-strata resulting from errors in interpretation
and/or inadequate site investigation. The latter has been
considered by Littlejohn (ref. 5) who specifically
highlighted the inadequate attention paid to gauging
groundwater levels and assessing the hydrogeological
conditions in site investigations.

CONTRACTUAL ARRANGEMENTS

6. Over the last 20 years the construction industry has
moved towards the increased use of specialist sub-
contractors. Dewatering is no exception to this rule. The
use of sub-contractors makes economic sense because
specialist companies can obtain better utilisation of
specialist plant and it is also easier to retain the all
important engineer and plant operator experience within a
smaller operating unit.

7. The vast majority of dewatering works are put out to
competitive tender by main contractors under standard FCEC
or BEC forms of sub-contract. These are basically 'back to
back' contracts so that the sub-contractor takes on all the
responsibilities and liabilities of the main contractor for
a specific part of the works. Occasionally dewatering works

are let as separate construction packages particularly on
projects where construction management contracts are in use.

8. In all cases the client/main contractor is responsible
for providing details of the excavation geometry by the
issue of appropriate drawings to the sub-contractor. The
main contractor is also responsible for defining the
construction programme and in particular the duration of the
dewatering requirements. The sub-contractor uses this
information together with the site investigation data
provided to design and cost an appropriate dewatering
scheme. The cost of dewatering works can be divided into
two elements, installation costs and running costs. The
installation costs are dictated solely by the volume of
equipment required for the works whereas the running costs
are also based on the duration of pumping, over which the
sub-contractor has no control. The main contractor
specifies the required duration of pumping and during
construction the pumping period will be controlled by the
main contractor's progress on the rest of the works.

9. The tender cost of dewatering works will rarely exceed
1 percent of total costs for large civil engineering or
building projects. For smaller projects, in particular for
trench works for services, dewatering costs can rise up to
around 10 percent of the total main contract value.
However, the dewatering works are a critical element of the
construction process and the potential impact on the main
contract works in terms of both delay and cost is
substantial, if for any reason the dewatering works do not
adequately control groundwater levels. Similarly any delay
in the construction of the main contract works will lead to
cost overrun on the dewatering sub-contract due to the
additional running period for the pumping plant.

DATABASE OF PROJECTS

10. A database has been set up of over 130 dewatering
projects carried out over the last 11 years. For each
project the following information has been recorded,

> start date
> type of project (wellpoint, deepwell, ejector)
> tender programme (installation and running)
> as constructed programme (installation and running)
> tender value (installation and running)
> final account value (installation and running)

11. For the purposes of this paper costs have been
converted to present day values using the retail price
index. Where a significant cost overrun is apparent the
primary cause or causes have been categorised as,

12. Additional equipment/works: This indicates an
extension to the areal extent or depth of dewatering. These
costs are often caused by the identification of additional
structures which require dewatering or changes to access

Table 1.   Analysis of projects used in database

a) Type of project

	No.	%
wellpoint system	77	58
deepwell system	46	35
ejector system	10	7
total	133	100

b) Final account value

	No.	%
0 to 5K	29	22
5K to 10K	21	16
10K to 50K	58	43
50K to 100K	15	11
100K to 500K	9	7
over 500K	1	1
total	133	100

c) Duration of running period

	No.	%
0 to 4 weeks	30	22
4 to 12 weeks	41	31
12 to 26 weeks	37	28
26 to 52 weeks	20	15
52 to 78 weeks	4	3
over 78 weeks	1	1
total	133	100

Table 2.   The average project

	Tender	As Construction
Installation period (wks)	2.3	3.2
Running period (wks)	10.8	16.1
Value (£000's)	37.3	50.4

Table 3.   Causes of cost overrun

	No.	% of total
Additional equipment /works	49	37%
Programme overrun	85	64%
Ground conditions	11	8%
Total number of projects	133	

In many cases more than one factor was apparent

arrangements or side support which have 'knock-on' consequences for the extent of dewatering.

13. <u>Overrun</u>: This indicates cost overrun due to an extension of the running period for dewatering due to causes other than changed ground conditions. Typical causes include poor progress on the main contract works or failure to fully appreciate the stability requirements of partially constructed structures. Very often where additional equipment/works is indicated extension of the running period is also evident.

14. <u>Ground conditions</u>: These costs are due to unexpected changes in the hydrogeological behaviour of the sub-soil at the site from those anticipated at the time of tender. In some cases the conditions encountered resulted in submission of a formal claim under the contract for changes in ground conditions which "could not reasonably have been foreseen". In other cases no formal claim was submitted because contractual responsibility was resolved prior to submission of valuations.

15. An analysis of the dewatering projects used to prepare the database is given in Table 1. It can be seen that of the projects considered 58 percent were wellpoint systems, and ejector systems which were only introduced into the UK in 1988 represent just 7 percent of projects. For over 80 percent of the projects the final account value was less than £50,000.00 and the project duration was less than 26 weeks.

COST OVERRUNS

16. The database of projects has been used to prepare Figure 1 which shows a comparison between the dewatering tender sub-contract value and the actual final account value. It can be seen that the final account value generally increased to approaching double the tender value. A few projects show greater increases. Cost decreases are apparent but are relatively rare. Those projects where unforeseen ground conditions influenced costs are separately identified but they do not stand out as being indicative of the more extreme cost increases.

17. The primary cause of the cost increase becomes more apparent when Figures 2 and 3 are examined. In Figure 2 the tender and final account installation costs have been compared. This indicates that installation costs often increase but generally by much less than 100 percent, although projects with installation costs of less than £6K do show a much wider scatter. It is also apparent that those few projects where unforeseen ground conditions influenced cost occasionally resulted in substantial increases in installation costs.

18. In Figure 3 the running costs are analysed. It is apparent that the as constructed running costs show a trend of a marked increase over the tender values. Typically running costs are double the tender assessment and in a few

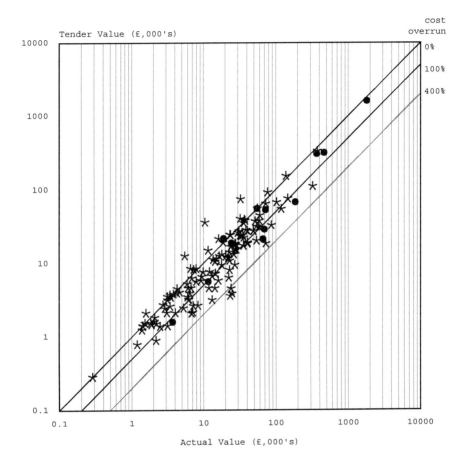

* cost change caused by changes to the scope of the
works and / or to the running period

● cost change significantly influenced by unforeseen
ground conditions

Figure 1 - Total sub-contract, tender verses final value

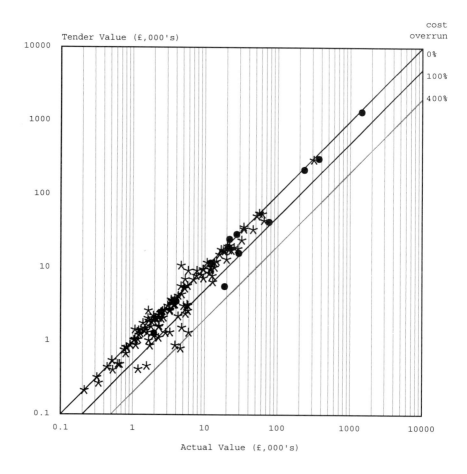

★   cost change caused by changes to the scope of the works and / or to the running period

●   cost change significantly influenced by unforeseen ground conditions

Figure 2 - Installation costs, tender verses final value

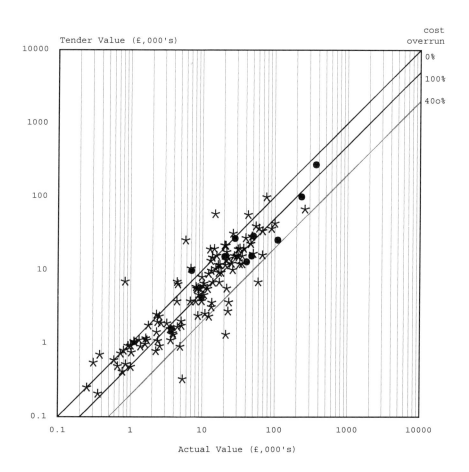

*   cost change caused by changes to the scope of the works and / or to the running period

●   cost change significantly influenced by unforeseen ground conditions

Figure 3 - Running costs, tender verses final value

cases are in excess of five times. This even applies to projects with running costs of over £10K, indeed the doubling of the as constructed cost and programme is most marked for such projects. Projects with a decrease in running costs or programme following tender are shown to be very much the exception. In Figure 3 projects where unforeseen ground conditions were identified fail to show a clear trend.

19. In Table 2 a summary of the projects in the database has been carried out to show the average of all 130 projects. The conclusion which can be drawn is that the majority of dewatering projects suffer cost overruns of at least 35 percent and a doubling of costs is not uncommon. The prime cause of this increased cost is extension of the dewatering programme rather than unforeseen ground conditions. This is a rather depressing conclusion since it implies that accurate project planning/programming in the UK is the exception not the rule. This conclusion is reinforced by Figure 4 which shows the cumulative frequency of cost overruns. The solid line is for all projects whereas the dotted line excludes projects where unforeseen ground conditions influenced costs. It is apparent that unforeseen ground conditions are of relatively minor significance to cost overrun.

20. The database and analysis are obviously open to criticism, the most serious of which include the following,

> The projects are all taken from the records of a single dewatering contractor and may well not be representative of the whole market.

> The costs shown represent the cost of the dewatering element of the works only. Knock-on costs due to change in ground conditions are not shown since this information is not readily available.

> The costs shown are in fact agreed valuations and not comparisons of the actual costs incurred by the dewatering sub-contractor. These could be significantly different although the sub-contractor concerned survived in business throughout the period under consideration.

21. These points have some merit but they do not negate the overwhelming correlation between increased costs and extended running period and the lack of correlation between increased costs and unforeseen ground conditions. This conclusion is summarised in Table 3 which lists the prime causes of cost overrun where over 64 percent were influenced by programme overrun whereas just 8 percent were influenced by unforeseen ground conditions. For half of the projects where unforeseen ground conditions were apparent the increased costs were relatively modest, however, for several

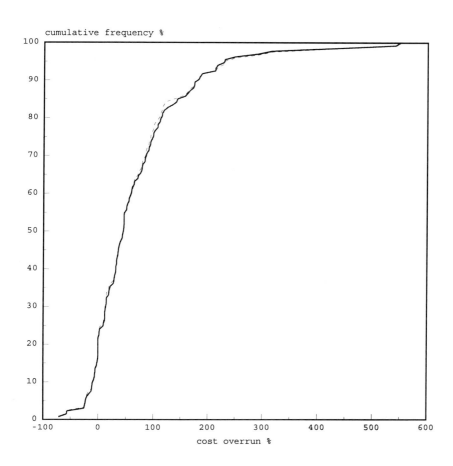

cumulative frequency %

cost overrun %

_____ all projects

..... projects excluded where unforeseen
ground conditions influenced cost

Figure 4 - Cumulative frequency of cost overrun

of these the knock-on costs to the rest of the works are known have been significant. This situation arises because under certain circumstances extension to the dewatering works may not be a viable solution to the unforeseen conditions encountered.

22.   Specific assessment of the projects where unforeseen ground conditions were identified as an important factor fails to identify any consistent explanation. The projects concerned cover a wide spectrum of system types, soil conditions and drawdown requirements. There is also no indication that unforeseen ground conditions specifically relate to cost cutting on the site investigation. For several of the projects concerned, comprehensive site investigations had been carried out which included pumping tests indicating that the difficult nature of the site had been recognised at an early stage. A point of significance is that although the difficult nature of the site was recognised and steps taken to carry out a comprehensive investigation this recognition was not extended to cover procurement and contractual arrangements.

CONCLUSIONS

23.   Cost overrun on dewatering projects is not uncommon. Unforeseen ground conditions which adversely effect construction works are experienced on approximately 8 percent of projects but this is not the main cause of cost overruns. The main cause of cost overruns is extension to the running period due to delay to the main contract works. On average the actual running period of dewatering works is virtually 50 percent greater than the tender programme. This implies that accurate project planning is the exception rather than the rule in the UK.

24.   It is striking that for several of the projects where unforeseen ground conditions impacted on costs the difficult nature of the sub-strata was identified and a comprehensive site investigation was commissioned by the client. However, no modifications were made to the standard forms of contract or competitive tendering procurement procedures. It is suggested that these arrangements create an adversarial relationship between the various parties to the contract which is not conducive to the quick development of least cost solutions as the works unfold and further information on the soil conditions becomes available.

REFERENCES
1. LEWIS G.F. The constructional history of the Kilsby tunnel. MSc dissertation, City University, Dept. of Civil Engineering, London, 1984.
2. POWERS J.P. Construction dewatering: New methods and applications, second edition. John Wiley, New York, 1992.
3. SOMMERVILLE S.H. Control of groundwater for temporary works. CIRIA, London, 1986.
4. ROBERTS T.O.L. and PREENE M. Range of application of construction dewatering systems. Groundwater problems in urban areas, Institution of Civil Engineers, London, June 1993.
5. LITTLEJOHN G.S. Inadequate site investigations. Institution of Civil Engineers, London, 1991.

22. Probabilistic risk analysis of slope stability to assess stabilisation measures

A. P. WHITTLESTONE and J. D. JOHNSON, Soil Mechanics Ltd, UK

SYNOPSIS. Conventional stability analysis of loosewall slopes on weak pavements is problematic. The use of probabilistic risk analysis (PRA) to overcome parameter value uncertainty and to quantify design reliability is discussed. Particular reference is made to employing risk analysis to compare slope designs using an economic approach. A cost-benefit analysis has been used to assess slope stabilisation requirements. The appropriate level of pavement treatment is selected by considering both the design safety and cost.

INTRODUCTION
1. The stability of loosewalls in open cast mines (Fig. 1) is critical to the success of the mining operation in terms of both safety and economics. Loosewalls constructed on weak pavements are potentially unstable. Although the loosewall slopes are often only temporary, stabilisation is sometimes required to effect adequate short term stability.

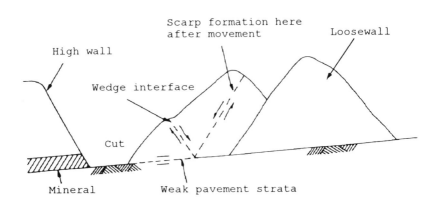

Fig. 1 Biplanar failure of loosewall slopes situated on weak pavements (ref. 2)

Risk and reliability in ground engineering. Thomas Telford, London, 1993

2. The stability of loosewalls is affected by the geometry of the slope, groundwater conditions, the inclination and operating strength of the pavement upon which it is cast and the strength of the rockfill itself. The predominant failure mechanism of loosewalls on weak pavements is a biplanar, active-passive wedge sliding along the pavement surface (Fig. 1) where the strength of the pavement strata is well below that of the rockfill.

3. Remedial measures commonly employed to improve the stability of loosewall slopes on weak inclined pavements comprise the reorientation of the cut direction to minimise the pavement inclination and treating the pavement by ripping or blasting to increase the frictional component of the pavement strength (ref. 1).

4. Loosewall stability and the effectiveness of different pavement treatment methods have been part of a study carried out by the authors. This study has been used in this paper to demonstrate the problems in using conventional Factor of Safety analysis and to discuss the use of Probabilistic Risk Analysis (PRA) results which enabled the assessment of loosewall stability and stabilisation measures.

CONVENTIONAL APPROACH

5. The deterministic approach to slope stability assessment enables the calculation of the Factor of Safety for assumed slip surfaces using limit equilibrium methods. The critical slip surface and minimum Factor of Safety can be determined for any slope geometry and the acceptability of design decided by comparison of the calculated Factor of Safety with an acceptable design value.

6. In many situations, uncertainty caused by the inherent variability in naturally occurring materials makes it difficult to calculate a singular value of Factor of Safety with confidence. This uncertainty in material parameter value can be caused by lack of knowledge or by recognised variability from laboratory or field measurement data. Sensitivity analyses can be carried out to identify the parameters to which the slope stability model is susceptible taking into account the engineer's assessment of parameter uncertainty.

7. Worst case values are typically adopted for parameters where large uncertainty exists or when the consequences of failure are significant. These values are selected by engineering judgement. Where the Factor of Safety is calculated from such pessimistic parameter values, the result is commonly recognised as a somewhat cynical measure of the design's suitability and the 'acceptable' design Factor of Safety is reduced accordingly. However, there are no strict guidelines or criteria for selecting a design Factor of Safety; values of 1.3 for temporary slopes and 1.5 for permanent slopes are commonly adopted to indicate safe slopes (ref. 3). Selection of the design criterion clearly depends upon the interrelationship between the engineer's judgement on parameter values and perception of the consequences resulting from slope failure.

8.   In the authors' opinion carrying out design assessment by
this   method   is   unsatisfactory.   The   approach   requires
unquantifiable judgements to be made which may not be readily
replicated   by   others   and   the   design   reliability   (or   risk
incorporated)   is   unknown.   The   engineer   can   attach   undue
significance to the calculated Factors of Safety and the
acceptable design value (ref. 4) to the extent that a result is
considered a safe or 'no risk' design if it betters the design
Factor of Safety; the reliability of design is frequently assumed
to be 100%.   Whilst it can be shown that this is often not the
case (refs 5-6) it can also be argued that a design approach that
seeks to eliminate risk entirely is not good engineering practise
either   as   it   results   in   excessive   cost   design   and   stifles
innovation (ref. 7).

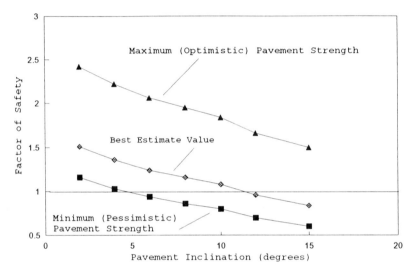

Fig 2. Variation in factor of safety before pavement treatment
with pavement inclination and selection of pavement strength
parameter value

9.   The   analysis   of   loosewall   stability   using   conventional
deterministic methods highlights precisely these problems.   The
variation and uncertainty in the material strengths, especially
the strength of the pavement strata, makes assessment of the
Factor of Safety difficult. By way of an example, Fig. 2 shows
the results of deterministic calculations for the stability of
a dry 40 m high loosewall at different pavement inclinations,
considering a typical variation in pavement strata strength. The
effect of variation in pavement strength value was evaluated by
using extreme optimistic and pessimistic values in the Factor of
Safety calculation. As the figure shows, the stability measured
by a Factor of Safety depends upon the value of pavement strength
selected;   results   vary   from   indicating   instability   where
pavements are inclined at more then 4°, to stability at all
pavement inclinations. The selection of a single best estimate

268

strength value, such as indicated on Fig. 2, clearly cannot account for the possible parameter variation and therefore incorporates either risk or pessimism into the design which cannot be quantified.

10.   In identifying the acceptable design Factor of Safety and thus the slopes which require pavement treatment a dilemma exists – consider the short design life against the substantial economic consequences of loosewall failure. These consequences include possible loss of life, loss of or damage to plant and disruption to mining resulting in a loss of revenue. What design Factor of Safety is acceptable?

11.   Rational assessment of the effect of pavement treatment on loosewall stability in our study was hindered because of parameter uncertainty and, more importantly, the very definitions of 'safe' and 'unsafe' were unquantifiable. The combination of conservative parameter selection to mitigate the problems of uncertainty and a high design Factor of Safety to counter the perceived risk, results in over-design by the selection of extensive pavement treatment which significantly increases the mining costs.

12.   To determine the stability of the loosewall on inclined pavements and rationally assess pavement treatment an alternative approach was followed.

PROBABILISTIC APPROACH

13.   Probabilistic risk analysis (PRA) allows the quantification of design reliability or risk by mathematically modelling the variability and uncertainty of parameter values, and assessing the outcome resulting from parameter value variation. Whilst not widely used in geotechnical engineering at present, probabilistic techniques are commonplace in financial/investment decision making and some branches of engineering. Application of the techniques to geomechanical problems is perhaps most active in the assessment of slope stability (refs 4, 6, 8-11).

14.   PRA in engineering, including the assessment of slope stability, is based on well-established deterministic algorithms and typically results in the determination of a Factor of Safety distribution rather than a fixed value. The probability or risk of failure is typically given by the proportion of the Factor of Safety distribution that lies below unity (ref. 2). This probability provides a quantification of the design reliability taking into account parameter value variability.

15.   The authors have developed a risk analysis approach for slope stability assessment which employs Latin Hypercube sampling (ref. 11) to perform probabilistic risk analysis. The approach uses commercially available software packages to provide the environment for the deterministic algorithm, perform the sampling iterations and determine the distribution of Factor of Safety (ref. 10).

ANALYSIS OF LOOSEWALL STABILITY USING PRA

16.   A two-dimensional biplanar, active-passive wedge analysis was used by the authors as the algorithm for the PRA to assess

the stability of loosewalls cast on weak inclined pavements. To analyze various slope geometries the parameters of rockfill bulk unit weight, rockfill strength and pavement strata strength were assumed to be stochastic variables conforming to normal distributions. The properties of normal distributions are well documented and generally accepted as viable for naturally occurring phenomena (ref. 12). Truncated normal distributions were used for each of the stochastic variables to prevent the generation of unrealistic extreme values during sampling. The selection of the distribution mean, standard deviations and truncation limits was made from published data and laboratory testing carried out as part of the study. For the parameter of pavement strength the mean value selected for the distribution corresponded to the best estimate value used to calculate the Factor of Safety values shown on Fig. 2 and the distribution truncation limits conformed to the maxima and minima values. For the situation analysed the loosewall was assumed to be dry.

17.   The upper line on Fig. 3, denoted 'Before Pavement Treatment' shows the results of PRA for the same slope geometry, range of pavement inclinations and variation in pavement strength shown on Fig. 2. The probability of failure results shown on the graph represent the assessed risks of slope failure for the 40 m high slope considered assuming that the continuous planar failure surface along the pavement exists. The figure shows that the relationship between stability and pavement inclination is similar to that shown by Factor of Safety (Fig. 2).

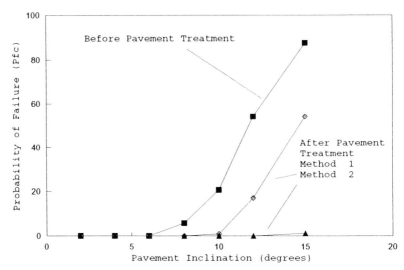

Fig. 3   Variation in probability of failure for 40 m high loosewall on weak inclined pavement

18.   The calculated risk of slope failure (Fig. 3) incorporates the variability and uncertainty of the pavement strength, but the results are a function of the probability distribution functions assumed for the stochastic variables. Altering the form of these

distributions, and the assumptions made concerning the other parameters, will affect the risk values calculated. In general terms the risk evaluated for a situation will be increased if broader distributions, representing more uncertainty, and/or more biased distributions, representing conservatism say, are used to represent the stochastic variables. Thus it can be considered that the risk calculated is an assessed risk incorporating both the perceived uncertainty of the parameter values and, to some extent, the judgement made on the form the parameter variation takes.

19. Using the PRA technique the assessed risk of loosewall failure was calculated for the variety of loosewall geometries and pavement treatment methods pertinent to the study undertaken.

ASSESSMENT OF STABILISATION MEASURES

20. From the results of the conventional and PRA analyses above it is apparent that some slopes require stabilisation to ensure stability. The pavement treatment methods appraised comprised pattern blasting of the pavement strata on various regular grid spacings prior to the casting of the rockfill to form the loosewall. The effect of pavement treatment on the pavement strength was assessed geometrically and was incorporated into the PRA by altering the distribution of pavement strength. In general the more closely spaced the blast pattern, the higher the mean value of the distribution and the more skewed the truncation limits were toward a higher frictional strength of the pavement.

21. Fig. 3 shows the effect on the assessed risks of loosewall failure for a 40 m high loosewall by treatment at two different blasthole grid spacings. Method 1 (indicated on Fig. 3) comprises a wide spaced grid which is less effective in treating the pavement than Method 2, but is significantly cheaper. The improvement in safety resulting from the different treatment methods is readily apparent as a reduction in the assessed risk (an improvement in the design reliability).

22. To reach a decision as to which pavement treatment is the most appropriate requires the definition of an acceptable level of risk for the design. Acceptable levels of risk for slopes in civil engineering and the mining industry have been discussed by several authors (refs. 9 and 13) and published by Kirsten (ref. 5). However, the selection of an acceptable risk of failure is a subjective judgement not dissimilar to the selection of a design Factor of Safety, discussed previously, and is similarly unquantifiable. This may be a contributory factor to both the non-usage of risk assessment and the non-application of PRA techniques in geomechanics design. The assessment of an acceptable risk for loosewall stabilisation design was impracticable in this case and therefore the authors adopted an approach that considers the economic factors of slope construction which determines an acceptable level of risk based on economic and safety criteria (ref. 14).

23. The general equation for the total cost of a slope (C_t) is (ref. 6):

$$C_t = C_c + p_f.C_f \qquad (1)$$

where C_c is the cost of slope construction, p_f is the probability of slope failure and C_f is the cost consequences of slope failure. The quantity $p_f.C_f$ represents the expected cost of slope failure.

24. Using this equation the acceptable risk for the design can be quantified by considering the consequences of failure in terms of the expected economic value into which safety can be included represented by a financial cost. The decision of design suitability then becomes financially controlled. This technique was considered ideal for the assessment of loosewall stabilisation as economic consequences of a loosewall failure are significant and should therefore form part of the engineering design approach.

25. For the situation examined the construction of a loosewall on a weak pavement had four possible outcomes; the probability notation for the likelihood of the events is shown in parentheses:

i   No failure (p_{nr}).

ii   Failure of the loosewall by a biplanar mechanism (p_{fl}) resulting in disruption of the mining operation (p_d), loss of mineral reserve (p_m), damage or loss of high cost plant or a life (p_p); or a combination of the previous events.

26. To determine the probabilities of event occurrence the sequence of failures were represented and interrelated using an event tree (ref. 15). Each branch of an event tree diagram can be assigned a probability representing the likelihood of occurrence and the probability of any particular outcome is derived by the product of the probabilities of each of the intervening steps. The event tree for loosewall construction in this particular situation was straight forward (Fig. 4); more complex situations can also be appraised using this approach.

27. The event tree analysis permits Eqn. 1 to be re-expressed specifically for the loosewall stability assessment studied:

$$C_T = C_{pt} + p_{fl}(p_d.C_d + p_m.C_m + p_p.C_p) \qquad (2)$$

where C_{pt} represents the cost of pavement treatment, p_{fl} represents the probability of a failure within the loosewall and C_d, C_m and C_p represent the financial consequences of the various failure events.

28. The consequences of loosewall failure (C_d, C_m and C_p) clearly depend on the location of a failure along the loosewall crest length. As the results of the PRA in this study were calculated using a two-dimensional model, which is independent of slope crest length, the slope cell approach (ref. 16) was adopted. The probability of failure was assumed to apply to a section of loosewall with a crest length equal to the slope height (a slope cell) and assigned the notation p_{fc} (the probability of failure of a 3D loosewall cell). The likelihood of a failure event in the loosewall (p_{fl}) was determined by considering the slope as a system of slope cells:

$$p_{fl} = 1 - (1 - p_{fc})^n \qquad (3)$$

where n is the number of slope cells occurring in the operational loosewall crest length.

29. Eqn. 3 was used as the basis for determining the probability of certain sections of the slope failing enabling the calculation of p_d, p_m and p_p. For example, the probability p_m was determined by assessing the number of slope cells which, if one or more of them failed, would affect the unrecovered mineral reserve. These probabilities were also adjusted to incorporate plant operational cycles as appropriate. Care was required to ensure that the probabilities determined were exclusive and conformed to the relationships defined by the event tree (Fig. 4):

$$p_{fl} + p_{nf} = 1, \quad p_d + p_m + p_p = 1 \tag{4}$$

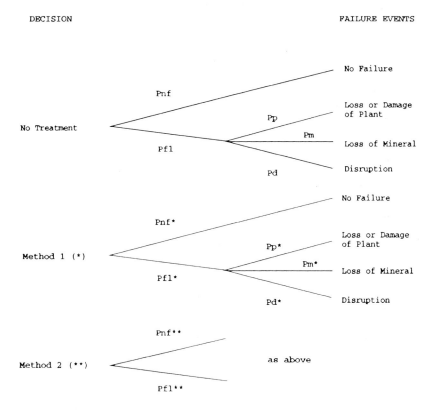

DECISION   FAILURE EVENTS

Note: Event tree can be expanded to include any number of methods.

Fig. 4 Event tree showing possible outcomes of loosewall construction

30. The economic cost consequences of the various possible events (C_d, C_m and C_p) were composed of the following costs (after ref. 8):

- The cost of clearing and reinstating the failed material, related to the volume of failed material (ref. 6) and including the cost of deferred income for the period of reinstatement.
- The cost of unrecovered mineral reserve lost in a failure.

• The cost of loss or damage to plant affected by a failure.
• The cost of loss of life.

31. These costs were determined from operational rates, unit costs and liability and insurance values. Where such cost information is not available arbitrary costs could be assigned to investigate the impact of the cost on the design suitability.

32. By evaluating Eqn. 4 the most appropriate pavement treatment method for a particular loosewall design could be selected based on the minimum acceptable cost of loosewall construction. The level of acceptable risk has clearly become a financial decision.

33. Fig. 5 illustrates schematically how the results of the study were interpreted. The figure shows the combinations of slope height and pavement inclination which require pavement treatment to effect economically safe loosewall construction.

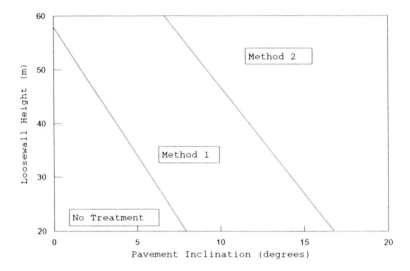

Fig. 5 Illustrative design chart for loosewalls indicating appropriate pavement treatment for situation studied

34. The results conform to the general relationship between risk and these parameters noted previously. As the risk of slope failure increases, the expected cost rises so that the more expensive and effective treatment method (Method 2) is economically viable. In low risk situations the most cost effective approach is no treatment; the decision not to treat the pavement is an acceptable financial risk.

CONCLUSIONS

35. In the assessment of slope stabilisation measures a number of factors have to be taken into consideration to effect a safe and economic design. The most difficult question to be addressed is what is a safe design and how much risk is acceptable for any given situation. Although conventional analysis enables the engineer to investigate the factors which are critical by sensitivity studies, the approach does not allow the uncertainty

in natural parameters and their effect on the design to be quantified. The selection of appropriate designs and slope stabilisation measures requires unquantifiable engineering judgements. These judgements are not easily integrated into cost-benefit studies to optimise design.

36. As demonstrated by the above assessment of loosewall stability on weak inclined pavements the assessment of stabilisation measures by PRA in conjunction with an event tree results in a methodology that:

- Quantifies the judgements made in the assessment of parameter uncertainty.
- Enables the comparison of designs considering design reliability.
- Permits the appropriate treatment method for a given situation to be selected by considering the cost implications and the likelihood of slope failure.

37. By using sound engineering judgement in the selection of analytical models and in assessing the parameter variability, a PRA approach and the use of event trees enables an economically 'safe' design to be adopted which incorporates slope stabilisation where appropriate. The safety of the design and the level of acceptable risk are delimited by economic criteria. This systematic and rigorous design methodology results in safe and economic design for situations where natural parameter variability limits the use of conventional approaches.

REFERENCES

1. Hughes D B and Leigh W J P : 1985 : Stability of excavations and spoil mounds in relation to opencast coal mining. Institute of Quarrying Transactions. Quarry Management, Vol 12, 4, pp 223-229, 232.

2. Nguyen V U and Chowdhury R N : 1984 : Probabilistic study of spoil pile stability in strip coal mines - two techniques compared. International Journal of Rock Mechanics, Mining Sciences & Geomechanics Abstracts, Vol 21, 6, pp 303-312.

3. Hoek E and Bray J W : 1981 : Rock slope engineering (third edition). IMM, London.

4. Priest S D and Brown E T : 1983 : Probabilistic stability analysis of variable rock slopes. Transactions of the Institution of Mining & Metallurgy (Section A : Mining Industry), 92, Jan 1983. IMM, London.

5. Kirsten H A D : 1983 : Significance of the probability of failure in slope engineering. The Civil Engineer in South Africa, Jan 1983, pp 17-27.

6. McMahon B K : 1974 : Design of rock slopes against sliding on pre-existing fractures. 3rd ISRM Congress on advances in rock mechanics, reports on current research, Denver. Vol IIB, pp 803-808.

7. Duddeck H : 1993 : Safety analysis and risk assessment for underground structures. ISRM International Symposium on Safety and Environmental Issues in Rock Engineering, Eurock '93, Lisbon (Eds. L Ribeiro E Sousa and N F Grossman). A A Balkema.

8.   Call R D : 1985 : Probability of stability design of open pit slopes. Rock Masses Symposium (Ed C H Dowding). Geotechnical Engineering Division of ASCE.

9.   Kirsten H A D and Moss A S E : 1985 : Probability applied to slope design - case histories. Rock Masses Symposium (Ed C H Dowding). Geotechnical Engineering Division of ASCE.

10. Whittlestone A P : 1991 : An application of probabilistic stability analysis in the design of rock slopes. MSc thesis, Camborne School of Mines, unpublished.

11. Nathanail C P and Rosenbaum M S : 1991 : Probabilistic slope stability assessment using latin hypercube sampling. 7th ISRM International Congress on Rock Mechanics, 2, pp 929-934. A A Balkema.

12.   Harr M E : 1987 : Reliability-based design in civil engineering. McGraw-Hill.

13.   McCracken A and Jones G A : 1986 : Use of probabilistic stability analysis and cautious blast design for an urban excavation. Conference on Rock Engineering and Excavation in an Urban Environment, pp 231-240. IMM, London.

14. McMahon B K : 1971 : A statistical method for the design of rock slopes.   1st Australia-New Zealand Conference on Geomechanics, Melbourne, Vol 1, pp 314-321 and Vol 2, pp 558-559. Institution of Engineers, Sydney.

15. Crossland B, Bennett P A, Ellis A F, Farmer F R, Gittus J, Godfrey P S, Hambley E C, Kletz T A, Lees F P : 1992 : Risk: analysis, perception and management. Royal Society, London.

16. Coates D F : Pit slope manual chapter 5 - design. CANMET Report No 77-5. Canada Centre for Mineral and Energy Technology.

ACKNOWLEDGEMENTS

The authors wish to thank the Directors of Soil Mechanics Limited for their permission to publish this paper. The encouragement and advice of Mr D R Norbury during the preparation of the paper is also gratefully acknowledged.

23. Calibration of safety factors for the design of piers in expansive soils

C. FERREGUT and M. PICORNELL, University of Texas at El Paso, USA

SYNOPSIS. Structural design optimization is taken to mean the minimization of the expected present value of the sum of the initial cost of a foundation and the expected losses incurred due to the foundation entering a certain limit state. Expressions are derived for the optimal central safety factor for designing bored piles in expansive soils.

INTRODUCTION

1. Bored piles are commonly used to support heavy structures on expansive soils. The main role played by the piles is to isolate the structure from the active swelling zone. However, as the soil swells, opposing shear stresses are generated on the pile perimeter through adhesion of the surrounding soils. The upper part of the pile is subjected to stresses that tend to extract the pile, while the lower part is subjected to stresses that tend to retain the pile in place. The result of these actions is that the pile is under tensile stresses and the pile head will heave to some extent.

2. A reliability based design methodology of bored piles to account for these effects has been proposed (ref. 1) using an ultimate state and a serviceability state functions. The ultimate state function limits the maximum axial stress in the pile to not exceed the ultimate tensile cracking stress of the pile sections. The serviceability state function limits the pile head heave to some allowable displacement. The interaction pile-soil was assumed linearly elastic. This analysis was later expanded (ref. 2) to include a linear elastic perfectly plastic model for the interaction soil-pile.

3. The design methodology requires considerable amounts of site specific data, and even job scheduling information about construction activities, in order to produce a deterministic design. In general, some of the design parameters can be reasonably estimated for each site; however, other site or job information might be effectively unavailable in engineering practice. These considerations suggest the necessity to approach the design of bored piles from a probabilistic point of view.

Risk and reliability in ground engineering. Thomas Telford, London, 1993

SAFETY FACTOR OPTIMIZATION

4.The lack of information about the behavior of foundations in service combined with the use of codes containing high safety factors can lead to the view, still held by some civil and geotechnical engineers as well as by many members of the public, that absolute safety can be achieved. Absolute safety is of course unobtainable, and such a goal is also undesirable, since the attempt to achieve absolute safety would consume too much of our finite resources.

5. Accordingly, it is now widely recognized that some risk of undesirable structural performance must be tolerated. This leads to the debated and open question of how to select structural risk levels for foundation design in order to obtain optimal structural performance, taking into account the available economical resources and competing demands.

6. During recent years, a new generation of probability-based design codes has been formulated. In most cases the reliability levels for these codes were selected on the basis of intuition influenced particularly by the current, good or bad, level of performance of existing structures. The load and resistance factors in these codes are functions of the coefficients of variation of the basic random variables, and this reflects a certain safety level differentiation with respect to the uncertainty in the values specified in the code. In some cases so-called "importance factors" have been introduced as a practical, although intuitive means of achieving differentiation of safety levels. Importance factors usually consist of multiplicative values to be applied to the standard design values of the actions or to the specified values of the resistance in order to modify the probability of failure of a particular design.

7. A practical rationale for the selection of safety factors for different types of structures is essentially lacking in the theory of codified design; this is specially true in the context of geotechnical structures. This paper takes a closer look at this problem and proposes ways to put its mathematical aspects into a simple formulae. Specific discussions focus on bored piles in expansive soils.

8. The safety parameter of a structural design standard is practically optimum if it maximizes the expected present value of economic benefits, and minimizes that of economic losses for society. For simplicity, in this paper, central safety factors and their corresponding safety levels (probabilities of failure) will be the code provisions to optimize.

OBJECTIVE FUNCTION

9. Any rational economic optimization study demands the assessment of initial costs, C, and potential future damage costs,

L, due to structures entering limit states. In the case of foundation structures these costs may encompass the following component costs:

Initial Cost
      a. Design costs
      b. Materials costs
      c. Construction costs
      d. Cost of supervision

Potential Future Damage Costs
      a. Cost of investigation
      b. Cost of strengthening
      c. Damage for injury or death
      d. Loss of revenue
      e. Legal costs
      f. Cost of removal
10. Thus an appropriate objective function to minimize is:

$$C_T = C + L \qquad\qquad (1)$$

where C and L are the respectively expected present values of initial costs and losses, due to structures entering limit states. Eq.(1) implies that changes in benefits derived from the structure's existence due to changes in design are incorporated into C, L or both.

Initial Cost Function
11. Let the central safety factor θ be defined as the ratio of the expected resistance R and the expected load effect, S. In conventional foundations little error is induced by assuming that the initial cost, at the neighborhood of the optimum is a linear function of the safety factor. Accordingly the expected present value of the initial cost C may be expressed as,

$$C = c_0 + c_1 \theta \qquad\qquad (2)$$

where c_0 and c_1 are constants that depend on the type of foundation.

Damage Cost Function
12. Actions on foundations include mainly the weight of the super structure, live loads, temperature effects and in the case of foundations on expansive soils the effect due to the shear forces that develop on the foundation due to the soil swelling. Most of these actions vary with time. Sometimes, however, it is easier

analyzing matters as if the structures were subjected to these actions at a fixed time during their life spans. If it is further assumed that the response of a foundation can only take place at a fixed time and that the only mode of structural damage or failure is a single limit state, the loss, H, at the time of failure, could be represented by a step function of the central safety factor say at $\theta = 1$. The expected present value of the loss due to failure or damage is obtained by multiplying this loss by the probability $P(\theta)$ that the limit state be reached, then:

$$L = HP(\theta) \tag{3}$$

10. If there is a series of possible limit states, either independent of each other or in cascade, or continuously varying with θ the loss function could take any of the mathematical expressions proposed by Ferregut(ref. 3). In this paper however attention will be concentrated to the case of a single limit state.

OPTIMAL SAFETY FACTOR

13. After substitution of Eqs. 2 and 3 in Eq. 1, the function to be minimized may be rewritten as,

$$C_T = c_0 + c_1\theta + HP(\theta) \tag{4}$$

or equivalently, in terms of a normalized cost $Z = (C_T - c_0)/c_1$, the following function may be minimized,

$$Z = \theta + IP(\theta) \tag{5}$$

where the relation $I = H/c_1$ is a relative measure of the cost of failure with respect to the initial cost of the structural foundation, and $P(\theta) = P(R/S < 1)$ is the probability of reaching the limit state or, in other words, the probability of failure.

14. The following approximation to the probability of failure has been proposed (ref. 4),

$$P = \alpha \exp\left(\frac{-\beta}{\ln(R/S)}\right) \tag{6}$$

where α and β are constants. Eq. (6) is a good approximation, valid in the range of relatively small failure probabilities for a wide variety of probability distributions of R and S. If both of these variables have lognormal distributions, in the range of probabilities from 10^{-6} to about 10^{-2} then $\alpha = 460$ and $\beta = 4.3$. If the following variables are defined:

$$\sigma = (lnW_R W_S)^{\frac{1}{2}} \qquad (7)$$

$$\alpha' = \alpha \left(\frac{W_S}{W_R}\right)^{-\frac{\beta}{2\sigma}} \qquad (8)$$

and $W = 1 + V^2$ (where V means coefficient of variation), Eq. 6 may be transformed into,

$$P = \alpha'\theta^{(\frac{\beta}{\sigma})} \qquad (9)$$

Equating to zero the derivative of I (Eq.5) with respect to θ gives the optimal central safety factor θ_o as a function of the importance ratio I, then,

$$\theta_o = \left(\frac{I\beta\alpha'}{\sigma}\right)^{\frac{1}{\frac{\beta}{\sigma}+1}} \qquad (10)$$

APPLICATION

Soil Pier Interaction Model

15. The magnitude of the shear stresses that develop at each section of the pile is determined by such soil properties as the perimeter shear modulus G, and the relative displacement between the pile section and the surrounding soil (displacement w). The displacements of the pier sections are governed by the following ordinary differential equation (ref. 5):

$$A \cdot E_c \cdot \frac{d^2u}{dZ^2} + G \cdot P(w - u) = \gamma_c A \qquad (11)$$

where

A = cross sectional area of the pier,
P = perimeter length of the pier,
E_c = elastic modulus of the composite section of the pier,
γ_c = unit weight of the pier, and
Z = depth below the soil surface.

16. The perimeter shear modulus G is a function of depth and the relative displacement w - u between the soil and the pile section. The soil heave in free-field w is also a function of depth. The solution of this differential equation for different input functions of G and w has been accomplished with a finite element program. To aid in the assessment of the heave profile for a site, the technical

literature was searched to identify published "w" heave-profile records of swelling soil deposits. These records were analyzed and compared to assemble a data base of heave versus depth that was used to develop an analytical model to describe heave with depth. To compare all these records, it was convenient to describe the heave versus depth profile in terms of dimensionless relative heave and relative depth. This was accomplished by dividing the depth by the depth of the active zone and the heave by the surface heave reported. The expression originally proposed elsewhere (ref. 1) to model the dimensionless heave profile is the following:

$$\frac{W}{W_{surf}} = \left[1 - \left(\frac{D}{D_{max}} \right)^a \right]^b \tag{12}$$

where

W	=	heave at depth D,
W_{surf}	=	surface heave,
D	=	depth,
D_{max}	=	depth of the active zone, and
a,b	=	parameters.

17. The uncertainty (variability) in the relative heave profile can be taken into account by considering all the parameters in Eq.(12) to be random variables. This considers that the sources of the uncertainty may be due to the uncertainties in the physical and analytical parameters a, b, W_{surf}, and D_{max}. Statistical data for each of these parameters were compiled and analyzed to model their variability. Final statistical parameters and the distributions chosen to model each of these random variables are listed in Table 1. A detailed description of these analyses can be found elsewhere (ref. 6).

18. A data base of surface heave-versus-time has also been compiled and analyzed. To facilitate the comparison of the different sets of data, the profiles were described in terms of dimensionless relative surface heave and relative time. The expression proposed by Pendones to model the resulting normalized curves takes the following form:

$$\frac{W}{W_{max}} = 1 - \left[1 - \left(\frac{T}{T_{max}} \right)^c \right]^d \tag{13}$$

where

W	=	heave at time T,
W_{max}	=	maximum surface heave,
T	=	time,
T_{max}	=	time at maximum heave, and
c, d	=	parameters.

TABLE 1   Statistical Characteristics of Variables and Parameters that Influence Pier Response

VARIABLE	NAME	DISTRIBUTION	MEAN VALUE	COEFFICIENT OF VARIATION
W_{max}	Surface Heave	Gamma	2.9 in	0.88
D_{max}	Depth of Active Zone	Lognormal	141.86 in	0.62
T_{max}	Time at Maximum Heave	Uniform	48.73 month	0.32
a	Parameter in Equation 2	Lognormal	0.54	0.59
b	Parameter in Equation 2	Lognormal	0.951	0.54
c	Parameter in Equation 3	Gamma	0.925	0.31
d	Parameter in Equation 3	Gamma	1.73	0.31
G_{max}	Asymptotic Value of Perimeter Shear Modulus	Normal	100 pci	0.10
$W_{surf} = \Delta W_{max}^{1}$	Surface Heave for the Unloaded Condition	Exponential	0.34 in	1.00
$W_{surf} = \Delta W_{max}^{2}$	Surface Heave for the Loaded Condition	Exponential	2.5 in	1.00
T_1	Time Pier is Casted	Normal	3 months	0.16
T_2	Time Pier is Loaded	Normal	6 months	0.083
E_c	Pier Elastic Modulus	Normal	3×10^6 psi	0.15
f	Parameter in Equation 4	Uniform	0.125	0.3464
L	Length of Pier		1299.2 in	
D	Diameter of Pier		41.34 in	
W_{crit}	Maximum Allowable Relative Displacement		0.15 in	

19. As in the previous model, the sources of uncertainty can be considered to be the uncertainties associated with each of the variables in Eq.(13), W_{max}, T_{max}, c, d. The statistical parameters and the selected probability distributions for each variable are shown in Table 1.

20. The load transferred to the pile sections is basically governed by the perimeter shear modulus G. The earliest attempts considered a fixed G for each pile section but increasing asymptotically with

depth Z to a maximum value G_{max} (ref. 5). This type of variation can be represented analytically by the following expression:

$$\frac{G}{G_{max}} = 1 - \left(\frac{1}{1+Z}\right)^f \qquad (14)$$

21. To allow slippage at the pile contact, the method used in the present study provides the continuous variation of Eq.(14) but limits the possible shapes of the f-w curves. For this purpose, a critical displacement, w_{crit}, is chosen. If the relative soil-pile displacement is smaller than w_{crit}, then the shear modulus is decreased relative to the value given by Eq.(14). The resulting f-w curve is shown in Figure 1. The shape of this curve forces the need to solve the differential equation (1) through an iterative process. In this sense, if the relative soil-pier displacement w_i exceeds w_{crit}, then the perimeter shear modulus G given in Eq.(14) would be reduced to G' indicated in Figure 1 for the following iteration.

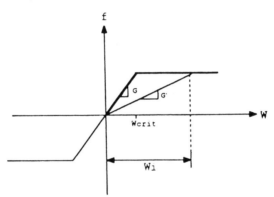

Fig. 1. Conceptual Sketch of Proposed Backbone Curve

22. The parameters involved in this approach are G_{max}, f and w_{crit}. These parameters can be obtained from field records on piers when simultaneous measurements of axial stresses in the pier and free-field heave have been reported. However, only four instrumented piers were identified. A complete analysis of these cases has been reported elsewhere (ref. 6). The low number of cases identified did not permit the formation of appropriate histograms; thus, a uniform distribution was adopted in the range of values obtained in the analyzed cases.

23. Upon casting, piles go through three distinctive phases: (a) remain unloaded; (b) load increases progressively; and (c) loaded with the constant dead weight of the structure. The swelling of the

subsurface soils can start before or during any of these stages. The possible variability can conceivably cover a very wide range of possibilities. Therefore, the analyses of the effects due to the construction schedule can best be implemented after the construction schedule has been defined. The designer will be in a reasonable position to estimate the time of construction T_1 of each pier and the time T_2 when the full dead load would have been applied on each pier. For the purposes of the illustrative examples, it has been assumed that times T_1 and T_2 are random variables with a normal distribution.

The method of analysis considers the two following pier conditions:

1. Unloaded: This first condition extends from the day of casting until the day when the dead load has been applied (i.e., from time T_1 to time T_2). During this time, the pile is assumed to be unloaded and the soil surface is experiencing a surface heave of ΔW^1_{max}.

2. Loaded: The second condition considers that the pile is loaded with the full dead load from the day of casting until the soil swelling is completed (i.e., from time T_1 to infinity). During this time, the soil surface will be experiencing a surface heave ΔW^2_{max}, which is equal or greater than ΔW^1_{max}. The most critical (i.e., largest pile head heave or largest tensile stress along the pier) of these two conditions is then used to design the pier.

25. Since the times T_1 and T_2, and the swelling process parameters, W_{max}, T_{max}, c, and d, are all random variables, the surface heaves ΔW^1_{max} and ΔW^2_{max} will also be random variables. The distributions of ΔW^1_{max} and ΔW^2_{max} have been found from a Monte Carlo simulation based on all distributions of the intervening parameters as described elsewhere (ref. 6).

Probabilistic Analysis

26. The computation of the uncertainties in the pier response due to uncertainties in the soil and material parameters was accomplished using a Monte Carlo simulation approach. The information summarized in Table 1 was used for the simulation of each of the input random variables. A preliminary simulation was conducted to determine the statistics of the two surface heaves ΔW^1_{max} and ΔW^2_{max}. For this purpose, Eq.(13) was used. The results show that the uncertainty on both heave increments can be modeled using exponential distributions (ref. 6). The calculated parameters are also shown in Table 1.

27. For illustration purposes, a drilled pier 1,299 in. long and 41.34 in. in diameter is considered. Two cases are studied: in the first case the pier remains underlined, and the soil surface swells ΔW^1_{max}; in the second case the pier head is loaded with 50 psi in compression, and the soil surface swells ΔW^2_{max}. The two pier

conditions described were analyzed using the statistical information of Table 1 for the problem variables and the Monte Carlo simulation approach previously described.

28. A summary of the results of the simulation for the <u>loaded</u> case is shown in Figure 2. These results indicate that the distribution of tensile stresses and axial displacements at any section are unsymmetrical and that the corresponding standard deviations are functions of depth. An example of the histograms of the response of the pile are illustrated in Figure 3. The histogram of maximum tensile stress suggests an exponential distribution; while, for the pile head heaves the histogram suggests a gamma distribution. A summary of the coefficients of variations of all combinations of limit states and case of analysis are presented in Table 2. These values were used to derive optimal central safety factors using Eq.(10) for four importance ratios (1,10,100,1000). Lower values may correspond to situations where the total cost of the foundation is very sensitive to its structural capacity and whose failure may not entail consequences far beyond the cost of replacing it. Larger values represent foundations of structures whose failure may induce collapse of a building and possible cause the injury or death of people.

Table 2. Summary of Coefficients of Variation

LIMIT STATE	UNLOADED CASE	LOADED CASE
Tensile Stress	1.132	1.271
Pile Head Heave	0.516	1.0

29. For the tensile cracking limit state, central safety factors were computed for several assumed coefficients of variation of the tensile strength of concrete. Large values were used, for these coefficients, to reflect the inherent statistical variability of the strength of concrete in tension, and the difficulty of conducting quality control when the concrete for bored piles is casted. Figure 4 shows the results for the unloaded case. It is readily observed that the values of the optimal central safety factor is highly influenced by the values of V_R and I used. For I = 1 the computed values are similar to those used in practice. However for larger values of this ratio the typical values used in practice are not appropriate. The larger values of θ_o used computed are mainly due to the large values of V_R used. Results for the loaded case were very similar.

30. The optimal central safety factors computed for the serviceability limit state are shown in Table 3. Again, these values vary greatly with the importance of the foundation. Due to the

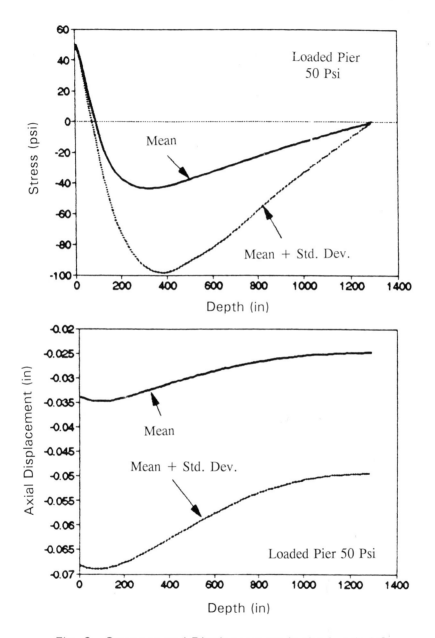

Fig. 2. Stresses and Displacements in the Loaded Case

287

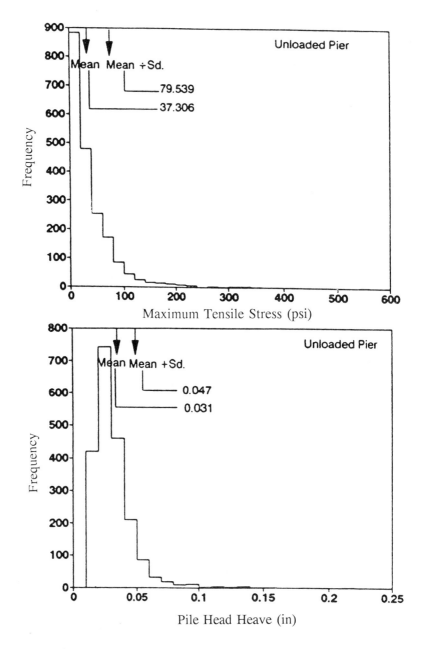

Fig. 3.   Histogram of Maximum Tensile Stress and
          Pile Head Displacement for the Unloaded Case

larger coefficient of variation estimated for the pier heaves when the pier is loaded the optimal central safety factors are larger for this case than for the unloaded pier.

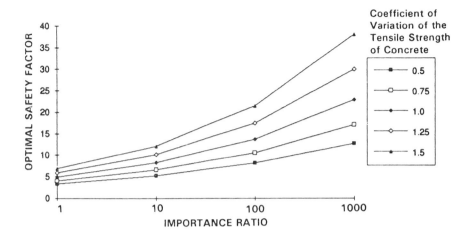

Fig. 4. Optimal Safety Factors Against Exceeding the Tensile Cracking of the Pile

Table 3. Example of Optimal Central Safety Factors for Checking Against Excessive Pile Heaves

IMPORTANCE RATIO	UNLOADED CASE	LOADED CASE
1	2.1	2.6
10	2.6	3.8
100	3.3	5.6
1000	4.2	8.1

CONCLUSIONS

31. Selection of optimal safety factors depend on the value taken by the importance ratio (failure consequences) as well as on the values of the coefficients of variation of the loads and resistance of the structure. These conditions are not currently recognized in design standards for geotechnical structures. The subject is very broad and with many facets that will require special studies and new techniques. The authors hope that this work will encourage further research along this direction.

ACKNOWLEDGEMENTS

32. The work reported in this paper was supported by Grant No. 3661-022 of the Advanced Research Program of the Texas Higher Education Coordinating Board.

REFERENCES

1. C. FERREGUT and M. PICORNELL. "Reliability Analysis of Drilled Piers in Expansive Soils." *Canadian Geotechnical Journal*, Vol. 28, No. 6, Dec. 1991, pp. 834-842.

2. C. FERREGUT, M. PICORNELL, and J.A. PENDONES. "Analysis of Uncertainties Related to Response of Piers in Expansive Soils." Proceedings of the 7th International Conference on Expansive Soils. Dallas, Texas, August 1992, pp. 477-482.

3. C. FERREGUT. "Methodologies for the Selection of Safety Factors and Safety Levels in the Design of Marine Structures." Proceedings of the Marine Structural Reliability Symposium. October 5-6, Arlington, VA, pp. 133-142.

4. E. ROSENBLUETH and L. ESTEVA. "Reliability Basis for Some Mexican Codes," ACI Publication SO-31, Detroit, Mich. 1972.

5. R.L. LYTTON. Foundations in Expansive Soils. In *Numerical Methods in Geotechnical Engineering* (C.S. Desai and J.T. Christian, eds.). McGraw-Hill Book Co., New York, N.Y., 1977, pp. 427-457.

6. J.A. PENDONES. *Analysis of Uncertainties Related to the Response of Piers in Expansive Soils*. M.S. thesis. University of Texas, El Paso, 1992.

24. The management of dynamic ground parameter uncertainty for nuclear facilities

C. I. ROBERTSON, Sir William Halcrow & Partners, UK

SYNOPSIS. The seismic analysis of nuclear facilities and other large or sensitive structures requires an assessment of dynamic soil structure interaction. The parameters governing the influence of the ground are dynamic modulus, damping ratio, Poisson's ratio and density. The moduli and damping ratios for the various strata at a site also exhibit strain dependency. The sources of uncertainty in the parametric values and the management approach to control this uncertainty are discussed. A case history is then presented which illustrates the influence that alternative strategies could have. Finally, conclusions are drawn as to the most effective approach.

BACKGROUND

1 The probability of a significant earthquake in the United Kingdom is relatively small, nevertheless the consequences of a seismically induced failure in a nuclear facility are far reaching. Therefore, in common with more seismically active areas of the world, a seismic load case is included in the design basis for nuclear facilities in the UK.

2 Seismic design processes traditionally follow a deterministic approach, with ground motions being defined by reference to a design response spectrum normalised to an acceleration level set according to the risk of occurrence. (The concept of a response spectrum is outlined in Appendix A).

3 The earthquake selected for design has a probability of occurrence of 10^{-4} per annum; this level of earthquake has typically been taken in the past to give peak horizontal ground accelerations of 0.25g. This is not dissimilar to the acceleration levels used in more seismically active regions.

4 The 10^{-4}pa event has been selected on the basis that with the current seismic design approach, structural failure has a 1 in 10^{-3} probability of occurring. This gives a joint probability of failure of 1 in 10^{-7}.

5 In civil engineering terms the seismic design methodology for nuclear facilities is unusual in the rigour that is applied at each stage, these being:

   (a) Site investigation and justification; including fault appraisal for possible continuing activity
   (b) Definition of the design earthquake (Response Spectrum and peak ground accelerations)
   (c) Determination of the seismic design criteria
   (d) Structural Layout   }
   (e) Static and Dynamic analyses }   Iterative Phase
   (f) Structural Design   }
   (g) Detailing
   (h) Assessment by the Safety Authorities (eg NII).

6   Current research and site specific studies are concentrating on reducing both the level of peak ground acceleration and the maximum acceleration responses as defined by the response spectrum. Pressure is mounting for the Nuclear Installations Inspectorate to accept Uniform Risk Spectra [Ref 1] in place of the Principia Mechanica Ltd (PML) spectra which have been in use since the early 1980's [Ref 2].

7   Welcome though these initiatives are in reducing the onerous nature of the seismic load case, the influence of other parts of the design process can also be equally onerous on the totality of the design. This paper will examine one such area, namely the methodology for determining and using the dynamic ground parameters. These have a direct influence on the earthquake motions within the free field, the foundation motions as determined for structural analysis purposes, and also importantly on the dynamic behaviour of the combined ground-structure system.

8   Figure 1 illustrates the seismic analysis and design approach. Following definition of the earthquake, typically at a rock outcrop, site response studies are undertaken to determine free field motions within the soil and at rockhead. These motions are then used to determine the foundation response of the coupled ground-structure system using a simplified representation of the structure. The calculated foundation motions are then input into more detailed structural models to determine member forces for design and internal responses for sub-system design.

9   One of the significant distinctions between seismic and other load cases is that changes in stiffness (and hence frequency) do not just alter the internal distribution of the loads but also can radically affect the magnitude of the total loading on the system. This can be seen by inspection of Figure 2 which shows a typical response spectrum. Changes in frequency alter the spectral acceleration, which is a measure of the load on the system. The sensitivity to frequency is such that errors in the stiffness estimates for the ground could render designs unsafe under hazard conditions or alternatively, cause them to be uneconomic. It is therefore incumbent on the designer to establish as good an estimate as possible of the dynamic ground parameters.

SOURCES OF UNCERTAINTY IN DYNAMIC GROUND PARAMETERS

10   There are many factors which contribute to the uncertainty in the dynamic ground parameters, some of these are shared with the more conventional parameters used to describe static soil behaviour.

Briefly, but not exhaustively, these are:

- (a)   Configuration of the ground strata as interpreted from the site investigation
- (b)   Errors associated with sampling disturbance and laboratory measurements
- (c)   Difficulties in interpreting in-situ measurements
- (d)   Relationship of measurements to previously published data
- (e)   Variation of ground properties with strain
- (f)   Non-linear model used to describe behaviour
- (g)   Influence of ground water in the propagation of seismic motions
- (h)   Three-dimensional effects.

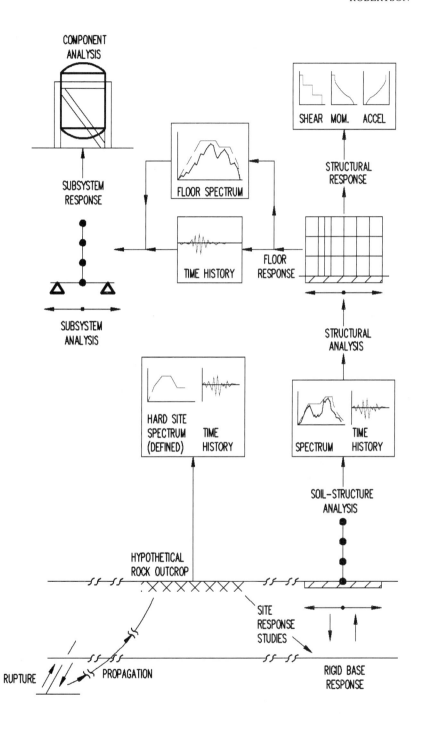

Fig. 1.   Overview of Seismic Analysis Process

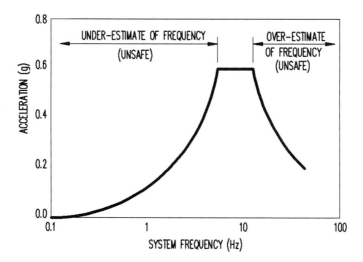

Fig. 2. Sensitivity of System Response to Error on Stiffness and Frequency Estimates

11 If these factors are examined in more detail, then the picture becomes very complex indeed. For example, the stress strain behaviour of soil is strongly non-linear, anisotropic and loading path dependant. This last influence is dependant on not only the previous loading history of a particular strata but also on the construction process itself. At the analysis stage the construction methods are usually not known.

12 The real dynamic behaviour of soil is sufficiently complex that only gross simplification will render the analytical problems tractable. The commonest approximation is to model the ground as a quasi-linear visco-elastic continuum, with moduli chosen to reflect the "effective" strain level at that location. The "effective" strain is a measure of the weighted average strain over the cycles of loading experienced during the earthquake. This model is relatively simple, but has the advantage that it can be incorporated readily into finite element routines, albeit with iterations to enable moduli and strain levels to be rendered compatible.

13 Other models have been used with varying degrees of success. However, the discussion provided in this paper will assume the quasi-linear model although much will also be applicable to other representations.

14 In practical terms the effects of the uncertainties are not strictly quantifiable. Nevertheless, it is necessary to adopt a systematic approach to limit uncertainty and to provide bounds on the possible range of values.

CONSIDERATIONS IN THE FORMATION OF A MANAGEMENT PLAN
Configuration of the Ground Strata

15 Because of the sensitivity of both the structural loading and response to the dynamic behaviour of the site geology, it is desirable to limit uncertainty of the ground configuration to as low as reasonably possible.

16 For these reasons, it is normal practice to carry out an intensive programme of borehole investigation for nuclear facilities. The interpretation can be further enhanced by a geophysical survey covering the site and its immediate

environs.   (This can have unexpected "benefits" as the
geophysics on one site revealed a potential shallow hydrocarbon
source).

17 Modern computer techniques for solid geometry modelling
facilitate the interpretation and subsequent presentation of
large amounts of data. The presentation of this data can also
then be correlated with analytical models which eases the
approval procedure with the relevant safety authorities.

18 It is worth noting that the effect of a particular
stratum is dependant on its relative stiffness and thickness.
For example a 10% variation in the thickness of a thin soil
layer can lead to a 50% variation in impedance value [Ref 3].
Soil layering can therefore be an important consideration on
the dynamic soil structure interaction analyses.

19 The objective should therefore be to provide an overall
configuration of the strata which also identifies their
relevant physical properties. This configuration is then used
in the analytical models. Localised pockets with different
characteristics and other inhomogenities can be catered for
within the analyses by parametric studies on the soil
properties, see paragraphs 36 and 37.

Physical Properties of the Strata

20   Field investigations yield information on the
configuration of the strata and provide samples for laboratory
testing. In addition, some of the dynamic properties can be
measured in-situ. These must be correlated with values from
the laboratory and with previously published data to enable a
full interpretation to be made and to give the maximum amount
of credibility and reliability to the values recommended for
subsequent use.

21 The parameters most usefully measured in-situ are the
compression and shear wave velocities. Taken with the mass
density they yield the relevant elastic moduli and Poisson's
ratio. Some skill is required in the interpretation of the
data obtained from a given layer, as adjacent strata with
higher wave velocities can distort the apparent wave velocity.

22 Both downhole and crosshole geophysics can be used,
although the latter normally gives more reliable results as
disturbance due to the borehole itself is less significant, and
transmission paths can be longer, which makes errors less
significant.

23 Laboratory tests can be used to determine low strain
shear moduli. Unfortunately, these are often a factor of two
or three less than those measured in situ due to sample
disturbance. Even with rock, reliable data cannot be obtained
probably due to the opening of micro-fissures as the in situ
stresses are relaxed. Although procedures do exist to adjust
laboratory values back to predicted in situ values [Ref 4]
further uncertainty is nevertheless introduced.

24 In addition to conventional laboratory testing, special
tests such as cyclic triaxial, cyclic shear and resonant column
tests are often undertaken to determine the strain sensitivity.
The normal representation of non-linear behaviour requires
information on the strain degradation of shear modulus and the
equivalent viscous damping for cyclic strains. These are
usually defined as shown in Figures 3 and 4.

Modelling of Soil Behaviour

25 As stated earlier, the commonest model is a quasi-linear
approach in which moduli and damping values are estimated
iteratively and related to the strain levels.

26 Damping is generally modelled by viscous damping because

295

of its mathematical convenience. The energy dissipation per cycle being made equivalent to the area of the hysteresis loop at a given level of cyclic strain.

27   The modulus at a given strain level is the average slope of the stress strain curve over the cycle.

28   Figures 3 and 4 indicate the level of dispersion of data from published sources for materials of a similar nature from different sites. Where published data for a given material is abundant and apparently reliable it is possible to use this without recourse to laboratory measurements. However, this introduces an uncertainty which may require explicit consideration at the design stage by parametric studies. The uncertainty may then have to be covered by designing against an envelope of possible properties.

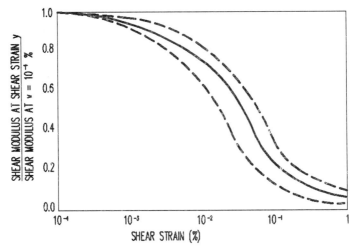

Fig. 3.   Typical Strain Degradation Curves for Shear Modulus of Sands

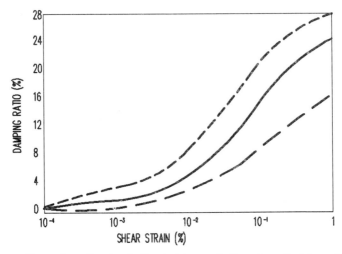

Fig. 4.   Typical Variation of Damping Ratio with Strain for Sands

29 Widening the bounds of design parameters may in turn lead to capital cost increases, which could outweigh potential savings in the costs of obtaining and testing samples. A judgement has therefore to be formed on the quality of the available information in relation to what is known of the strata and the potential sensitivity of the design to the strain degradation of these strata. Where appropriate this can be tested by very simple and approximate models.

Factors Impinging on Site Investigation
30 As with more conventional jobs, forward planning is essential and decision making should be based on as much useful information as possible. Desk studies will therefore form part of the planning process for the site investigations, which will obtain data for conventional engineering properties as well as the dynamic ground parameters. In addition, the site justification will need to address the seismicity of the locality and data for this will also be required.
31 One of the unusual aspects of nuclear projects is the depth to which some boreholes have to be sunk to gain data, a 100m into rock is not uncommon. At the site investigation stage the design of the facility may not be very advanced, but some idea of the mass and stiffness distribution of the structure is required to enable judgements to be made as to the appropriate depth of the boreholes. Nuclear facilities are often very massive and very stiff and therefore can interact significantly even with a rock foundation. With large raft foundations the bulb of influence can extend to 100m. Obviously the sensitivity of the facility to the properties of a given strata become less with increasing depth and a balance has to be struck between cost and quality of information.
32 Knowledge of the analysis and design requirements allow collection of data to be geared to these requirements. For example, if the simple quasi-linear soil model is to be used then laboratory experiments are designed to provide information on the strain degradation properties as shown in Figures 3 and 4. If it is planned to use more sophisticated models then the tests themselves have to become more sophisticated.

OUTLINE OF MANAGEMENT PLAN
General
33 It is essential that the data requirements and the form of presentation are properly defined at the outset. Further, it is necessary to have a proper appreciation of the design and analysis procedures so that there is confidence that the data provided will meet the known requirements and also potential developments through the design process. It should also be noted that not only must the designers be satisfied, but also that the Safety Authorities, as final arbiters, must be satisfied, this latter normally being somewhat harder to achieve.
34 These requirements are fed into the planning process for the site investigation. The distribution and density of boreholes, the depth and discrimination requirements of geophysical surveys, the specification for in situ and laboratory testing and other requirements can then be determined.
35 Once the raw data has been obtained, it is manipulated and interpreted to provide recommended design data. Part of this process will include reference to published data for similar materials which have undergone comparable geological processes. This places the data in its appropriate context and gives confidence that the values obtained are properly

representative of the material as a whole.

36   The recommended design values are best estimates with a band of uncertainty on either side of the estimate.   It was noted earlier that errors in the stiffness estimates can be potentially unconservative.   To guard against this possibility, it is necessary to consider what effect the errors in the dynamic ground parameters could have on the design.

37   It is therefore appropriate to investigate the response of the coupled soil-structure system for a range of properties either side of the best estimate.   Typically, the range of moduli investigated might be -50% to +100%, although tighter bounds are possible depending on the quality of the data obtained, and also its variability across the site.

38   Although there are several parameters with potential influence on the response, a systematic parametric study on each one in turn is a task not to be taken on lightly because of the complexity of the individual analyses and the difficulty of interpreting and using the large amounts of data generated. The parametric studies are therefore typically reduced to a variation in moduli alone and these are used as a vehicle to encompass all the other uncertainties.   It is worth noting that these uncertainties also include the ability of the analyst/designer to properly represent the behaviour of the structure within the various models.

39   British practice in this regard is not well defined. Historically it has been the practice to undertake the structural design against a smoothed and broadened spectrum, which is obtained from the envelope of motions from the parametric study.   Recent studies have suggested that this is unduly onerous and the case history presented below illustrates this.

The Plan

40   Bearing in mind the various points discussed in the previous sections, it is worth summarising the process required for obtaining the dynamic parameters and managing the uncertainty.

    (a)   Definition of Requirements
                (Parameters required, relationships to
                modelling and design processes, depth of
                investigations, etc.)
    (b)   Input Into Overall Plan for Site Investigation
                (Implications on geophysical survey, borehole
                density and requirements for
                crosshole/downhole testing, laboratory
                testing, etc.)
    (c)   Undertake Site Investigation
                (Obtain raw data from in situ laboratory
                tests.)
    (d)   Manipulate and Interpret Data and Formalise
          Recommendations
                (Relate values obtained to published data.)
    (e)   Perform Analyses and Undertake design
                (Undertake parametric studies to determine
                sensitivity of design to variation in dynamic
                ground parameter values.)

CASE STUDY
Preamble

41 Although the geotechnical aspects of determining dynamic ground parameters presents many features not encountered in more conventional works, there is available much published information on them.   In contrast there is little information

on the significance of uncertainty in the values and how this should be managed. This is perhaps a reflection on the boundary between geotechnical and structural disciplines. Nevertheless, it is an area where what constitutes good practice is not well defined and is therefore the focus of the discussion below.

Description of the Coupled Soil-Structure System

42   The structure in this case history is founded on rock, which consists of a series on interbedded sandstones, mudstones and siltstones with occasional bands of limestone. At a depth of about 90m there is a dolerite sill. Above the rock there is typically 12 metres of glacial till. This is topped by about 8 metres of rock fill. Figure 5 shows the variation of shear modulus with depth.

43   The structure for which results are presented consists of two massive concrete walls, approximately 14m wide and with a clear distance between them of 36m. These walls contain a number of service subways and are founded on a 5m thick foundation slab which also supports the internal columns of buildings located between the walls. The external load bearing elements of these buildings are founded on top of the walls. A typical cross-section is shown in Figure 6. These walls are not in contact with the strata above bed rock.

44   The earthquake was defined as the Principia Mechanica hard ground motion at a hypothetical rock outcrop in the free field. The dynamic ground structure interaction analyses were undertaken using the program FLUSH, which is a two-dimensional program operating in the frequency domain and uses the quasi-linear model for the soil as previously described.

45   A parametric study was undertaken in which the responses to ground moduli variations were investigation. The moduli used were best estimate (BE), BE -50%, BE -25%, BE +100% and BE +50%.

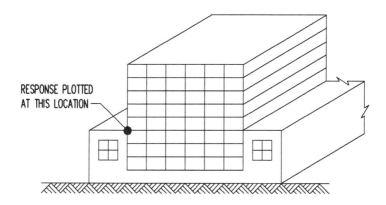

RESPONSE PLOTTED
AT THIS LOCATION

Fig. 6.   Case Study: Schematic Part View of Structure

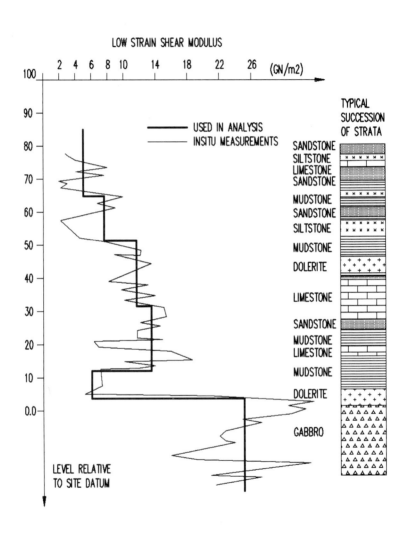

Fig. 5. Case Study: Variation of Shear Modulus with Depth

Results from the Analyses

46 Although the structure is founded on rock, its mass and stiffness is sufficiently high that significant interaction with the rock occurs. This is illustrated in Figure 7 which gives the response spectra at the top of the wall for three of the five conditions investigated. The spectra illustrated are a measure of the motions at the top of the wall. They show the peak acceleration of hypothetical single degree of freedom oscillators against natural frequency when the oscillators are attached to the top of the wall.

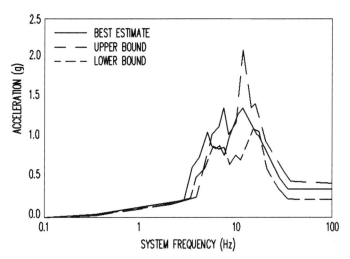

Fig. 7. Case Study: Response Spectra at Top of Wall for Best Estimate and Lower and Upper Bounds

47 The spectral accelerations at 40Hz and upwards correspond to the structural accelerations at the top of the wall, ie the oscillator is sufficiently stiff that it moves exactly with the wall. The peaks in the spectra correspond to the modal frequencies of the combined ground-structure system. If a system is attached to the wall whose frequency coincides with that of the wall, very strong amplification of the motions will occur as illustrated by the peak spectral accelerations.

Discussion of Results

48 The spectra show that with increasing ground stiffness the fundamental frequency increases. They also show that there is strong interaction between structural modes and ground modes associated with the site stratification. This is particularly noticeable when comparing the best estimate response to the upper bound response.

49 The historical approach adopted in the UK to cover for uncertainty in the parametric values was to apply peak broadening of ±15% to the envelope of results and to produce a smoothed and broadened spectrum.

50 For the circumstances illustrated here where the structure is sensitive to the parametric values, the parametric bounds will tend to control the width of the design spectrum and in this case the peak of the spectrum is controlled by the upper bound. This peak gives very onerous values compared to the best estimate.

51 This approach, whilst recognising that variability and uncertainty exist, implies that subsequent structural design is

undertaken on the assumption that the effects of upper and lower bounds are co-existent. Whilst definitely conservative, it also gives rise to spurious results.

52   An alternative approach is to recognise that the best estimate is just that, and to give some weight to the other values obtained from the parametric study a reasonable alternative procedure is to average the results from the various runs. Figure 8 gives the results from such a process. For comparison, also plotted are the best estimate and the best estimate results peak broadened by ±15% with some smoothing applied.   Apart from two relatively minor excursions, the broadened best estimate provides an envelope to the average of the parametric study.   Although only one set of results are presented here, other results from different models have given a very similar outcome.

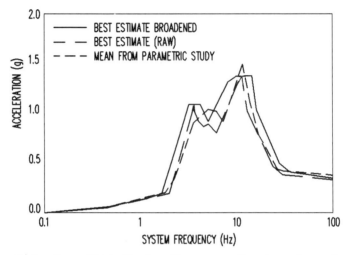

Fig. 8.   Case Study: Response Spectra from Averaging Process, Best Estimate and Best Estimate Broadened

53   Studies reported in Reference 5, show that spectra generated for equal probability of exceedence have lower but broader peaks than those generated deterministically.   One contribution to this is that the random variability of properties as experienced in situ effectively detunes the system from a well defined resonance.   The averaging process carried out on the results has a similar effect.

54   In situations where a large number of analyses have to be performed, for example to investigate different load states, then undertaking parametric variation on each condition becomes difficult due to the large amounts of data.

55   The following procedure is therefore proposed:

(a)   For situations where only a limited number of analyses are required then parametric variation studies should be undertaken for each condition. The generated response spectra should then be averaged, broadened and smoothed before being input to a design.

(b)   For situations where a large number of conditions are to be analysed, then parametric studies should be undertaken on a typical condition and the results averaged. If this demonstrates that the best estimate broadened spectrum is reasonably representative, then the remaining analyses can be undertaken solely on best estimate properties. Minor adjustments to peak spectral values or the incorporation of additional broadening to the final broadened and smoothed spectra can be applied if judgement suggests that this would be appropriate.

SUMMARY AND CONCLUSIONS

56   The sources of uncertainty in the determination of dynamic ground parameters for seismic analysis and design has been reviewed and the process to manage this uncertainty has been outlined. A procedure for averaging analysis results from parametric studies has been proposed as offering a realistic method for accounting for the uncertainty which does not introduce unreasonable levels of conservatism such as might result from an enveloping procedure.

REFERENCES

1   Mallard D.J. et al.   Recent Development in the Methodology for Seismic Hazard Assessment. Conference Proceedings, Civil Engineering in the Nuclear Industry, p65 et seq.   Institution of Civil Engineering, 1991.
2   Principia Mechanica Ltd.   Seismic Ground Motions for UK Design, April 1981.
3   Wong H.L and Luco J.E.   Identification of Sensitive Parameters for Statistical Simulation of Soil Structure Interaction, UCRL-15493, NUREG/CR-3044.   Lawrence Livermore Laboratory, 1981.
4   Seed H.B. and Idriss I.M. Soil Moduli and Damping Factors for Dynamic Response Analysis, EERC 70-10, University of California, December 1970.
5   American Society of Civil Engineers ,Structural Analysis and Design of Nuclear Plant Facilities, Ch5, ASCE, 1980.

APPENDIX

Figure 9 demonstrates the derivation of response spectra. In essence the peak accelerations of a series of one degree of freedom oscillators resulting from the input of a seismic accelerogram is plotted against the resonant frequency of the oscillator. For design purposes it is convenient to allow for the range of possible earthquakes within a single design spectrum. This is usually achieved by generating a spectrum to meet the mean plus one standard deviation derived from responses to a large series of accelerograms.

The response spectrum is a convenient representation as individual structural modes of vibration can be treated as single degree of freedom oscillators. The response of each mode to an earthquake is thereby easily estimated and the modal responses combined to give the total structural response.

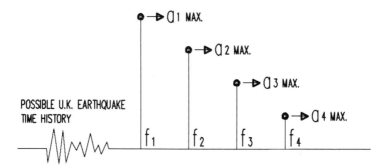

Fig. 9a.   Calculation of Peak Acceleration Response in a
Set of Single Degree of Freedom Oscillators from a Single
Time History

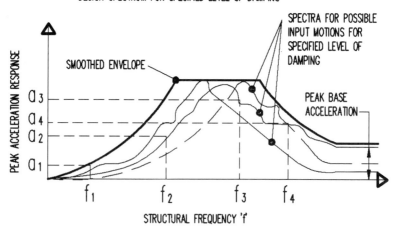

Fig. 9b.   Smoothed Envelope Design Spectrum Generated
from an Envelope of Possible Time Histories